T A N

D0716668

W-R-E-C-K-A-G-E :

an Encyclopaedia

of COLLISION on the

Public Highway

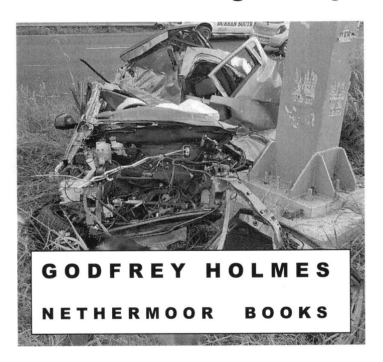

GODFREY HOLMES

NETHERMOOR BOOKS

NETHERMOOR BOOKS
"St. Elphin"
12 North Promenade
Withernsea
HU19 2DP
Telephone : 01964-615258

Contact the Author : Godfrey.holmes@btinternet.com

Twitter = @Godfrey_Holmes

Facebook = Godfrey Holmes Profile [Withernsea]

BRAKE Telephone Number = 01484-559909
BRAKE VICTIM HELPLINE = 0808-8000401
Brake is also on Facebook & Twitter @Brakecharity

Although Royalties from the sale of this Encyclopaedia will be donated to BRAKE, the Charity has had no direct input into - nor bears responsibility for - this Book's Content

dedicated   to
the   memory   of
my Neighbour [living   opposite]
JESSICA   IDDON

killed at Stonedge
near Chesterfield
Sunday June 2nd., 2008
age : just Seventeen

What will the Emergency Services
find ? ?

Who knows ?

AN ENCYCLOPAEDIA OF

COLLISIONS ON THE PUBLIC

HIGHWAY

AUTHOR's NOTES

As far as the Author is able to trace,
TANGLED WRECKAGE is the *first ever*
comprehensive Encyclopaedia on the Subject of
Collision on the Public Highway.

The *Public Highway* referred to throughout is taken to be that existing in England, Wales, Scotland & Northern Ireland; but the Author earnestly hopes many entries, also much discussion, within, might apply to other nations: calamitous Collisions wherever they happen.

If another A to Z exists in print, that will be duly acknowledged in future Editions.

Also, to the best of the Author's Research, any Laws & Statistics within are as up-to-date & as accurate as accessible in June 2020. The Author apologizes in advance for any factual inaccuracies, *all unintended*, which, again, will be duly corrected in future Editions.

So it is: *TANGLED WRECKAGE* is a new Journey: literally. And the Author welcomes any Feedback from any Reader, any Organization anywhere....

An ENCYCLOPAEDIA of

COLLISION on the Public Highway

DEFINITION of
a COLLISION on the PUBLIC HIGHWAY

<< The OCCASION of ONE or more ROAD-USERS
SUFFERING LOSS or SHOCK or INJURY or DEATH,
SHORT-TERM or LONG-TERM STRESS or DISTRESS :
because THEY HAVE STRUCK
- or BEEN STRICKEN BY -
ONE or more OTHER ROAD-USERS
or by ANY OBJECT FOUND on that HIGHWAY >>

Notes:

++ **"Road-User"** to include, in order of frailty: baby carried or in a pram; disabled person needing, or not needing, using, or not using, assistance; young child Pedestrian or Passenger; older child or teenaged Pedestrian or Passenger; older Pedestrian or Passenger; Bystander; young Pedal-Cyclist; older- perhaps more experienced- Pedal-Cyclist; Horse-Rider whether mounted or not; Rider of Moped or Motor Scooter; Motorcyclist; Car-Driver; Minibus or small Van-Driver plus Passenger; Driver of a Campervan plus Passenger; Box-Van Driver; Bus or Coach Driver; Fixed-Chassis Lorry-Driver;

Juggernaut Driver: to include the Driver of a connected or disconnected Tractor & Trailer.

++ It is quite possible for one or more of these Road-Users to be more secure, "safer," than someone appearing to be *stronger* on the Public Highway : for instance a properly strapped-in baby might suffer less injury than her father driving that car; a Moped-Rider might be more protected through slowness than a far more powerful, more protected, *Harley-Davidson* Motorcyclist; or a Van Driver might be injured swerving out of the way of an uninjured 15-year old Pedal-Cyclist. This is called leapfrogging of risk.

++ For the purpose of this Definition: a "**Public Highway**" is any road or carriageway where a member of the public is reasonably expected to be without seeking permission, except where that Highway has had to be closed or Tolled;

++ these "Highways" to include remote country lanes, green lanes and wide bridleways where a member of the public is allowed to proceed without seeking explicit permission, yet still subjecting themselves to local by-laws;

++ *and* for the purposes of our main Definition: wayside laybys, verges, coppices, ditches, dykes, rivers, hedges, also cliffs: all easily accessible, at speed, away from the actual tarmcadam;

++ and - again for our purposes-: a "Highway" to include a Petrol Station, Service-Station, & a "private" or public Car Park.

++ Finally: *an Object* is taken to be any piece of detritus, brick thrown, load shed, loosed tyre, street furniture or front wall.

LIST of the MAIN CAUSES of COLLISIONS on the PUBLIC HIGHWAY:
in order of RELATIVE FINALITY

Vehicle-Pedestrian Collisions

| | |

Overtaking Collisions

| | |

Loss of Control Collisions

| | |

Right Turn Collisions

| | |

Road Junction Collisions

| | |

Roundabout + / or Nose-to-Tail

| | |

Opening-of-the-Door Collisions

| | |

Moving-Across Collisions

| | |

Left Turn Collisions

| | |

Manoeuvering Collisions

| | |

Unstable Load Collisions

EXCLUDING WHOLE JUGGERNAUT SLEWING OVER THE CARRIAGEWAY

| | |

Public Service Vehicle Collisions

EXCLUDING FIRE or ROLL-OVER; MINIBUSES or TOP-DECK SLICED OFF

| | |

Meeting-an-Obstruction Collisions

INCLUDING ONE DRIVEN VEHICLE SWIPING
AN UNOCCUPIED PARKED VEHICLE

| | |

Animal-on-the-Carriageway Collisions

EXCLUDING HORSE-WITH-RIDER

| | |

Street-Furniture & Gatepost Collisions

EXCLUDING TREES, LAMP-POSTS & SUICIDES

****

NB : THIS HIERARCHY TAKES LITTLE ACCOUNT OF FREQUENCY: IN WHICH
CASE *JUNCTION COLLISIONS* WOULD OUTSTRIP ALL OTHERS...
NOR CAN IT EVER EXCLUDE THE POSSIBILITY -
AS WITH A PILE-UP - THAT NOSE-TO-TAIL MIGHT ASCEND TO THE TOP;
OR BOMB PLACED IN A MOTOR-COACH GO OFF THE GRID ALTOGETHER.
MOTOR INSURERS HAVE THEIR OWN HIERARCHIES
FOR THE PURPOSE OF REINSURING: eg. CAR DERAILS PASSENGER TRAIN

TANGLED WRECKAGE :

an ENCYCLOPAEDIA of

COLLISIONS

on the PUBLIC HIGHWAY :

PART ONE :

an A to Z of

CAUSE & CAUSATION

***

*** over 320 entries ;

*** many more cross-references ;

*** an award of up to 5 %%%%% - s

for *seriousness / potential for calamity* ;

& *** an award of up to 5 @@@@@ - s

for *likelihood* of ever encountering this.

+ + + + + + + + + + +

11

ABANDONED VEHICLES

% @

The main risk with abandoned vehicles is where they have been before being abandoned! Have they been in a Police chase? Or used to commit a crime? Have they been caught by a speed camera? Or shepherded there by a Drunk Driver? Then the question of "torching" arises - so hazardous for passing Pedestrians.

See : Taking Without Owner's Consent; Police Chase

ABSENCE OF FOOTBRIDGE AND/OR PEDESTRIAN UNDERPASS

%%%%   @@@

On a busy Trunk Road, the absence of alternative ways of crossing - Footbridge or Underpass - greatly endangers Pedestrians. In fact, in rush-hour - occasionally during *all* waking hours - some Pedestrians find certain crossings absolutely impossible. This impossibility increases exponentially where (i) the road to be crossed is either adjacent to a busy Roundabout; (ii) where two lanes need crossing at the same time; (iii) where there are no pedestrian lights; (iv) where there are *three* lanes needing crossing; and (v) when nobody, nobody at all, signals GO. We are all familiar with crossings from Hell; worse where one's route cannot be adjusted to a safer place to cross. Of note, sometimes the traffic-engineer has actually laid down Pedestrian dimpling or a Pedestrian pavement-dip - yet still that Highway is totally un-crossable.

See : Pedestrians from Nowhere; Speed; Footbridges

ACCESS ONLY
%%% @@@

Particularly near High Street shops; near football & entertainment stadia; also along short-cuts & rat-runs; a probable majority of vehicles are quite deliberately ignoring "Access Only." Worse, errant Drivers always seem to have a plausible excuse. Where a side-road is half-a-mile or less from the named Town Centre or other attraction, sceptical or intimidated local residents live in constant fear of those many seekers who probably never deserved "Access."

See: Rat Runs; No Entry; Narrow Roads; U-turns; Reversing.

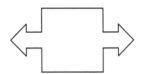

"ACCIDENT-PRONE" DRIVERS & RIDERS
%%% @@

Labelling somebody "accident-prone" minimizes, in a way, the chaos they are causing on the Highway. There is academic research into this supposed phenomenon which links "strings of accidents" to a Driver or Pedestrian's low self-esteem, poverty, strained finance, or sleeplessness. All very relevant. But if a fleet finds one of its Lorry Drivers or Minicabs or Hire-Cycles is involved in more mishaps than anyone else: it is wiser to send that person away for re-training - or in the case of a very elderly Driver, retirement - than to rest on possibly spurious theories that they *were born* to attract calamity.

See: Bad Insurance Risks; Elderly Drivers; Inexperienced Drivers; Pedestrians from Nowhere….

ADVERTS TIED TO LAMP-POSTS

% @@

When an advert is tied to a Lamp-Post, the Rider or the Driver momentarily strains to read it. That applies to a greater degree to *big* adverts on hoardings or in shop-windows, also to banners strewn right across the road from Left to Right. Nobody wants of miss out on a treat or an offer. One or two Councils restrict - even ban - wayside advertizing.

See: Distractions; Motorway Adverts; Loss of Concentration

AGENCY DRIVING

%% @@

Agency driving is very different from *employee* driving. Levels of commitment to both the commissioner of that agency & to the general public could be far lower here than where someone drives for employer or self. Sometimes the Agency-Driver has a clouded, or incomplete, driving-history.

See Fleets; HGVs...

AIR-BAGS DEFECTIVE

%%%% @

Unbelievably, a manufacturer's Air-Bags can be proven defective for year after year, yet not replaced as a part of any potential mass recall or imminent emergency. Also there is little *testing* of possibly defective Air-Bags. Functioning Air-Bags are eminently superior to either no Air-Bag at all or Air-Bags that *could-be* all right. In the event of Collision, a good Air-Bag helps prevent, or reduce, facial & pulmonary injury.

See: Air-Bags Exploding; Steering-Wheels

AIR-BAGS EXPLODING
%%%% @

Exploding Air-Bags are nearly always catastrophic upon impact.
See: Air-Bags Defective; Steering Wheels; Emergency Stops

AQUAPLANING
%%%% @

Aquaplaning is a very specialized type of skid: where pools of standing or running water overwhelm the four- or six-tyre capacity of a vehicle to maintain a straight line. Nor is Aquaplaning dependent upon many *hours* of rain. It can happen *20 minutes* after a cloudburst, always exacerbated by preparedness, overall speed - or speed of approach.
See : Tyre Pressures ; Speed; Overtaking; Rainfall; Skids

AIRPORTS
%%% @

For nearly every Driver whether going on holiday; coming back from holiday; dropping off and collecting other families going on holiday; or attending a business meeting, the Airport is a hostile environment: full of unexpected signage, roundabouts, slip-roads, holiday hotels - & terminals apparently allowing no stopping whatsoever. Additionally, an Airport's many Multi-Storeys themselves cause, or host, Collisions, not least because of time constraints. And a direct cause of those many extra Collisions is the tired or worn-out Driver who is still in a holiday mood; hasn't slept for the whole of his or her journey; who had to get up early at a faraway Seaside Resort; and needs to get home in a hurry. Then there are those air passengers more used to driving on the Right than on the Left. And, if matters could get worse, the very existence of family Meet-&-Greet *doubles* the amount of traffic using Airports because it needs 4 journeys to get that family or a single traveller away, not two.

See: Impatience; Time Limits; Taxis; No Entries; Multi-Storey Car Parks; Tiredness....

ALCOHOL INTAKE
%%%% @@

Although Britain's permitted Driver Alcohol Intake is much higher than in other countries, *any* alcohol at all taken by a Driver or Co-Driver is hazardous. Alcohol impairs decision-making and speed of reaction to traffic. Alternatively, noisy Passengers might be drunk even when their Driver is sober. And as if that were not depressing enough, careless or inadequately-illuminated Pedestrians might be drunk.

See: Drink Driving; Teenage Passengers; Lack of Concentration; Boy-Racers...

ANIMALS ON THE ROAD
%% @

Animals ahead generally means sheep or cattle. These herds crossing field-to-field are relatively easy to spot. Just switch off the engine. More troublesome is the one stray sheep or cow, worse the one stray horse that might portend more stray horses ahead of that. Most dangerous of the larger animals is the deer at night. These deer have little road sense. They are also in a hurry. At best they dent a passing car; at worst the deer - or horse - goes straight through the windscreen, potentially killing the driver or front-seat passenger.

Much smaller animals are also a hazard. Everyone wants to save someone's pet dog or pet cat. But it is only safe, or safer, to do an emergency stop if the rest of the road is entirely clear. Otherwise Police & Insurer alike will look dimly on multi-party Collisions directly or indirectly caused by stray pets.

See: Emergency Stops; Lack of Concentration

APPROACHING A ROUNDABOUT
%% @@@

Lots of Collisions happen on or after approaching a Roundabout. And because every single event on that Roundabout is determined by the speed and the mindset - also the signalling - of those Drivers who are approaching it.

Chance is: a Road-User may never get onto the actual Roundabout because of a Collision at the starting-line. Maybe a following Driver imagined the vehicle immediately ahead has already opted for entry. Or maybe another Driver swops lane in order to gain maximum advantage once on the Roundabout.

The Highways' Agency frequently erects high barriers to deter all Drivers or Riders from proceeding without first halting completely. Such barriers are homicidal. Everyone needs the fullest preparation for decision-making that starts as early as 100 metres before the Roundabout itself.

See: Roundabout Discipline; Leaving a Roundabout; Mini-Roundabouts; Change of Mind...

ARGUMENTS
%%%   @@

No research has taken place - or perhaps *could* take place - into the rôle of domestic arguments in poor Highway behaviour. But there is circumstantial & narrative evidence that a Driver in the middle of an argument; or hearing argumentative children on the back seat; or harbouring anger towards a spouse or work colleague; or recovering from "a domestic"; or worst of all: still angry with another Road User, is prevented from competent driving by the wrong attitude, a mindset out of kilter.

See: Road Rage; Impatience; School-Run.

BABY ON BOARD
%%   @

The notice "Baby On Board" doesn't always change the behaviour of vehicles in pursuit of said newborn baby. The Newborn Baby can really only travel in a mother's arms or in a Moses' basket: neither of which is especially safe at the moment of Collision or emergency braking - or in an adapted child car-seat. The worst outcome is said Baby or Toddler propelled through the windscreen.

See: Car Seat Safety; Emergency Braking

BACK-SEAT PASSENGERS
%%   @@@@

To be a Back-Seat Passenger is both an enviable and a blighted position to be in : happy because one has been offered a lift;

and could be marginally safer in the event of a head-on Collision; or when the front-seat Driver is in rear Collision with an HGV. But this Passenger has a number of *disadvantages* possibly outweighing his or her "sense of security." First the Back-Seat Passenger is in a inferior position to become a "Back-Seat Driver" than the main front Passenger. The controls are also further away - with $360°$ vision hampered. Nor will the Driver necessarily welcome either physical or knowledgeable nudges from immediately behind. Additionally, Back-Seat Passengers might also be less well strapped-in through the necessity of a third Back-Seat Passenger Adult needing the "Child's Seat-Belt" in an uncomfortable middle. Fourth, not every saloon car has 2 escape doors to the rear. Fifth, there are *specific* Collisions: eg. HGV or White Van rear Collisions, side-impacts or pirouettes, where Back-Seat Passengers will be killed or seriously injured while the two at the front live to see another day.

See: Rear Collisions; Head-On Collisions; Seat-Belts; Teenaged Passengers; Shifting Load within Cabin... etc.

BAD INSURANCE RISKS
%%%% @@

By definition, bad Insurance Risks cause Collisions; or fail to react quickly enough to somebody else's careless driving. Bad Insurance Risks include Drivers & Riders with a multiple claims' past, Disqualified Drivers, Drunk Drivers, 19-year old Boy Racers. But the actuarial science is imprecise because the "worst" Drivers & Riders display little or no concern for anybody else on the Highway; and will continue to drive while disqualified; will usually be uninsured; will drive in order to pursue or entrench their general criminality; and will drive away from Collisions without staying round. Nobody can rescue them - or their victims.

See: Road Rage; Impatient Motorists; Driving while Disqualified; Dishonest Driving; Crash for Cash.

BANKING
%%%% @

Banking is specialized Roadcraft born of Motorcycling skill. The angles, possibilities, and centres of gravity are amazing. But the Rider is perpetually only seconds away from death or injury. Sometimes the Rider's own boots are scuffed!

See: Motorcycles; Speeding; Wrong Side of Road; Lack of Concentration... etc.

BLACK ICE
%%% @@@

Black Ice happens when there has been rain or spray the day before, then overlaid, perhaps at dark-fall, by white frost. The result is a largely invisible hazard - & potential for skidding. Everyone relies on the road-gritters - yet the gritters themselves might only have had access to a wrong weather forecast - or been unable, or unwilling, to come out that night. Thus Black Ice is the greater difficulty the *earlier* in the day one walks or travels. It also upends Pedestrians.

See: Icy Roads; Weather Conditions; Skidding; Swerving; Snow

BOLLARDS ERECTED TO BRING DOWN SPEED

%% @@

Superficially, it sounds great to erect one, two - or a series of Bollards: good to bring down speed on fairly long & straight town by-passes or to encourage a fairly low-cost crossing for Pedestrians. One would imagine these islands - because the bollards have to be mounted on an island - always do what they are supposed to : separating once and for all traffic moving in opposite directions.

Unfortunately, some racers who have already committed themselves to being on the "wrong" side of the road cannot get back onto their portion because of the bollarded island. Result : Head-On Collision. Also worth consideration: the late night "game" of Bollard-Bashing, deliberately reversing into as many Bollards as possible with an S.U.V.

See : Speeding; Overtaking; Head-On Collisions; Refuges; Wrong Side of the Road

BOREDOM

%%%% @@@@@

It is impossible to overestimate the contribution of Boredom or Over-Familiarity to Collision on the Highway. The bored Driver or Rider is a hazard to both self & wider public. Boredom arises not only from Over-Familiarity but also from Commuting, Traffic-Jams, Tiredness, or road-type. And by its very nature, Boredom is as internalized as it is universal.

See: Commuting; Tiredness; Long Journeys; Motorways - *plus several other entries.*

BRAKE FAILURE
%%%% @

Brake Failure is thankfully relatively rare - and sometimes an alternative form of braking such as hand-brake or the mounting of a grass verge becomes available. But when Brake Failure happens at speed or on a downward gradient: a car, or worse, a Motorcycle or Lorry, loses all direction, soon ploughing into anything & everything , *everyone*, in its path.

See: Failed MOTs; Poorly Maintained Vehicles; Swerving

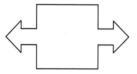

BRAKE LIGHT MALFUNCTION
%%% @@@

Brake Lights are confusing enough without any malfunction. Very few are the Drivers or Riders who regularly test their Brake Lights - or even understand where these differ from Side-Lights or Dipped Headlights. Yet Drivers & Riders who are following a vehicle, more so in darkness, depend on perfectly-functioning Brake-Lights for their survival. More confusing, if that were possible, several vehicles are now fitted with fourth, fifth or sixth Brake-lights: fitted, for instance, at the foot of the rear window.

IF fitted, all these extra Brake-Lights *should* function and *shouldn't* dazzle; nor are Brake-Lights, however good, a replacement for cautious driving.

See: Fog-Lights Left On; Dazzle; Rear Collisions; Sudden Braking….

BRIDGE STRIKES
%%%% @

Network Rail reports - & despairs - of an estimated 50 Bridge Strikes every single week - with many lorry drivers, perhaps foreign lorry drivers - declining or refusing to stay on the scene lest they get into trouble. Most Bridge Strikes happen beneath railway bridges, some of those bridges never having carried a train for years. But where there *is* a train service above, Bridge Strikes are *calamitous* delaying hundreds of trains, thousands of passengers. Then there is the danger to *oncoming* vehicles while lorries shed part of their load; or skew across the opposite lane; or desperately try to reverse, do a U-turn ... and beat a retreat.

See: Low Bridges; Unfamiliar Route; Foreign Driver[s]; U-turns

BOY-RACERS [so-called]
%%% @@

"Boy-Racers" is a general term given to young and middle-aged Drivers, Passengers & Spectators who gather, encased in souped-up hatchbacks: in big public car-parks or industrial sites after hours or shopping-estates to perform stunts on the Public Highway: speeding, overtaking, wheelies, sudden braking, U-turns, tandem-riding, whatever.

Although Boy-Racing is technically - as well as patently- *illegal*: the Law is rarely enforced . Instead Boy-Racing is seen as fun, a hobby, free-entertainment: often accompanied by loud beat music and the cussing of any unwary passer-by.

See: Pursuit; Speed; Rowdy Passengers; Loss of Control

BROKEN MIRRORS
%%% @

Mirrors are so important, whether equipped to cars, lorries or motorcycles that they must be intact; also correctly adjusted.

See: Visibility; Overtaken on the Offside; Hidden Cyclists

BULL BARS
%%% @

Bull Bars are rather out-of-fashion: some newer fittings actually illegal - but it can be fairly said that, when Bull Bars were all the rage in the late 20th. Century, in one foul swoop they put Road Safety back 40 years. Bull Bars were and are enormous & intimidating; worse often fitted to enormous & intimidating SUVs. Even now the remaining Bull Bars are supposed to be "Pedestrian-friendly." Forget it. They aren't. Bull Bars might *originally* have been useful nudging out of the way herds of cows on a farmer's footpath - but are now literally past their sell-by date.

See: Road Rage; U-turns; Pedestrians from Nowhere; S.U.V.s.

BUS LANES RUNNING OUT
% @@

Bus Lanes are not without their problems as soon as they are opened... closed? They are cheap to paint, fairly cheap to police - but far too narrow; and far too confusing. That's because every Bus Lane has to Run Out! And when they disappear, Cyclists, Motorcyclists & Drivers must suddenly swop lane in preparation for some stretch of road or some roundabout *not* gifted with a Bus Lane.

See : Lane Swop; Buses; Pedestrians from Nowhere; Undertaking.

BUSES & BUS-DRIVERS
%%   @@@@@

By their very nature, Buses stop more often in urban areas: therefore act unpredictably. Buses are also bulky. Buses, of course, *do* need to overtake both cars & other Buses where hazard is multiplied for any Pedal-Cyclist or Motor-Cyclist at the front, on the inside of, or on the outside of that Bus. Finally - and it often *is* final - due consideration has to be given to Pedestrians having just alighted; Pedestrians running in order to board; & unseen Pedestrians passing near or passing by the Bus.

See: Coaches & Coach-Drivers; Parked Cars; Cyclists Unseen; Pedestrians from Nowhere

BUS STOPS
%%   @@@@@

Bus Stops are a hostile environment for anybody but a Bus Driver. Too often they're used a temporary car parks. As bad is the Driver or Rider who tries to beat the Bus by overtaking it while it is picking-up or dropping-down. Then children appear from nowhere at the front or back of the waiting or leaving Bus. On the approach to certain towns & cities, it can be argued there are far too many Bus Stops, too closely bunched, and allowing *embarkation* instead of simpler alighting.

See: Buses; Overtaking; Anger; Impatience; Pedestrians from Nowhere

CABIN LOAD UNSAFE
%%% @

We are used to the hazard of trailer loads unsafe or lorry loads unsafe - or roof loads unsafe. Less often considered is the [internal] cab or saloon load unsafe: DIY materials; cans of paint; tools and power-tools; planks; children's toys; groceries; unsecured bottles or six-packs of beer or cola. In fact *any* unsecured load, blunt or sharp, becomes a powerful projectile in the event of emergency stop, near miss, Collision. And the person first & most dangerously struck by an object flying at 40- or more mph is the Driver: soon to be the distracted, stunned or concussed Driver. More obliquely, an unsecured load can hem a Driver in without hitting him or her - or simply obscure the centre-mirror.

See: Unsafe Loads; Roof Loads; Emergency Stops; Pets; Distractions; Mirrors not Adjusted

CAMPER TRAILERS & BUILDERS' TRAILERS
%% @

The most common form of Trailer on the road are the Artics. But the word also applies to any towed Camper Trailers & Building Materials' Trailers: some of the latter transporting small garden machinery, compressors, plate-compactors, boarding, power-tools, ladders - even racing motorcycles & small saloon cars. These Trailers are best towed correctly by Range Rovers, cautiously steered, at a low speed.

See: Trailer Safety, Caravans, Speed; Swerving

CAR CARRIERS
% @

Car Carriers are very unusual on most highways. Yet they are almost as much of a problem empty as full. Full: the Car Carrier has to be extremely carefully loaded so that no car gets dislodged. Empty: there is rattle, perhaps sway. And because of their *length,* Car Carriers take a lot of overtaking.

See: Overtaking; Slipping Backwards; Unsafe Loads

CAR LEASING FINANCE
%% @@@@

This fairly novel form of car finance has a delayed impact on Highway Collisions by making motoring far more affordable [far too affordable?] for people who maybe shouldn't be driving or riding at all. On the up-side, Leasing brings on to the roads far newer vehicles than might otherwise be purchased outright or handed down the food-chain. On the down-side, this Finance is a chimera. It leads to treble vehicle ownership in families who could well manage with *two* vehicles; then encourages people to upgrade to larger cylinders Drivers who are having difficulty enough steering simpler saloons.

See: Excessive Mileage; Generated Traffic; Traffic Jams

CAR PARKS
%%% @@@@@

Were a Collision consultant attempting to manufacture a Collision opportunity, [s]he would definitely devise a Car Park. Car Parks are happy hunting-grounds for scratching, scraping, denting, smashing into other vehicles - rarely requiring the leaving of a note. Also the temptation to reverse towards, or over, unwary Pedestrians.

These hazards witnessed nowhere more than in tight, timed, Car Parks - worse if these Car Parks are *unfamiliar* - where chance is Drivers & Pedestrians alike have something else on their minds. Additionally, shopping has to be put in boots, trolleys returned to trolley-bays, snow cleared from roofs. It's not as if Car Parks are *well-lit*. The atmosphere feels hostile.

Not mentioned yet is the uneasy *legal* status of the Car Park. No owner of a venue or superstore or workplace wants to cover loss or damage arising through parking. Nor will any provider, these days, wish to provide *wide* spaces. Conversely, their narrower spaces take no account of more numerous supersized or 4-wheel-drive vehicles.

Technically, good road manners on the Highway should transfer to the Car Park. But the classic outcome in the event of Collision is 50/50. Everybody, without exception, gets out and says: "You came from nowhere; I just didn't see you." And what of the Driver parking in the face of a different hazard : too late for a conference, a rendezvous, or for catching a train.

See : Impatience; Tight Deadline; Reversing, Road Rage, etc.

CARELESS PEDESTRIANS [RECKLESS PEDESTRIANS]
%%%%% @@@@

Again allowing for Pedestrians *always* being the weaker party of the Highway, there is a reasonable expectation Pedestrians - like on-coming Drivers - will exercise degrees of caution. Ideally, Pedestrians should not jay-walk or play chicken, nor step in front of distant vehicles - nor, at worst, lie down in the road. There will always be a difference between most Pedestrians *unexpected* Pedestrians & most the rashest of *careless* or *reckless* Pedestrians.

See: Loss of Concentration; Speed; Pedestrian from Nowhere

CARELESS DRIVING
%%%%   @@@@

Careless Driving is a label rather carelessly applied. It can even pertain to Manslaughter ["Causing Death by Careless Driving"]: behaviour or behaviours the man in the street would have no hesitation calling *dangerous* - or *reckless* - driving. Yet Police & prosecutors alike prefer to plea-swop until they discover the lowest-tariff offence that will clear the Courts.

In fairness, the formal charge of *Careless* Driving sometimes follows minor distraction: changing a CD, calming an unruly child, or reaching on to the back seat for a humbug.

See: Distractions; Dangerous Driving; Lenient Sentences

CHICKEN … Playing Chicken, or the Dare
%%%% @

Playing Chicken takes many forms : wheelies, taking a pillion on a pedal-cycle, lifting the front-wheel of a motorcycle for 50 or 60 yards, negotiating the full circle of a roundabout at 45mph, lying on top of a white van's luggage-rack- or simply running in between moving lanes of traffic. Responding to the challenge of a dare: pleasing?   delighting?- one's mates. Boasting achievement. *The idea* is to scare passing Motorists, Bus-Drivers & passers-by more than self. *Until denouement*.

See: Boy Racers; Pedestrians from Nowhere; Bollards

CHILD SEAT [& CHILD-SEATBELT MALFUNCTION]
%%%% @

Custom-built child seats strapped within cars & vans are a wonderful invention. So are special seat-belts or booster-cushions for under 15-year olds. The only difficulty is: these must all be fitted - & adjusted - extremely accurately & knowledgeably.

And so much goes wrong. Here are just a few of the hazards: absence of special seat for that particular journey / or vehicle ; makeshift car-seats; loose Moses'-baskets; child seated wrong-way round; insecure anchorage; tampering; loose grip; car-seats fitted too hurriedly; child *enthroned* too hurriedly; child well-versed in undoing his or her car-seat; seats second-hand; worn out seats... child car-seats by their very existence making the Driver drive faster or more recklessly than advisable.

See: Children in Cars; Commuting; School Drop-Off

CHILDREN AT PLAY
%%% @

We Road-Users may hardly ever meet Children at Play - because their parents or guardians have told them not to. Instead, children are strictly reined in or deposited in their [safer?] bedrooms. Nevertheless: in less-privileged areas of a Town or City - or during Weekends & School Hols - Children at Play will be in far greater evidence. Most have no gardens to play in: so they come out onto the street. Fine in the 1950s-but there is now 5 times the volume of passing traffic as 70 years ago. And by definition, Children at Play are not terribly attentive to passing vehicles seeking a short-cut or rat-run.

See: Rat-Run; School Run; Commuting; Pedestrian from Nowhere

CHILDREN CONGREGATING
%%%% @@@

Especially in conurbations; & especially near blocks of flats; especially along the route of suburban rat-runs: children and teenagers will be socializing with each other. Hence the high number of "incidental" Pedestrian injuries & deaths before school, after school and in twilight. Car manufacturers advertize child survival rates if a saloon car hits a child or teenager at 20, 30, 40 or 50mph. [See Part II of this Encyclopaedia]. Cinemas, sports' fixtures & pop festivals are particular draws for excitable [?] older children congregating.

See: Rat- Runs; Access Only; Reversing; Parked Cars; Festivals; Loss of Concentration; Pedestrians from Nowhere.

CHOPPER BIKES
%%%% @

Raleigh's 1969 ramped-up production of Chopper Bikes doubled overnight the number of child Riders presenting themselves at A&E. Choppers were less stable and trickier to ride than conventional boneshakers - with far more wobbles. Parts of the problem were the slower & heavier frame; the positioning of the gear-lever; the width of the rubber tyres; also a distorted centre of gravity. Modern-day transport should not be a fashion accessory.

31

See: Cycle Safety; Hidden Cycles; Young Riders; Children at Play; Unseating

CLIPPING THE PAVEMENT
%%% @

Clipping the pavement either starts a Collision - or results from a Collision. Or maybe that clipping happens when or where there is poor parking technique. The danger here is more to Pedestrians & to other Road-Users than to the vehicle itself or unoccupied vehicles parked nearby. *Pavements* - like bollards - are quite a foe for Drivers & Cyclists: not something to quarrel with; unhappily not a foe for Lorry-Drivers who hardly feel the bump - *or ascertain the risk.*

See: Careless Driving; Kerbside Parking; Speed; Lack of Concentration; Pedestrian from Nowhere

CLEARANCE TO THE LEFT
%%% @@@

Knowing how much clearance to give a Horse or a Cyclist or a Pedestrian - even a parked vehicle - on the UK Left is often learnt only over time. But experienced Cyclists and Equestrians nearly always report *far too little* Clearance is given. That's because on a normal single-carriageway road most Drivers hope road space will not run out in the face of an oncoming car or white van. The truth is: space *does* run out, principally to the repeat disadvantage of he or she who was given woefully tight Clearance. Worse, Right-hand Drivers have pitifully poor visibility on their nearside.

See : Overtaking; Seeing Oncoming Vehicles; Pedal-Cyclists; Pedestrian from Nowhere

COACHES & COACH-DRIVERS
% @@@

Surprisingly, Road Hazard surrounding Long-Distance or Privately-Hired Coaches is not identical to that attaching to Single- & Double-decker Buses. Coach-Drivers are *always* pressurized by the clock, and tormented by traffic-jams. Additionally, they are highly likely to be as weary as they are wickedly underpaid. Very, very, few Coach-Drivers are awarded according to the degree of their responsibility. They are expected to be doctors, nurses, couriers, guides, arbiters, social workers: everything, as well as Drivers round or through holiday - & Central London - traffic. Nor are their comfort-breaks anywhere near frequent enough in keeping with current legislation.

Three problems *not* publicized enough are the swing a Coach needs to negotiate the tight angles of a Roundabout; the complexity of a Coach-Drivers Sat-Nava; & a very high potential for Driver Boredom.

See: Boredom; Buses & Bus-Drivers; Tachographs; Intercom

COINCIDENCE
%%%% @@@@@

All Collisions on the Public Highway are the result of Coincidence: often a series of Coincidences happening in a gap of between 2 & 10 seconds before impact. Afterwards, all *surviving* participants & onlookers say : "It only! If only!" Yet in Part II, I shall be explaining how Coincidental circles, ebbs, flows & "unforeseen" consequence *can* be interrupted.

See : Loss of Control; Loss of Concentration; & All Other Entries

COMMUTING
%%% @@@@@

Even where a Driver or Rider is not commuting, he or she will encounter Commuters. Commuters not only suffer from tiredness, boredom & over-familiarity; they are also forced to drive against the clock at both the beginning and the end of their shift, meeting or workday. *Additionally*, the Commuter might then face parking difficulty; problems & deficits occurring in the non-driving elements of their work roles; *and* imminent transfer to an employer-owned vehicle. Worse, not a few Commuters have to combine a daily obligation to arrive at or depart their place of employment on time with the stressful School-Run.

See: Boredom; Over-Familiarity; Traffic Jams; the School-Run

COMPETING FOR ROAD SPACE
%%% @@@@@

The umbrella term: "Competing for Road Space" applies to nearly all dangerous events on the Highway. Road space is finite. It cannot be otherwise - except at 2am on a Winter Wednesday morning - and, even then, HGVs will be heading to or from Felixstowe & Holyhead.

When we do compete for road space, we swop lanes, or growl, or become impatient, or overtake on the nearside, or push in, or jump lights. As Drivers & Riders, we become chancers, gamblers. We hardly stop to weigh up what would happen if *we* obtained that precious time advantage - rather than a rival vehicle. Will we get away with it? Perhaps not?

See : Overtaking; Undertaking; Impatience; Road Rage

CONVOY   [Driving in Convoy]

%%   @

Fixed Convoys with Highways' Agency pilots are very *safe*. *Unsafe* is the habit / yearning to stick together; to drive in Convoy over a fairly unfamiliar route towards a shared destination. Fine until the Convoy is held up, out-of-sight, interrupted. Convoys never appear more visible - also stately - than those following a Hearse to the Crematorium: in which case it is very bad manners to split that Convoy in two!

See: Unfamiliarity; Queues; Time Limits; Overtaking

COURIER-DRIVERS COMMENTATING

%%   @

Certain Coach-Drivers taking Passengers on holiday have the *additional* task of providing a running-commentary for those Passengers: whether that be local history, beauty-spots, highlights, refreshment stops. All this through a microphone. Better by far to have that role given to the Co-Driver - because the imparting of information is bound to adversely impact on a Coach or a Minibus Driver's Roadcraft.

See: Distractions; Loss of Concentration; Coach Travel

CRASH-for-CASH

%%%   @

Despite, or because, of its comparative rarity, Crash-for-Cash succeeds by *imitating* ordinary with-fault Collision. Only it just happens it is always the selected Driver's fault, not the criminal's! Perpetrator(s) often own a 9-year old hatchback that has seen better days. And, handily, there are always impartial "Witnesses" in the lead vehicle. It only remains for that lead vehicle to slam its brakes on - maybe in the midst of a Roundabout - then berate the following Driver for colliding. Worse, the following Driver has possibly been specially chosen by age, gender, or hoped-for apology. The criminal's narrative is as indisputably plausible - as is the lifelong "whiplash" subsequently suffered by any or all of the perpetrators. Most Insurers would rather settle than expose the trickster for what he's up to. After all, the fault might in actuality be two-sided?

A little-exposed Sister to Crash-for-Cash is Pedestrian Fraud- where a Pedestrian arranges to be filmed falling on uneven paving-stones or tree-roots showing up above the tarmac. Or tripping on a Pothole. Again, the aim is £000s in Compo. However, such trickery not only denies cash-strapped Councils cash - but also makes them inattentive when there really *is* a danger to Pedestrians, which is often.

See: Dishonest Driving; Leaving a Roundabout; Road Rage

CRAWLING TRAFFIC
%%%   @@@@@

Driving in concert with Crawling Traffic isn't nearly as easy as it sounds. This aspect of Roadcraft demands unlimited patience and understanding. Two main approaches are possible: to gently accelerate in the hope that modest acceleration will always be just enough - but not too much - to maintain the flow; *or* to go a little further each 30 seconds, then brake. Good brake-lights in slow-moving traffic are an essential safeguard: the more the better. Also no distractions or misting-up within the saloon or cab. Even smoking or inserting a CD amidst the Crawl is hazardous. Watch out too for the U-turns of Drivers further along; also for hidden Pedestrians mistakenly thinking the Crawl is stationary.

See: Patience; Just-in-Time; Commuting ; Hill-Starts; Distractions; Sudden Braking; Pedestrian from Nowhere

CRITICIZNG THE DRIVER
%%%% @@

Whenever & wherever a Driver is criticized there is likely to be trouble: trouble born of injured feelings or perceived insult. Therefore, even in the event of that Criticism being justified - which it often is; even in the event of that Criticism being from a dearly loved one - which again it often is; even where the Driver him- or herself is on the point of criticizing their own performance, Criticism from any other quarter is inconvenient, unconventional, unexpected- & distinctly *un*welcome.

Criticism - if at all - most frequently emanates from the front-seat Passenger / or Navigator. Worse, that Criticism might come from *the back-seat* - Heaven Forbid *from a child*! And even worse, where Criticism arises - however mute or unintentional or oblique that comment - from another Road-User or a passing Pedestrian, the result is frequently an episode of Road Rage. *Crucially*, the Driver's scarcely suppressed anger lasts for hours *after* the Criticism, making both Roadcraft & speed that bit more erratic.

See: Anger; School Run; Road Rage; Back Seat Riding ; Loss of Concentration; Pedestrian from Nowhere

CROSS-OVERS
%%%%% @

Vehicles crossing over from an opposite carriageway have always proved hazardous beyond description. Yet all Motorways & dual-carriageways were originally constructed without barriers. Only when consequent deaths & injuries reached unacceptable levels did barriers appear. And even then, nobody could determine which barriers became part of the problem rather than part of the solution.

Dark rumours circulated, many authenticated, that the Ministry of Transport had to have a specific number of deaths & injuries before they would erect any barrier.

Yet Cross-Overs are occasionally *demanded* by the Highways' Agency: where all other options to keep traffic moving have been exhausted. There is another hazard rarely talked about: the Cross-Over of cargo or spare tyre where the entire oncoming vehicle actually stays on course. Pretend that oncoming load is a loosened Mobile Home and cargo Cross-Over becomes sheer calamity.

See: Unsafe Loads; Motorways; Swerving; Head-On Collision

CROSSROADS WITHOUT TRAFFIC LIGHTS
%%% @@@

Thousands of roads not of Motorway standard have Crossroads - sometimes five or six on a 2-mile stretch. Admittedly, these Crossroads are often well-signed, and signed *well-ahead* - but costs forbid each & every Crossroads - even on a Trunk Road - being Light-controlled. Lights aren't the answer to everything: but Collisions await Crossroads as much as Crossroads await Collisions. And very many speeding vehicles overtake just where a Crossroad lies ahead.

See: Remote Crossroads; Speed; Overtaking; Unfamiliar Route

CRASH HELMETS OFFERING LITTLE OR NO PROTECTION
%%%% @@

Crash Helmets are a wonderful accessory for Motorcyclists: so good that, on pure logic, all Car Occupants should always wear them in order to minimize brain injury in the event of Crash!

Nonetheless all Crash Helmets ought to be really carefully chosen & maintained: brand new for that Rider; no stickers; no past scuffing or deterioration; a visor both providing and enhancing visibility; expensive. Should a Motorcyclist be unseated for any reason, the Crash Helmet takes a terrible bash.

See : Motorcycles; Cycle Helmets; Impaired Visibility; Unseating

CUL DE SACS
%% @@

Cul de Sacs throw up all sorts of hazard not present on through roads. Parking is very limited: leading to hostile competition for available spaces; moreover all those vehicles have got to turn round somehow. Which is difficult without a dedicated turning-circle - or where that turning-circle is itself occupied by parked vehicles.

See: U-turns; Pedestrians from Nowhere; Parking; Competition for Road Space

CURTAINED LORRIES
% @@

Curtained Lorries [or Trailers] are built that way to allow forklift trucks free access for loading & unloading. Many Curtained Lorries are easily robbed of that load in the middle of the night - but real danger to *other* Road Users arises from a Wind-Tunnel. In a gale, that makes the Curtained Lorry flip over, especially upon high or long bridges and flyovers.

See: Lorry Safety; Wind Tunnels; Slipstreams; Dishonesty

CUTTING CORNERS
%% @@@

Drivers cut corners in order to avoid changing down gear; wishing to maintain uniform speed; or aiming to enter a side-road at a more convenient 45°-angle instead of the recommended 90°. Cutting corners is especially hazardous where the road ahead appears to be hairpin bend after hairpin bend or where an emerging vehicle does not expect it.

See: Unpredictable Driver Behaviour; Speed; Impatience; Pedestrians from Nowhere

CYCLE HELMETS OFFERING LITTLE OR NO PROTECTION
%%%% @@

As with Motorcycle Crash Helmets, Cycle Helmets *should* be worn - although that is not the law - and must be of the latest, perhaps most expensive, construction. Cyclists stand almost 100% chance of being unseated at some time in their riding careers - often more than half a dozen times.

See: Crash Helmets; Cycle Wobble; Chopper Bikes; Unseating

CYCLES IN TRANSIT

%   @

Hardly any Cyclist is aware of the correct fitting & fixture for a Pedal Cycle in Transit - where a van or SUV cannot accommodate it inside or on a trailer. The correct - & safest - positioning is on a specially-purchased roof-rack - with each Cycle facing the same way as the car or van. As it is, Cycles stick out either side of a vehicle boot and obscure both the number plate *and* rear vision. The *haste* of their strapping down could lead to problems further down the road.

See: Roof Racks; Cycles; Wide Loads; Unsafe Loads

CYCLE WOBBLE

%%%% @@@

Wobbling Pedal-Cycles are presently a far greater problem than wobbling Motorcycles. That is because Pedal-bikes have little weight, also a different centre of gravity.

Cycle wobble is caused by wind; by wind-tunnel; by poorly reinstated roadworks; by active roadworks; by potholes; by black ice; by sludge; by tram-tracks; or simply by the need to decelerate quickly in the face of hazard or traffic standstill.

It is absolutely essential Cars & Lorries look out for - more important, *allow for* - Cycle Wobble. Wobble could happen at a single second's notice, resulting in almost instant unseating.

See: Potholes; Tram Tracks; Slipstream; Cycle Helmets; Chopper-Bikes; Unseating

DANGEROUS CARGO
%%%% @

Most Tankers delivering hazardous substances have a sticky label on them to indicate what's inside the tank. Petrol Station lorries are by definition hazardous. But so are open skips, unsecured heavy machinery, pipes and brickettes of nuclear waste. In the event of Collision on the highway, dangerous cargo becomes twice. thrice, as dangerous.

See: Motorways; Lorry Safety; Unsecured Loads

DANGEROUS DRIVING
%%%%% @@

For Police to label someone's driving Dangerous, it has to have been *really bad*: overtaking on a blind bend, overtaking on an upward hill, jumping lights on red, driving under the influence of drink or drugs, or mounting pavements. And no end are the Collisions resulting from Dangerous Driving. Occasionally, the Crown Court hands down a really long prison sentence for Dangerous Driving - but more often there is leniency.

See: Manslaughter; Overtaking; Careless Driving; Drink-Driving; Driving while Disqualified... etc.

DARES & DARING
%%%% @

Daring might come from an onlooker, a kerbside friend, a work colleague - or -most commonly - a front- or back-seat Passenger. The Dare could be to sit two-to-a-saddle, to dodge between lanes of moving traffic, to get to a destination double-quick, to escape Police pursuit - or simply to drink one more pint, one more measure of gin or spirit before going home. Dares can mean tragedy: all round…. *& do on next time*.

See: Chicken; Police Pursuit, Speeding, New Drivers…

DARK CLOTHING
%%% @@@

If a Cyclist, Jogger or Pedestrian is wearing dark clothing - especially accompanied by twilight, nightfall, recent rainfall or sodium lighting - he or she is much more difficult for an on-coming Driver to spot. White or hi-visibility clothing provides greater protection. One trouble here is that the endangered other Road-User - usually a Pedestrian merging with the drizzle and the tarmacadam - is completely oblivious to the hazard.

See: Twilight; Grimy Windscreens; Pedestrian from Nowhere

DAZZLE
%%% @@@@@

Dazzle arises from conditions not all meteorological. Dazzle *could* come from a tractor or road-repair vehicle being lit *too well*. Or Dazzle might result from the neon lighting of passing shops or hoardings. Equally, Dazzle might come from one's own spectacles; from one's own interior cabin light; from piercing sunshine bouncing off recent heavy shower; or, wantonly, from some child on a Motorway bridge directing a laser towards each approaching Driver.

By no means uncommon, September, December, February of May Dazzle happens when strong sunlight is lower in the sky

than one's visor. Or where another Driver carelessly leaves fog-lamp or full-beam on unnecessarily. A more recent hazard is the newer pair of headlights dipped, but appearing full-beam. This occurs where a vehicle manufacturer has fitted as
See: Weather; Fog-Lights; Rainfall; Grimy Windscreen

DEBRIS IN THE CARRIAGEWAY
%%% @

Whether it is bricks, planks, cardboard, uneaten fast food - or somebody's house clearance: debris in the carriageway - particularly if that is also *a Motorway* - causes problems of swerving as well as necessary running over of the object or objects. Maybe it's a load of nails; maybe broken glass; assorted rubble damaging the tyres simply by its irregularity. Or boxes that might be empty or full. Debris means sudden decision and an instant alteration of driver-behaviour. Worst if this is a dead human or animal body run over by a previous driver. An absolute nightmare. Therein is the clue: a desire to skirt the obstruction without, by swerving, causing other Drivers who have not necessarily seen the debris to swerve...
See: Motorway driving; Swerving; Lane swop

DEFECTIVE VISION
%%%% @@

Defective Vision is a phenomenon different from *obscured* Vision. The term "defective" applies to Drivers - Drivers over 65 in particular - whose eyesight is failing with their not having informed family, GP, DVLA less so: in case they have to stop driving. A slightly different category is the Driver driving Igloo or a Driver driving whilst weeping.

Not apocryphal is the Driver who assured his nervous Passenger: "I've been diagnosed with Sight Loss, but when I see something dark on the Left, I move to the Right;" & when I see something dark on the Right, I move to the Left."

27% of all Drivers have Defective Vision: the majority of this population dreading driving at night, dusk or dawn. Few, if any, *doubt* the standard & efficacy of their full-daylight driving: hence those Collisions where "I just didn't see..."

See: Unclear Visibility; Grimy Windscreen; Elderly Drivers; Reversing; Pedestrian from Nowhere

DISHONEST DRIVING
%%% @@

Dishonest Driving covers a multitude of sins: a multitude of categories of risk to other Road-Users. A short summary of dishonesty affecting Roadcraft follows : Drunk Driving, Drug Driving, tampering with the Tachograph; going to commit a crime; coming away from committing a crime; using the vehicle itself to achieve robbery or injury; ram-raiding; carrying stolen goods; carrying contraband goods; carrying illegal immigrants or asylum-seekers; saying there was sun on the windscreen when there was not; saying the Driver sneezed when he or she didn't; saying the Passenger is ill when he or she wasn't; overloading a van or lorry; pretending to be coming back from a deeply-upsetting Granny Funeral; driving an unlicensed Taxi; driving while disqualified; driving with impaired vision; driving while telephoning using a handset; texting at the wheel; driving against doctor's instruction; driving a company-car for unauthorized private business; driving after being anaesthetized; hit-&-run; leaving the scene of a Collision prematurely; stopping another Road-User for no reason except to upset that Driver, rob him or her, alarm him or her or assault him or her; driving to deal in illegal drugs; driving to collect debt by intimidation; stealing a cycle or a vehicle; driving knowing oneself to be exhausted; abducting a child; enticing a child or estranged wife or girlfriend into a moving vehicle in order to torch them or drive them over a cliff; driving a mother or father or friend's vehicle claiming to be occasional Driver where one is the actual owner; & crash-for-cash. And that list is only half of what could be called profoundly *Dishonest* Driving.

Yet dishonesty is not enough to obtain a conviction - because dishonesty might be in the mind only. Onlookers, judges, Innocent Passengers, Traffic Police, Insurers, whoever, must establish that Dishonesty increased the chance of Collision - or led to a Collision or a near-miss.

The answer to this escapism is that motoring skill is *always* likely to be impaired by implicit or explicit Dishonesty. A vehicle or powerful motorcycle is as bad as a gun - or worse. Yet there is no threshold of either motive or competency for taking to the Public Highway.

Therefore, as sure as night follows day, there will be far more Collisions when the Driver is evading something or someone; far more Collisions when a Driver or Rider couldn't care less; far more Collisions enticing the Police into a chase; or far more Collisions where Collision is intentional, to order: part of the exercise, integral to the excursion.

See: Anger; Impatience; Road Rage; Crash-for-Cash; Driving while Disqualified; Police Chase... & nearly every other entry in this Section

DISTRACTIONS
%%%% @@@@@

No Driver or alternative Road-User can afford to be distracted. Yet foreseeable Distractions are too numerous to list: chief among these being screaming children; bystanders waving; loud music; telephones; the smoking of cigarettes; eating at the wheel; changing radio station; Sat-Navs, & roadside advertisements. To name but a few...

See: each & every entry relating to impaired concentration

DOG-WALKERS
%%% @@@

It's not at all clear whether a car is more scared of encountering a Dog-Walker - or a Dog-Walker more terrified of encountering that car. Dog-Walkers often need to walk their canines twice a day, not once - so either session might be conducted in darkness, depending on the time of year. Motorists should always be prepared for Dog-Walkers, on either side of the road ahead. Yet Dog-Walkers - especially those without Hi-visibility jackets - usually come as a surprise. Hence injury or death: the more so when a Driver coming up from behind does not allow clearance on the Nearside.

See: Animals on the road; Pedestrians from Nowhere; Loss of Concentration; Clearance; Swerving; Sudden Braking; Speed

DOUBLE-PARKING
%%   @@@@

Double-Parking is a menace: usually the product of houses, especially terraces, having been built decades before car ownership was ever conceived: let alone such a preserve forming a widespread ambition. Double-Parking on either or both sides of the road undoubtedly impedes emergency vehicles. It is also very threatening to the local resident who craves to be able to look out from their front windows & see their personal vehicle somewhere or other; alternatively in a pretty environment *to see no vehicle at all*. And because Double-parking invariably causes *dispute*: the practice of such inconsiderate parking sets everybody off on a wrong note at the beginning - or end - of journeys already hazardous.

See: Impatience; Pedestrians from Nowhere; *Cul-de-Sacs*; Kerbside Parking; Pavement Parking; Emergency Vehicles

DRINK-DRIVING

%%%%% @@

Drink-Driving is a huge subject fully deserving of a book all of its own. As such an outstanding danger, Drink-Driving - directly responsible for 9000 deaths & serious injuries on the Highway each twelvemonth - has already attracted *50 years or more* of controversy, re-visiting social disgrace, ruined careers, frightening near-misses, lots of special pleading.

Ever since Transport Minister Barbara Castle brought in her upper limit of 80mg-of alcohol to-every 100 millilitres of blood [the limit in Scotland later reduced at 50mg/100ml.] Drivers and voters alike have either thought these numbers realistically plucked from nowhere far too high or far too low as as an acceptable or negotiable threshold.

The truth is: *any upper limit* is artificial, therefore probably too generous. A meaner, but electorally suicidal, alternative would be no alcohol to be drunk where driving is to take place less than 16 hours hence. Of significance, whenever Bus-Drivers are tested on private airfields, their speed of reaction; their ability to avoid bollards or red lines; *their finesse*; is altered for the worse by even 100ml of wine, or one glass of low-strength cider. And only an outsider can see that danger.

Sadly, lessons are *unlearnt* as well as learnt. It's difficult to opt out of a Party: easy to convince oneself one will get home without incident at the end of the day, end of shift, or end of celebration. Even *sensible* employees, husbands, daughters are tempted to have a drink - just one - before returning to the wheel of a car. And with awful consequences. Our image of the

Drunk-Driver is one totally incapacitated, struggling to get into whatever seat he or needs to get into or onto, staggering along, at the same time spewing up all over. The reality is different: a smartly-dressed business leader returning from a successful sales' conference; the President of the Golf Club; a Teacher at the end of term; a Dentist rather than Publican.

See: Drinking at the Wheel; Drug-Driving; Lack of Concentration; Driving while Disqualified; Police Chase; Pedestrian from Nowhere

DRIVING ON THE WRONG SIDE OF THE ROAD
%%%%% @

Driving on the Wrong Side of the Road is most calamitous - & most common - among British Drivers going overseas or overseas' Drivers coming to Britain. Research indicates that a single night's sleep, a single ferry journey, a single coffee-stop, *a single lapse of concentration*, can push a vehicle onto the Wrong Side: maybe for miles on end.

But overtaking, speed, swerving, ignoring One-Way street signs- even avoiding a cat! - can push a Driver or Rider onto the wrong side of the carriageway. Hence head-on Collisions.

See: Overtaking; Foreign Drivers; One-Way Streets; Crossovers; Unfamiliarity

DRINKING AT THE WHEEL
%% @@

Just as with eating and smoking at the wheel, so drinking at the wheel or handlebar is hideously dangerous: not that it's *alcohol* being drunk at the wheel on each & every occasion -

though some alcohol *is* drunk in transit. By adding up the number of Collisions: a bigger problem than *consumption* of bottles of water & tins of cola is *reaching* for them, unscrewing or uncapping them, then tipping them up without spillage or interference with a whole myriad of controls.

See: Eating at the Wheel; Smoking; Distractions; Loss of Concentration; Swerving

DRIVING ABROAD
%%% @@

Driving Overseas presents so many new challenges: unfamiliar rules of the road, unfamiliar hazard warnings, unfamiliar routes, unfamiliar speed limits, unfamiliar road-signs, whatever. There are also hairpin beds, roads not gritted or salted - and local Drivers & Riders seemingly beyond reproach or prosecution. That's all without the added responsibility of towing a Caravan or camping-trailer!

See: Speeding; Unfamiliarity; Wrong Side of the Road

DRIVING WHILE DISQUALIFIED
%%% @

Driving While Disqualified is automatically illegal - but it happens. And it isn't very easy to spot just by number-plate recognition. These Disqualified Drivers may well have been speeding or driving under the influence of drugs or alcohol in the recent past - so are very unlikely to be insured *or* to care about any other Road-User [nothing to lose?]. Hence more Collisions, worse during a Police Chase.

See: Police Chase; Dishonest Driving; Crash-for-Cash

DRUNK PEDESTRIANS
%%% @@

Beware Friday & Saturday Party Nights, Christmas, New Year. Currently, there are no breath-tests for living Pedestrians, just the offence of being Drunk & *Disorderly*.

See: Speeding; Drink-Driving; Pedestrian from Nowhere

DYKES & DITCHES
%%%% @@

Roadside Dykes & Ditches are *always* a danger, even where there is a Hard Shoulder in between. A car or motorcycle can easily be undiscovered for a full week in a hidden Ditch or Coppice. Furthermore the vehicle or machine can flip over, falling on top of those trapped or unseated beneath. No barrier can surround *every single* Dyke or Ditch in the land. And beware Counties like Lincolnshire, Norfolk, East Kent: where Dykes are a commoner being a more necessitous means of draining the land.

See: Motorcycles; Speed; Unseated; Swerving; Skidding

EATING AT THE WHEEL
%%% @@

Eating at the Wheel of a car or lorry is not by itself against the law - although the practice might be discouraged or banned by one's employer. Also Police might reasonably charge the nibbling, gorging Driver with either driving-without-due-care-&-attention or Careless Driving. *Eating* actually needs a lot of skills: choosing the food, opening its often-hard or heat-sealed wrappings, dividing it, conveying it to the mouth without spillage, then digesting it and disposing of the grease. A procedure probably best not attempted in the first place. Nevertheless, several Mums, reps, deliverers and commercial travelers are so tight for time they'll be tempted to have a meal behind the wheel: particularly during a long traffic-jam or whilst waiting till road works can be passed on green.

Drive-Through [drive-thru'] Restaurants should possibly be banned - as if any facility endorses and encourages Eating at the Wheel, worse in darkness, it is this misguided option.

See: Smoking at the Wheel; Fast-Food Delivery; Distractions; Loss of Concentration

ELDERLY DRIVERS
%% @@@@

Although many elderly drivers are statistically safer on the Highway than 18-37 year-old drivers or riders, when an elderly or centenarian driver is involved in Collision, the scene is likely to be more chaotic. Additionally, elderly drivers are far more likely to collapse at the wheel or depress the wrong foot-pedal than drivers under the age of 65. Of interest, Collisions caused by - or not averted by - Elderly Drivers do not automatically diminish in automatic saloons.

See: Young Drivers; Illness at the Wheel; Driving while Disqualified; Defective Vision

EMPTY LORRIES
%   @@

Empty Lorries are, by definition, in a hurry because they are not full. Their Drivers have free rein to drive a little less cautiously than when the Trailer or Box they towed was heavily loaded. That makes Empty Lorries difficult to overtake. Also by their being empty for hundreds of miles, they are failing to do what another Lorry Driver somewhere else is bound despite expense and expedience to do : to take a load in the opposite direction that could have been taken by Lorry Number One. That makes roads more cluttered and, indirectly, leads to more Collisions.

See: HGVs; Swerving; Time Pressures; Wind Tunnels

EXCEEDING THE STATED WEIGHT-LIMIT
%%%%   @@@

Lots of Lorries & Trailers & white vans exceed their Stated Weight-Limit. They do this mostly hidden, non-disclosed. Such Drivers & Agencies hope there will be no Local Authority Weighbridge; no burst tyre; no shedding of the load; no random Police checks. So it is rogue Drivers wish only that they'll merge effortlessly and indistinguishably with correctly-laden Vehicles.

Yet the consequences of overload are as fearful as they are fatal: more fatal when that overload is insecure - as it frequently is. No Tractor & Trailer with 6 axles should exceed a cargo of 44,000 kg. Where weights are higher, braking is far less assured; nor can the juggernaut keep to its chosen path.

The entire vehicle changes its integrity. Quite apart from not making it up any hills.

See: HGV Crashes; One Way Streets; Agency Drivers; Tachographs

EXITING A TOLL-BOOTH
%%   @

Toll Booths positioned at the beginning or the end of a Bridge throw up lots of challenges, not least finding the right money in time! Then, immediately after paying, Drivers are instructed to condense down from up to 8 separate lanes of traffic at up to 8 booths to a single, at most double, line of traffic going forward. Hence all those blind-spots & the side-swipes.

See: Swerving; Loss of Concentration; Blind-Spots; Side-swipes.

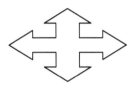

ELECTRIC BIKES [*Rear-Wheel Electrically-Assisted Cycles*]
%% @@

Electric Bikes first became common in the 1950s & 1960s when car ownership was lower than nowadays. Then from the 1990s forward, they had a revival on hills & mountains. Finally, more *ordinary* Cyclists chose Electric Bikes as their commute/ leisure outing of choice. They are legal - but subject to all the dangers of clearance & blind-spots common to unassisted Bicycles.

See Cycles, Clearance, Blind Spot, etc.

EMERGENCY VEHICLES
%%% @@@@

It is ironic that the very Emergency Vehicles that keep the Public safe - from burglary, theft, fire, injury, falling masonry, snow, whatever - also have potential to harm the Public through negligence or coincidence. Not uncommon is unpreparedness, also inability or refusal to give way to said Emergency Vehicles.

See: Overtaking; Pursuit; Speeding; Jumping Lights; Double Parking

END-OF-MATCH
%%% @

When a football match ends at exactly 16-49 on a Saturday or Sunday, 20-49 on a Monday night, hundreds & thousands of fans spill out of the Stadium at exactly the same moment: crowding the Pavements, also the actual roads leading to that Stadium. Similar phenomena occur at the sudden end of a Cricket or Snooker match or day at the Races. Here is potential for all sorts of Collision

See: Impatience; Congested Traffic; Pedestrians from Nowhere

END-OF-SHIFT, END-OF-WORKING DAY
%% @@

Whenever & wherever several hundred workers are discharged from a factory or warehouse at exactly the same moment, there will be a much greater chance of Collision, particularly impacting upon Pedestrians rushing home [for a few months in the dark?] - or workers looking for their lifts or aiming to retrieve their cars & pedal-cycles.

See: Heavy Traffic, Traffic Jams, Pedestrians from Nowhere

FAILING TO SIGNAL INTENT OR INTENTION
%%%   @@@@

Many Drivers think they'll be sent an electricity bill for using their Left or Right indicators. Yet in almost every instance of this restraint, this cussedness, other Riders, Drivers or Pedestrians cannot read the intent or intention of he or she unwilling to signal. So the Pedestrian might cross an exit road unaware of fast-approaching traffic; or a Motorcyclist might find his or her exit from a Roundabout blocked; or a Driver in the "wrong" lane of an unfamiliar road might not be able to obtain the "right" lane. In one very real sense, greater use of stricter road-positioning or sounding the hooter would help.

See: Lane Discipline; Speeding; Roundabouts; Competition

FAST-FOOD DELIVERY
%%% @@@

Fast Foods and motoring are an unhappy combination. At its simplest, Drivers drive miles till they see the Fast-Food joint they most wish to patronize. They then have to find an awkward parking-lot, or join the dreaded Drive-Thru' alternative. This Drive-Thru presupposes that first, the Driver is going to remain unfed ; second, that the Driver paying through the window can get all the way home before said fast-food loses its flavor, its heat - or both.

Bigger problems arise when those Motorists and Moped-Riders, also Cyclists, retained by Fast-Food joints deliver pizzas and pies to people's doors. These Couriers are in a hurry: impatient, ill-directed - their destination obscure - and very poorly paid. Worse, recipients tend to be ungrateful. That leads to double-parking and the forsaking of good road-manners.

See: Deliverers Delivering; Time Limits; Distractions; Eating at the Wheel; Impatience; Double-parking

ELECTRIC SCOOTERS [*for some time "banned" in Britain*]
%% @

Unlike abroad, Electric Scooters are a relatively rare sight in Great Britain: partly because obstacles surrounding licensing & insurance. But they are being trialed in certain Cities. As with Mobility Scooters, the biggest hazard is speed-without-control.

See: Mobility Scooters; Segways; Quad-Bikes; Youth

FERRIES [including CAR FERRIES]
%%   @

The time pressures - and sheer unfamiliarity - of travelling by Car Ferry overwhelms the Driver or Rider who does not know the rules: of which there are many. As well as parking promptly & properly, the vehicle owner / or Rider has to be brisk re-joining their means of carriage; also very familiar with ramps! Moreover a large proportion of Drivers & Riders must then negotiate a foreign country where not only the rules & regulations will be different, but also, most often, traffic will proceed on the wrong side of the road. Very many Collisions occur on the vessel or driving to or from the Ferry-Port.

See: Time Pressures; Wrong Side of the Road; Foreign Drivers; Driving Abroad

FAILED M.O.Ts
%%% @

Where Drivers continue to drive a vehicle that has either failed its M.O.T. or would fail its M.O.T., they become in charge of a slow-tapering bomb about to hurt very many innocent people as well as themselves. The fact that an M.O.T. isn't due quite yet - or, paradoxically, where the defective car or white van has recently *passed* its M.O.T. - does not excuse either the vehicle's owner or hirer or steward. Ideally, *no* vehicle with developing faults should ever leave its garage or car park till remedial action has been taken.

See: Brake Failure; Wipers not Working; Second-hand Vehicles; Lights not Working

FALLEN PEDESTRIAN
%%%% @

Where a Pedestrian falls unrelated to any Collision: the chance is magnified 10-fold that the Pedestrian will *then* be run over. Causes of Pedestrian Falls are pavement fighting; Pavement scuffles; running for the Bus; running out of the way of bullies; suicide; drunkenness; swoon - or high-heels. Even driven at 10 to 15 miles per hour, moving vehicles can very rarely stop in time where a Pedestrian has fallen. Braking takes too long to bring about a stop ahead of the body in the road.

See: Pedestrian from Nowhere; Impatience; Loss of Concentration; Drunken Pedestrian

FALLING TREES
%%%% @

The devastation caused by trees falling suddenly on a car or carriageway is arguably one of the most unpredictable events in a travelling environment where far too many events are incorrectly called:"Acts of God." The best one can hope for is few seconds of notice.

See: The Weather; Wind; Debris on the Highway

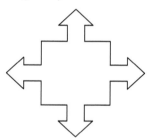

FIRE
%%%%% @

Fire engulfing cars, lorries & buses is most to be feared: not least because of petrol & other fuels on board, making even parked cars on fire a danger both to passing Pedestrians & Drivers rubbernecking. And sometimes vehicles do not carry an extinguishers - or warning triangles. Worse, certain vehicle manufacturers know their output is more susceptible to spontaneous Fire. Yet complaining owners are never told of other fires engulfing that particular model. Lastly, Fire is a well-documented component of suicide and murder/suicide.

See: Suicide; Defective Vehicles; Unsafe Loads; Rubber-necking

FLASHING

%%%   @@

Flashing full-beam headlights is almost always inappropriate: even where - perhaps most of all where? - the approaching Driver wishes to tell another Driver or Pedestrian that they can proceed in front, or simply rejoin the queue. Never take a Flash as Gospel! Not infrequently the Flash is used to warn another Driver or Rider that the speed-cops are round and about. *That* alert is as dangerous as it is illegal. Perhaps, most dangerously of all, Flashing is used to *confront* a Driver or Rider in the opposite direction that he or she should not be overtaking into a lane that properly belongs to the flashing Driver/ or Rider. Finally, the Flash is unpleasantly used to create *urgency* for the poor lead-vehicle to proceed much quicker This happens most on Motorways where a Driver ahead is conscientiously attempting to keep to the stated 40,50,60, or 70 mph limit.

Very, very, occasionally, a Flash is *helpful*: for instance to tell an HGV Driver that he or she can safely re-join a slower lane. Otherwise that Driver might be nervous of squashing the Flasher. Or a Flash might uniquely warn on-coming traffic that there has just been a Collision on their side of the road.

See: Speed; Impatience; Overtaking; Road Rage; Lane Discipline; Road works

FIGHTING

%%%   @

Although live Fighting is relatively uncommon, where it happens *inside* a vehicle, there will almost certainly be a Collision. And where it happens on the Pavement: the danger is that passing   Drivers will either rubber-neck or have to swerve to avoid a slumping body. Then there is the risk of Driving whilst in a bad frame of mind following an earlier fight.

See: Road Rage; Arguments; Fallen Pedestrian; Pedestrian from Nowhere; Rubber-necking

FLEETS
%%% @@@

Corporate behaviour is rarely the same as Corporate expectation, less so Corporate *Responsibility*. Some but not all Fleets have *all* their vehicles involved in a Collision averaging once every two or three years. Branded & Fleet drivers are usually driving against the clock or on just-in-time delivery. Worse, not every Branded Driver is directly employed by that Brand! When tiredness or boredom sets in - even on those rare occasions no other hazard of weather, bystander, newcomer, or approaching vehicle presents itself - there is residual risk of Collision. Many Fleets comprise Agency Drivers who might have driven for a competitor very shortly beforehand, or disembarked from a Ferry. No Fleet is exempt from the complacency that besets the Professional Driver.

See: HGVs; Boredom; Tiredness; Agency Driving; Time Limits, Traffic Jams; Loading On

FLIP-OVERS [*including ROLL-OVERS & CAPSIZE*]
%%%%% @

Flip-Overs happen most often, though not exclusively, where a road or railway or river or public footpath lies either beneath, or at an angle to, the carriageway or bridge that is positioned higher. Flip-Overs are universally calamitous; more likely, & with worse consequence: where the Road-User flipping over is a Cyclist, Motorcyclist or High-Sided Vehicle. Britain's worst Flip-Over *ever* was Great Heck, February 28th., 2001 when a vehicle towing a vehicle dropped over a low parapet straight onto not one but two active railway tracks.

Related Capsize is when a high-sided lorry or tricycle or light-weight SUV flips over at the bottom of a hill or slope or slipway- or on an exposed flyover.

See: High-sided Vehicles; Underpasses; Veering Out of Control; Towing; Speeding; Dykes & Ditches; Wind Tunnel; Flyovers

FLOWS OF TRAFFIC FROM ALL DIRECTIONS
%%% @@@@

Busy junctions allowing for four-way moving traffic - occasionally five - even six-way moving traffic - are confusing, therefore hazardous, to say the very least. The bewildered Pedestrian shorn of dedicated space scarcely knows what to make of all these [often unceasing] flows of traffic.

And behind the wheel, unmarked or unanticipated flows are baffling to any Driver from outside the area where such Flows are routine, permitted, indeed encouraged.

Then when one flow stops: there is Fools' Paradise when new flows start without any gap in between. Eventually the Pedestrian *is* allowed a look-in, but far too late to avert preceding danger.

See: Impatience; Pelican Lights; Jumping of Lights; Unseen Road Markings; Roundabouts; Pedestrian from Nowhere

FLYOVERS
%%% @

Flyovers - particularly those steep & elevated Flyovers high in the sky - are especially prone to fog, wind-tunnel, lack of hard-shoulder, speeding and loss of vehicle control. Flyovers are also subject to rubbernecking - because they tend to be built in interesting places. And where 4 or 5 Flyovers all lead into each other, there are so many chances for the inexperienced Driver or Rider to lose his or her way. Hence some very scary Collisions & Flip-Overs on Flyovers

See: Hard Shoulders; Flip-Overs; Veering; Rubbernecking; Confusing Signs; Unfamiliarity; Slipstreams

FOG
%%%% @@

Fog by itself does not "cause" Collision. What causes Collisions is poor *Driver-behaviour*. Truthfully, Fog happens less in the 2000's than most of the 1900's. Whether that is due to Clean-air Acts or some reduction of heavy industry is unclear. But thick Fog *will* still happen, particularly during October, November, December, January & February [the darkest months of the year]. Thus drivers must prepare for it: checking their fog-lights, being ready to crawl, being ready to be the lead-vehicle: so often the lot of the most cautious - not the most incautious - of Drivers! Readiness to abort, curtail, or *slow-down* a journey is essential in Fog. Beware, also, the Fog *inside* a car, not without. Whatever other road hazard or frost or black ice or excavation or incident exists: it will *always* be heightened by Fog, particularly "Fog from nowhere" - eg. a very lively bonfire or firework party. Fog has to be a menace: because the very first dotted matrix signs invented - those which had room only for the word E-N-D - used to say F-O-G.

See: Weather; Unclear Visibility; Fog-lights left on; Speed

FOG LIGHTS LEFT ON
%   @

Fog Lights are *rarely* needed and should never, ever, be used simply because it's dark outside. The real danger of illegally leaving Fog Lights on when there is no Fog, or dispersing Fog, is that Brake Lights will be misunderstood; worse, ignored altogether. Fortunately, the horrible dazzle of unnecessary Fog Lights makes any following Driver protest with a sharp reminder!

See: Fog; Brake Lights; Dazzle; Weather

FOOTBRIDGE OR UNDERPASS UNUSED
%%%%   @@@

Footbridges or Underpasses are constructed in order to hurry up - moreover to make much safer - crossings to a chosen destination. In reality it can look bolder, less cissy, less chicken, to the installation of Footbridge or Underpass altogether and make a dash across the busy Highway: in preference to that safer route. And the side-effect of this daring is an on-coming Driver or Rider simply not *expecting* the Pedestrian here is not where a Pedestrian is meant to be, with such a good, probably hard-fought for, alternative. Maybe the erring and impatient

Pedestrian distrusts the Underpass: smelly, confusing, beset by loiterers, also beggars; distrusting only a little less the Footbridge: too far away, too slippery, too unsuited for the pram or wheelchair.

See: Impatience; Absence of a Footbridge; Pedestrian from Nowhere; Speed

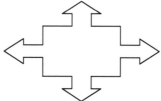

FORCING A VEHICLE INTO STATIONARY OR MOVING TRAFFIC
%%%%   @@

The act of forcing a Car or White Van, less commonly a Motorcycle, into a line of standing-still or crawling traffic is as unpleasant a gesture as it is dangerous. Moreover it leaves a bad flavour in everyone's mouth except the chancer's. First: there's unlikely to be *room* for the unwanted joiner. Second: the person forced - as opposed to willing - to give way will be brimming over with resentment. Third: the Driver forced to give way is, him- or herself, left stuck at the next traffic lights or road works. Fourth: the *un*successful Driver forcing his or her vehicle into traffic risks blocking the *operational* lane in the opposite direction: an act that then leads to a whole new round of anger, resentment and delay. Force dictates me-first, others later. Force is saying blow the lot of you!

See: Road Rage; Anger; Impatience; Pedestrian from Nowhere; U-turns; Temporary Traffic Lights; Queues

FORCING A VEHICLE TO SLOW
%%%% @@@

It can hardly ever be indicated, except by dazzle, but 1000s of times each driving or riding day, one vehicle or another is *forced* to slow down. A typical scenario is for the Driver or Rider to overtake on a blind hill - or foolishly trying to overtake a tractor or long lorry or whole stream of traffic on the downhill, or on the bend. In these circumstances, somebody has to give way - and it won't be the reckless Driver. So what happens if everyone runs out of road? Collisions through this cause definitely impact upon the "innocent" Driver and his Passengers as much as, if not more than, the aggressor.

See: Impatience; Overtaking; Road Rage; Speed

FOREIGN DRIVERS
%%% @@

Foreign Drivers are not dangerous of themselves but they are far more likely to be Right-hand Lane Drivers than Left-Lane. After a night's rest; after a long ferry journey; or after a simple comfort-stop, Left-hand steer Drivers are far more likely to revert to Right Lane than remember the Left Lane.

Foreign HGV Drivers face even more hazards - as do innocent road-users suddenly encountering a foreign HGV. Heavy Goods' legislation is different in Britain; mirrors require different adjustments; & road signs are different. And were a Foreign Driver ever to be caught for any lapse, or lapse of judgment, it is highly likely he or she will be back in their home country before the law catches up with them.

See: HGVs; Tiredness; Ferries; Lane-Switching; Tachographs

FOUR-by-FOURS
%%% @@@@@

4x4s & Off-roaders are now the 1st. choice of half of all car purchasers. The driving position is higher; the shell of the vehicle stronger; the capacity of the vehicle, roomier.

By definition 4x4s are quite protected where two of them are in Collision. The larger problem is side-, head-on, or rear Collision where an S.U.V. or its equivalent runs into *an ordinary* saloon or hatchback; to say nothing of the huge danger where that Collision is with Cyclist, Motorcyclist or Pedestrian. Many estimates confirm a *25-times* greater danger 4x4 Collision compared with Car/Car, Car/Pedestrian, Car/Cyclist. So watch out for those rigid girders built into the frames of 4x4s.

See: Driving Height; Side-Swipes; Impatience; Unseating

FOURTH LANE ADDED
%%   @

The Highways' Agency: in a vain effort to increase Road Space, thereby generating brand new traffic, frequently makes a 3-lane Motorway into a 4-lane Motorway. Riders & Drivers already in the *nearside* lane are suddenly confronted not with *merging* traffic from the Left but with *processional* traffic to the Left. Faced with such a surprise, the slower Motorist has no choice but to slot into that 4th. Lane, more-or-less blind. Later problems arise when that extra lane - whether a 3rd. or 4th. - is suddenly sacrificed.

See: Motorways ; Lane Switching, Pushing In; Slow HGVs

FRONT WINDSCREEN GRIMY ON THE INSIDE
%%%% @@@@

Laziness often prevails cleaning this awkward - less accessible - surface of dirt, sheen & dead insects, a screen sometimes reflecting straight back any paperwork resting on dashboard. So it is the unprepared or unwary Driver has impaired forward vision: especially in fog, rain, sharp sunlight or at night. Sobering it is to reflect on the hundreds of deaths or injuries that could have been avoided over the years for want of a fifty-penny clean & dry cloth to hand - or simply a worn-out pyjama.
See: Impaired Vision; Dazzle; Weather

FRONT WINDSCREEN MISTED ON THE INSIDE
%%%% @@@@@

This phenomenon is sometimes caused by driver & passenger breathing; more often by heavy rain or lowering temperature outside; complex & wrongly-set air conditioning inside. Misted screens are very, dangerous: exacerbated by grime or sheen.
See: Front Windscreen Grimy; Fog; Rain; Impaired Vision

FRONT WINDSCREEN OBSCURED ON THE OUTSIDE
%%%% @@@@@

Many are the conditions reducing Driver Vision on the outside - as opposed to the inside - of a front windscreen: ice, snow, freezing-fog, freezing-rain, dense fog, torrential rain, dirt, mud, squashed insects - or unaddressed light rain: this bad news for every single road-user or casualty impacted.
See: Weather; Fog; Snow; Igloo; Grimy or Misty Windscreen

FRONT WINDSCREEN WITH ICE
%%%% @@@

Several conditions can give rise to inside frosting of a vehicle's windows, front windscreen worst affected: outdoor parking in sub-zero temperatures; heating systems not yet working; freezing breath; heavy frost or snow outside; yesterday's rain icing over. The temptation is always to commence a journey prematurely - or to trust a frozen chamois, a plastic scraper - or a kettle full of steaming hot water. The recourse all too rarely available at the minute of most need is proprietary de-icer canister, amazingly cheap.

See: Grime; Mist; Fog; Rain; Igloo; Impaired Vision; Snow

FROZEN RAIN
%%%%% @

Frozen Rain - as opposed to black or white ice - is a phenomenon as frightening as it is unanticipated. Most Motorists, Cyclists, & Pedestrians might only encounter Frozen Rain once in 3 or 4 years. And when it happens, Frozen Rain: rain that only freezes upon settling, is far worse than the proverbial "skating rink." Nothing makes sense. And there's no salvation. Even school children will be propelling themselves forward and across the road on their bottoms. For those same Pedestrians in limbo, *compacted-ice* Pavements are almost as bad.

See: Skidding; Black Ice; Windscreen with Ice; Fallen Pedestrian; Rain

GAPS IN THE DUAL CARRIAGEWAY
%%% @

Gaps are left in some Dual Carriageways: created *not* for U-turns but for Right Turns into a side road and Right Turns from that same side-road. And the Gap often only holds 2 vehicles at a time: one in, one out. Try to put more there and an impatient queue begins to build on both the main road and the secondary road. A keen knowledge of Closing distances is thus essential for these Gaps. And this is one of very few occasions where the old hand-signal for slowing down [in a fast-lane] is really helpful.

See: U-turns; Closing Distances; Mirrors; Pedestrians from Nowhere; Hand Signals.

GENDER OF THE DRIVER OR RIDER
%%%% @@@@@

Male Drivers are twice as likely to cause death & injury on the road as Female Drivers: worked out on a mile-by-mile comparison. Also Male Lorry-Drivers are four times as likely to cause death & injury as their Female Colleagues: again on a mile-upon-mile comparison. With Motorcyclists, the gap is far greater: Male Rider against Female Rider. Several Motor Insurers hesitate to cover men aged 17 to 25, except with very high premium. In one sense, the Gender-gap is counter-intuitive. After all, many Mums are overburdened by the school-run, strapping in very young children, time limits - and that mythically sedate Roadcraft, feminine.

See: Impatience; Road Rage; HGV Safety; Motorcyclists; Youth

GENERATED TRAFFIC
%%%   @@@@

Generated Traffic is the technical name for building more Highways & Motorways which then generate traffic that might never have embarked upon their journeys but for the existence of those *additional* Highways. For instance, the M25 was, at first, intended to take traffic out of Central London. It still fulfills that promise 5-10% of the time - but the rest of its patronage is local London-Suburb to London-Suburb, North of England to South of England, or Gatwick to Heathrow, Heathrow to Gatwick traffic - where there might have been a very identifiable Public Transport alternative *had the M25 never been conceived*. In fact, were the Government to build every new road and bypass ever conceived, the result would mainly be more *journeys*, more Collisions... and - ironically - more Traffic Jams.

See: Additional Mileage; Traffic Jams; Long Journeys; Motorways; Airports; Queueing Traffic

GETAWAY VEHICLES
%%%%%   @

By their very nature: Getaways are not going to obey any law: whether a law regarding documentation *or* a law relating to actual driving behaviour. Getaways aren't always getting away from non-motoring crimes they have or have not committed. A number of Getaways are getting away from a Collision they have caused or been involved in; or from an intended or coincidental Police Patrol.

See: Dishonest Driving; Crash for Cash; Hit-&-Run; Police Chase

GOOD SAMARITANS
%% @

Good Samaritans are non-implicated Motorists & Pedestrians who - out of the goodness of their hearts - stop what they're doing or driving or carrying in order to be Good Witnesses, Nurses, Attendants, Raisers-of-the-Alarm. All very admirable!

Except.... Except being a Good Samaritan can quickly lead to multiple *added* danger, where the Samaritan cannot safely exit the vehicle he or she was in. Then there are *hoax-stops* in order to rob the Good Samaritan or take the Samaritan's vehicle! Not including yet *Road Rage* targeted at Samaritan & his or her nuisance value. Not every guilty party; not every drunk or errant driver; not every father beating up mother welcomes the Good Samaritan. And some Good Samaritans are run over straightway they leave wherever they were safer.

See: Witnesses; Pedestrian from Nowhere; Road Rage

GROCERY DELIVERY VEHICLES
%%% @@

Grocery Deliverers: shelf-to-shopper, are relatively newcomers on the Highway; and growing in number year-by-year. Very few Supermarkets co-operate with each other; thus it is possible for 5 Deliverers all to be delivering into a small village at the same delivery-slot. Grocery Couriers are frequently deprived of both rest and toilets. Moreover, the intended Householder will possibly be out-of-home - or even untraceable.   As if matters could not get worse, Grocery Deliverers are underpaid & forever working against-the-clock.

See: Parcel Deliverers; White Van Man; Tiredness; Over-familiarity with the Road; Time Limits; Impatience

GUILT
%%   @@@

It's perhaps an irony that Guilt might lead to Collisions - but it makes sense when one thinks of distractedness & preoccupation. Maybe a Driver is guilty about something that's happened at home or work or during school drop-off; maybe a deep relationship problem; more commonly on the Highway: Guilt surrounding a past Collision, Crash or Near-Miss. One would imagine that category of Guilt would lead to utmost caution. And in a way it does. But if any Driver or Rider becomes too cautious, they freeze behind the wheel or the handlebar, thus cannot integrate with other traffic so successfully. The Highway is Theatre: so every single factor comes into play as it would in a playhouse: especially self-referential factors. So on the Highway, Highway-related Guilt is uppermost; other deep regrets secondary.

See: Post Traumatic-Stress; Anxiety; Upset

HAND SIGNALS
%%   @

Hardly anybody uses Hand Signals these days - yet they are essential for Cyclists, Motorcyclists and for car manoeuvres which could easily be *mis*interpreted. The two Hand Signals most used to avoid Collision are Right Turn & Slowing Down.

See: Gaps in Dual Carriageways; Motorcycles; Cycle Safety

HGVs IGNORING PROHIBITION
%%%% @

Where a suburban street, country lane or short-cut bans, or limits, vans & lorries above a certain weight: dozens of HGV Drivers ignore the restriction claiming they needed "Access"; or were led astray by their employer; or by their satnav - or in the case of Bridge Strikes, by Act of God. The net result is the heavily-laden lorry running out of control - in the process harming Pedestrians & ill-positioned Car Drivers, also destroying street furniture.

See: HGVs; Reversing; Narrow Lanes; Bridge Strikes; Long Lorries; Pedestrians from Nowhere.

HAIRPIN BENDS
%%%%% @

Part of the problem of Hairpin Bends is unfamiliarity. Most Drivers, Cyclists & Motorcyclists are not used to Hairpins: especially abroad - where a Driver / Rider might also be on the wrong side of the road. The Hairpin needs a very specialized Roadcraft: ie. braking at exactly the right moment; accelerating at the right moment. Also doing Hairpins at speed is a well-known Dare

See: Speeding; Unfamiliarity; Driving Abroad; Banking

HARD SHOULDER COLLISIONS
%%%% @

It should be a contradiction of terms: a Collision on the Hard Shoulder. Because: before temporary suspension of Hard Shoulders for either road navvies or rush hour, Hard

Shoulders- planned in Britain from 1958 onwards - were intended to be the safest of sanctuaries. Then came a series of alarming Collisions *on the actual Hard Shoulder* as opposed to on those active lanes nearby. Someone, somewhere, must have been driving on auto-pilot, worse, driving where driving forward was usually prohibited. This resulted in the ploughing down of AA & RAC Patrols called out for roadside assistance. So it was the guidance changed: from Stay Inside Your Vehicle to *Stand Behind the Nearside Crash Barriers.*

See: Tiredness; Sleep; HGVs Out of Control; Snow; Skidding; Motorways; Crash Barriers

HEAD-ON COLLISION
%%%%% @@

Strictly speaking, Head-On Collisions happen because of road hazard from a different category: eg. Unclear Visibility, Overtaking, Speeding. But such is the devastation caused by Head-On Collision that it fully deserves an entry of its own.

Whether the Head-On is car-car, lorry-lorry, car-lorry, motorcycle-car, motorcycle-lorry, motorcycle-motorcycle, car-pedal-cycle, lorry-pedal-cycle, or any other combination, the result is nearly always worse than any other category of Collision - eg. sideways , swerve, brush, or damaging street or car park furniture.

Because *any* Head-On Collision: even one seen, mitigated, at the very last moment, is the addition of 2 speeds: speed of On-comer Number One added to speed of On-comer Number Two- with all the jolt, pulmonary injury, shattered glass, crumpled bonnet, broken neck anybody could anticipate through *not* having anticipated the danger of Head-On.

The truth is Head-On Collisions arise from two or more separate decisions: the amalgamation of those decisions, each misguided decision separately, then together, spelling disaster.

See: Speed; Unclear Visibility; Unlit Vehicle; Impatience; Overtaking; Third Lane; Tiredness; Time Limit

HEAD-RESTS
%%   @@@

Head-Rests are a problem area. In theory, they are great Collision-reducers due to the comfort they afford the Driver's head & neck - where the neck in particular must be relaxed throughout a journey. On the other hand, some Head-Rests are set far too high, too rigid, also, and crucially, still in position when nobody requires one: thus impeding field of vision.

See: Cabin Comfort; Tiredness; Rest Breaks; Mirrors

HEAVY FOOTWEAR [or UNSUITABLE FOOTWEAR - or NO FOOTWEAR AT ALL]
%%%   @@

Anybody who's been a Coach Passenger where the Driver is wearing hiking boots will need no reminder that Footwear matters. Footwear is so influential that a saloon car might be driven much more safely were the Driver to shed *all* Footwear. Flip-Flops and Sling-back shoes are an absolute nightmare. Hardly any pedal-control is possible in shoes that so easily lasso the foot-pedal rather than depressing it. Other unsuitable

Footwear include gentlemen's brogues [with shiny leather soles], deck-shoes [with slippery & un-dimpled rubber soles], high-heels, also bedroom slippers, wedges & thick platforms. Moreover, all driving behaviour is influenced by hovering over the brake or accelerator: the latter pedal in particular demanding exactly the right manufacture of shoe-sole, of exactly the right thickness.

See: Out of Control Vehicles; Swerving; Braking; Long Journeys

HEAVY GOODS' VEHICLE SAFETY
%%%% @@@@@

The loyal & conscientious Drivers of most HGVs can proudly turn to their own exemplary careers behind the wheel of Tractor or Lorry-Cab. But when HGVs also White- & Luton-Vans are involved in Collisions, the result is nearly always magnified above the risk of colliding with a hatchback or cycle: because Lorries - even unladen Lorries - have all that extra weight, force and clout. Also all those time constraints.

See: Lorries; Gender; Under-riding; Motorways -& most entries

HEAVY GOODS' VEHICLE STRENGTH AGAINST WEAKNESS
%%%% @@@@@

Although, statistically, HGVs might cause fewer Collisions than smaller vehicles, when there *is* a Collision, that event is far more likely to end in chaos, injury, death. For instance, allowing for never wanting the demise of even the most careless lorry-driver: where a non-HGV Road-User is hit by an HGV, the chance of *the weaker party*'s death or injury is at least 30 times than the chance of that HGV Driver's death or injury. So it is: every other Road-User - including competitor HGV Drivers - is daily and constantly forced to alter driving behaviour when confronted by an HGV.

See: Unusual Vehicles; Fleets; Agencies; Foreign Drivers; Tachographs; Just in Time; Overtaking

HIDDEN CYCLIST
%%%%% @@@

Cyclists *do* get hidden - and when they *are* hidden, they are so acutely in danger of being struck, then unseated, that they will then almost inevitably be injured or killed. Cyclists can be hidden in fog; hidden round a bend; hidden behind a Bus or Lorry; hidden in a busy supermarket car park; hidden *on* a Roundabout; hidden as straggler in a road-race; hidden with no lights; hidden with dim lights; hidden without high visibility jacket; hidden at twilight; hidden turning Right from a side road; hidden turning Left from a side road; & - most perniciously - hidden when, in darkness, they are crossing a Roundabout exit *lengthwise* when a car or van or lorry is about to exit from that same Roundabout, at exactly that moment, whether at an angle of 60°, 75° or 90°. And the *more popular* cycling becomes, especially in the wake of Corona Virus: in urban as well as rural situations, the more Collision opportunities there will be where the stronger Road-User is far more secure than the Cyclist as weaker Road-User.

See: Cycle Safety; Roundabout; Speed; Impatience; Loss of Concentration; Roundabouts; Road Rage

HILL-STARTS *[SLIPPING BACKWARDS]*
%%% @@

The Hill-Start is a tricky move at the best times: getting the balance right between hovering on the brake and hovering on the accelerator. Where Hill-Starts go wrong, the car, van or lorry slips backward to collide with whichever vehicle or Pedestrian is standing behind it. Not a few deaths each year are caused by owners vainly trying to halt a sliding parked vehicle! An additional concern is the Hill-Start begun before someone has overtaken the static vehicle; or the Hill-Start attempted half-way up a short suburban rise - where there is no accounting for an oncoming vehicle itself passing a parked car the other side of the hill.

See: Rolling Backwards; Braking; Reversing; Concentration

HIRE CARS
%%% @@

Car-Hire firms charge a considerable sum for Collision Waiver. That is part-acknowledgement of the propensity for Drivers hiring one of their vehicles to be involved in a Collision. And these Collisions are often as much the result of unfamiliarity with the area - or the very long journey for which the hire was necessary - as the unfolding calamity. On the other hand, impossible penalties sometimes make some transitional Drivers *safer*: for fear of having to pay that hefty surcharge. Which all skirts the other two problems with Hire Cars: the controls are awfully different; and the hiring itself might follow a notable Collision where the hirer him- or herself was the alleged cause.

See: Taxis; Courtesy Cars; Limousines; Foreign Drivers; Driving Overseas; Unfamiliarity; Time Limits; Long Journeys

HIT-&-RUN
%%%% @

Hit-&-Run is usually *totally* criminal - & not infrequently performed in order to commit a *non-vehicular* crime. However, Hit-&-Run can also be *incidentally* criminal: failing to stop; or swerving to avoid an animal on the Highway; exceeding the stated speed limit; not having the correct documentation; driving underage; driving a class of vehicle not on one's licence; or being perhaps needlessly afraid of a positive breath test or the appearance of a Police Patrol. Then there is the attested phenomenon of the Lorry Driver who arrives back at his or her depot 80 or so miles away blissfully unaware that the back of a long trailer or box has caused havoc.

Where a "minor" Collision happens in very heavy traffic, such as might be found on a congested Motorway; or conversely, where nobody at all is about in the middle of the night, the victim or survivor might have to rely on laboratory analysis of paints. As a rule, there is always a greater chance of avoiding awkward questions or Court by making a getaway than stopping to face the music.

See: Mounting the Pavement; Hidden Cyclist; Lack of Concentration; Dishonest Driving; Dangerous Driving; Telephoning; Drink Driving; Emergency Vehicles; Time Limits

HITTING THE BARRIER
%%%% @@

Until very, very recently, most Motorway barriers failed to cushion somebody swerving into them, or attempting to mount them. Until quite recently, railways or roads or rivers beneath a carriageway had no roadside barriers above them to stop the flip-over: the Great Heck flip-over, early in the morning on February 28th., 2001 being Britain's worst ever. Additionally, until the start of this Century, most roadside barriers had sharp contours at both ends: leading to the piercing of a saloon car, the spearing of a Cyclist.

See: Hard Shoulders; Dykes & Ditches; Flip-overs; Veering Out of Control; Underpasses; Speeding

HOOTING & HONKING
% @@@@

Hooting & Honking at other Motorists - less so, at Pedestrians - is strongly discouraged in this country, banned after darkfall. Hooting can be a sign or mere re-acquaintance or a cheap way of saying: "Goodbye!"- but it's still considered an unpleasant communication. Most unpleasant is Hooting *as Road Rage*; Hooting to intimidate other Drivers; Hooting at Cyclists;

Hooting on Motorways; even Hooting as a sign of celebration. The act of Honking upsets & confuses all Road-Users, leaving them less prepared for the journey ahead. And since the year 2000 we are Honking more like it would be on the Continent than the British way of doing things.

See: Impatience; Waving; Speeding; Overtaking; Forcing

HOVERBOARDS *[including Skateboards & Roller-skates]*
%% @

All micro-wheeled pavement-transport risks going out of control: veering away from the relevant verge, pavement or gutter. At that moment, the Hoverboard or its equivalent falls in front of, or beneath, the nearside back wheel of a chance passing vehicle. With disastrous consequences.

See: Mobility Scooters; Segways; Electric Scooters; Blind Spots

HORSES SPOOKED
%%%   @

Horses have every right to be on the Highway because most turnpike roads & drovers' roads were actually laid for single horses or the horse-&-cart, or, later, for the horse-&-carriage. But a car's hooter, a Motorcyclist's exhaust, or a low-flying aeroplane, can easily spook the Horse. The Horse then bolts, its hapless mount thrown into a ditch; worse onto the Highway itself - that mount vainly attempting to stay seated.

See: Animals on the Highway;   Too Little Clearance; Overtaking; Ditches & Dykes; Impatience; Unseating

IGNORING ONE-WAY STREET SIGNS [*incl. NO ENTRY*]
%%%% @

Ignoring the No Entry sign warning of a forthcoming blocked or one-way Street has disastrous consequences: because nobody expects a car or van or motorcycle to be there! Other vehicles -worse Cyclists- have to swerve out of the way. Another danger is a private vehicle entering a City's Tram Track route when that *isn't* permitted.

See: Unfamiliarity; Wrong Side of the Road; Trams

ICED PAVEMENTS
%%% @@

When the Pavement is too icy or slippery to use - Pavement maintenance is a very low priority - there will be only one consequence: children &/or their guardians will walk on the better-cleared road surface itself. That means Drivers, Cyclists too, are far from prepared for this new hazard. After all, Pedestrians are usually somewhere out of the way, *not in the way*.

See: Weather; Snow; Pavement Parking; Pedestrians

IGLOO DRIVING
%%%%% @@

Igloo Driving occurs when a Driver decides to proceed with a journey without fully clearing Front Windscreen, Side Windows - *nor indeed all external mirrors* - of snow, frost, ice & slush.

See: Front Windscreen Obscured on the Outside; Inside too

ILL DRIVERS
%%%% @@

Drivers do not have to be actually *dying* in order to cause terrible Collisions. The Illness or Impairment might be invisible or slow-developing, exaggerated every mile. The main Illnesses or indispositions that cause death & injury to both Ill Drivers *and* innocent parties are bronchitis, knee replacement, hip replacement, P.S.D, dementia, heart failure, stroke, cardiac arrest - and spondylitis; also any Illness or condition that led to insomnia the night before a Driver drives. Ill Drivers swerve more often: so endangering Pedestrians and anybody haplessly sitting in a parked vehicle. Ill or immobile Drivers also take an age to leave their vehicles in busy traffic - to say nothing of manoeuvering the Mobility Scooter out of the gutter.

See: Tiredness; Swerving; Loss of Concentration; Sudden Braking; Disability

ILL-ADJUSTED MIRRORS
%%%% @@@

It is easy to have the all 3 or 5 essential mirrors of a Vehicle - depending on the bulk of that Vehicle - ill-adjusted, non-adjusted, or poorly-adjusted. In each & every case, this prevents both driver & co-driver assessing correctly road hazard, wherever & whenever that hazard presents itself. It is often said *foreign* HGVs are unaware of their off-sides, British HGVs unaware of their near-sides. Yet *correct* mirror-adjustment is an art as well as a science: a practice that might have to alter halfway through a journey: perhaps for close pavement-parking. Many drivers towing a vehicle or trailer prefer panoramic mirrors to conventional fixtures.

See: Defective Vision; Windscreen Grimy; Pedestrian from Nowhere; Sharp Turn Left; Overtaking

IMITATION
%%   @@@@@

Imitation is a fairly constant presence on the highway. As Riders or Drivers we are, possibly, totally unaware of Imitation. But that ever-recurring Imitation flatters the bad Driver who is now joined by the *good* Driver or Rider! One vehicle forces itself into a line of stalled traffic; then the next one does. One Pedestrian dashes across the road outside the Railway Station, then the next one does. One car overtakes a Bus; the next does. One white van U-turns in a jam; then the succeeding vehicle does a U-turn as well. All these Imitations, copying bad Roadcraft rather than good, *double* the chance of injury or death because if it was unsafe initially, it's doubly unsafe now.

See: Daring; Impatience; Overtaking; Pedestrian from Nowhere

IMMEDIATE BRAKING
%%%   @@@@

Immediate - as opposed to emergency - Braking is an easy Driver behaviour into which to lapse. Gone are the days most Drivers & Riders of Motorcycles would change down gears, then slow down gradually. Indeed, some Roadcraft manuals actually *advocate* quick braking - in order better to prepare following Road Users. Contrarily: now brake-dust is seen more as an environmental hazard, the old habit of making brake-pads last most of the life of a vehicle might gain the credibility it deserves.

See: Animals on the Road; Brake Lights; Loss of Concentration

JACK-KNIFED LORRIES
%%%% @

Jack-knifing is a product of a Tractor-&-Trailer Juggernaut - or low-loader - skewing right across the carriageway, with all 8, 10 or 12 of its wheels locking in different directions to form a V-shape or L-shape.   Fine if nobody is following immediately behind; or if the skew or skid is controlled.   The danger is always - particularly on a Motorway - that a saloon car will be overtaking *at the exact minute* of wheel-lock.

 See: HGVs, Long-Loaders, Overtaking; Iced Roads

JUMPING LIGHTS   *[on Amber or Red]*
%%%%%   @@@

Too many Drivers & Motorcyclists, even Pedal Cyclists, jump traffic lights. Later they may claim that those lights changed *too quickly*. Very occasionally, the sequence of lights itself is ill-timed, therefore unpredictable - or not fit for purpose. That failure applies in particular to *temporary traffic lights*. These are erected round road-works or arbitrary excavations or re-surfacing of the carriageway. Drivers jump lights because they fondly imagine there is *a time-lag* in the lights, as seen from one end of the hazard or the other.

At busy & important road junctions, jumping the Amber or Red results in catastrophe: because other streams of traffic have already started to move; worse many Drivers pressing hard on their accelerators, glad of the break. Nobody- least of all the innocent Pedestrian - has time to pick up on the danger. The result: head-on crash, or near miss.

There is growing evidence that, in Town- & City-Centres, *Pelican* lights are set to favour the moving traffic, *not* the Pedestrian. Counter-intuitively that makes *the last* Driver before the Green Light for Pedestrians shows feel *entitlement* to proceed: simply because everyone else has!

See: Impatience; Commuting; Flows of Traffic; Pelican Lights; Pedestrian from Nowhere; Queueing; Speed

IMPATIENCE
%%% @@@@@

Impatience always has potential to result in Collision or Near Miss. At its most extreme, Impatience also leads to unforeseen U-turns, foul mouthing, erratic weaving, road-rage; and principally terrible Roadcraft. Ironically, Driver Impatience might not originate *on the road*. There might have been an argument inside a parked car, in the school, or pub, prior to travel; or unresolved tension in home or shop immediately before travel. Another spur to Impatience is tight deadline or being stuck in the proverbial traffic jam.

See: Road Rage; Arguments; Overtaking; Queueing Traffic; Crawling Traffic; Just-in-Time; also many other entries

IMPRISONED IN CAR or VAN
%%% @@

A car or white van - especially when it is moving - makes a perfect Prison. Those so imprisoned are children on their way to School; teenagers on their way to / from a party; women & girlfriends subject to terrible domestic violence; also estranged partners; and enemies or debtors *tricked* into getting into an unsafe vehicle: unsafe because its existing occupant(s) want quick repayment or revenge.

Less dramatically, but still a cause for distress: hundreds of friends & relatives desperate for a toilet or refreshment break are *imprisoned* in a moving vehicle because the Driver "cannot find" a suitable café or lay-by or pub or service station *"on the right side of the road."* Once inside a vehicle, a Passenger's protest - even a child's protest - maybe more if it's a child protesting - falls on deaf ears. A *frightening* situation for everyone except the rampaging Driver: one easily leading to Collision while the situation is not sorted out.

See: Deadlines; Service Stations; Lack of exercise; Speed; Tiredness; Dishonest Driving

INEXPERIENCED DRIVERS
%%% @@

All drivers are inexperienced in *some* Highway- or weather-conditions. Additionally, the only way to become an experienced Driver or Rider is to have been inexperienced! Collision statistics, like-for-like, usually reveal that car-drivers aged 18-24 have a 1 in 3 chance of Collision as opposed to 1 in 11 for age 55-64.

See: Teenagers; Boy-Racers; Speed; Weather; Darkness

JOY-RIDING   [so-called]

%%%%% @

This hobby - hugely entertaining to participants & performers, if not to the Police & wider public - is always dangerous; & by definition illegal. The question of Pursuit then arises.

See: Taking without the Owner's Consent; Driving while Disqualified; Driving without Insurance; Boy-Racers; Dishonest Driving

JUST-IN-TIME

%%% @@@

Just-in-Time is a fairly recent arrival on the Highway: the practice of not storing ingredients or parts or spares or packaging in the factory, but commissioning it so to arrive on the actual day it is most needed. This puts terrible pressure on Truck Drivers, also smaller Van-Deliverers. Hence Collisions when time is failing.

See: Impatience; Tiredness; Long Journeys; HGVs; Traffic Jams; Queueing Traffic; Unloading; Tachographs

LAY-BYS

%%% @

Lay-bys used to be called "Lie-Bays" by the Ministry of Transport - which was logical. These dedicated & paved cavities provided at regular intervals along major or trunk roads, or at very occasional intervals on Smart Motorways, give rise to lots of safety questions. What happens if a Driver or Rider hasn't *seen* the preparation sign quarter- or half-of-a-mile ahead? What happens if an exhausted Driver spots the

Lay-By too late to enter it safely. Worse, what happens when a car or lorry tries to judge the speed of rear traffic in order to crank up for exiting a Lay-By. UK Lay-bys are not pretty. In fact they are frequently used for the deposit of litter or for going to the toilet. Several HGV Drivers sleep in a Lay-By till Dawn.

Another question needing an answer is: "What would happen if a Lay-By is also home to a pop-up café, coffee-bar or burger joint? Many deaths and even more serious injuries have happened where, at speed, hungry Drivers suddenly see a welcome Café. Traffic following the hungry or thirsty one cannot - and do not - anticipate the sudden braking involved.

See: Emergency Braking; Smart Motorways, Closing Distances

LENIENT SENTENCING   *[for Road Traffic Offences]*
%%% @@@@@

Sentencing in the Courts, plea-swopping behind the scenes, roadside warnings, points on licences, whatever, all add up to a culture of leniency in "disposal." No way are Sentences with regard to moving-traffic offences commensurate with similarly harmful offences, equipped with illegal drugs or a gun, in the home, pub, school or supermarket. On average: the tariff is £50 per life; 3 points for an upset load blocking the carriageway; £90 for 5 miles above the speed-limit. Or complete *discharge*: no penalty whatsoever. The scare or shortfall or Near-Miss or Collision is deemed unavoidable: an "Act of God." Hence forgiveness

But why is Lenient Sentencing a *Danger* on the Road? Surely it aids Road Safety by giving penitent drivers & riders new insights, also a "second" chance?

The maximized hazard resulting from minimized Sentence sees that criminals of the road, or on the road, watch out for Sentences. Then weigh their options up. In other words, a culture of Leniency, a prevalence of diversion from the Courts, directly *and* *indirectly* encourages bad road behaviour. For instance low tariffs like £50-a-life reduce anxiety about causing Death by Careless Driving, Death by Dangerous Driving, also TWOC. Impunity soon filters down to driving-seat level. *What do 3 points matter when there are twelve to go at?* And literally adding insult to injury, many Drivers & offenders decline even to go to Court in the relatively rare instance where there is an actual Session. That leaves the erring Professional Driver in profit, because they lose no pay.

See: Careless Driving; Dangerous Driving; Police Patrols ; Police Pursuits; Speeding; Foreign Lorry Drivers

LACK OF EXERCISE
%%%% @@@

Very few Drivers on long journeys - or journeys made longer by traffic-jams - take frequent enough breaks in order to stay alert, & fully concentrating - so at peace with themselves & other Road-Users. Once every 90 minutes for 10 - 15 minutes is the *minimum* respite in order to relieve strain on the legs, back, neck and nerves. Passengers, too, need a break.

See: Lay-Bys; Deadlines; Traffic Jams; False Time Limits; Long Journeys; Imprisoned in a Vehicle; Cabin Comfort; Coaches

LACK of PROFICIENCY or PRACTICE in EMERGENCY BRAKING
%%   @@

Emergency Braking is an essential Roadcraft Skill. And a bit like the Penalty Shoot-out in Football: the procedure needs practice, then more practice. On the other hand, there are hardly any circumstances outside immediate hazard when that drill *can* be practised! In other words, the skill is honed in crisis & past crises recalled. Behind the wheel or the handlebars, there are usually far too many distractions, or preoccupations, for Emergency Braking to begin until a second or two too late. Furthermore, Emergency Braking is always impacted - and deferred - by alcohol intake large or small.

Bus Drivers necessarily practice Emergency Braking weekly. It is surely time for other road-users *to follow* their example.

See: Fallen Pedestrian; Coincidence; Pedestrian from Nowhere; Speed; Lack of Concentration; Animal on the Road.

LANES BLOCKED
%%   @@

Whether it is a Crash, a stalled vehicle, standstill, a parade or demonstration or road-works: there are bound to be Lanes Blocked. A Gantry - where built - can be useful informing Drivers & Riders of this event; but even the swiftest & clearest matrix might not spell out the real reason for the blockage. Hence sudden lane-switching and/or rubber-necking.

See : Queueing Traffic; Crawling Traffic; Smart Motorways; Impatience; Rubber-Necking; Road-Works

LANE SWITCHING
%%%% @@@@

Lane Switching causes death & injury because it is often "forced" on a Driver or Rider by sudden circumstance: a stalled vehicle; an impending Bus Lane or Tram Track; an obscured or missing Road Direction Sign; being boxed-in within a wrong Lane; careless or forbidden parking; traffic snarled-up in an intended Lane; unfamiliar Roundabout, whatever.

And many Drivers are *not* good on Mirrors. So a sudden change of Lane is bound to interfere with a hidden vehicle or flow of traffic on the Left or a hidden vehicle or flow of traffic on the Right. The temptation, on the spur of the moment, is to hope for the best! The cumulative evidence is that Lane Switching happens most at complex Roundabouts or busy 4-way Junctions. Then on Motorways, it is rife: as everybody attempts to get a move on, however that is achieved.

See: Lanes Blocked; Impatience; Side-Swipes; Mirrors Ill-Adjusted; Queueing Traffic; Unclear Signs

LEAVING A ROUNDABOUT
%%% @@@@

In order to leave a Roundabout successfully, a Driver or Rider must not be squashed, hemmed in, or hit, from either nearside or offside. One common hazard is that another Road-User switches intention at the last minute, deciding to use a different exit or a different lane at their pre-selected exit. Another common hazard is stalling on the Roundabout itself or immediately upon exit. Traffic following then has no alternative but to freeze active traffic already on the

Roundabout: but needing either a different exit or a different lane from the same exit. Then there's the Crash-for-Cash merchant to consider, also the Coach or HGV that cannot maintain *a curved* line on the Roundabout, that mythical line able to be kept to by ordinary cars.

See: Roundabout Discipline; Crash-for-Cash; Switching Lane

LIGHTING-STANDARDS, LIGHTING COLUMNS, LIGHTING GANTRIES

%%%% @@@@

At least 80 Road Users a year are killed through either hitting a Lamp-Post or its equivalent or by that Lamp-post falling onto them. More imaginative ways of lighting the Highway such as end-to-end cables or light-brackets fixed to people's homes have hardly ever been attempted. Nor has the rubberized, fully-bendable, Lighting Column yet come on stream. The best one can hope for in a Collision is that there will be a guard round the foot of the standard.

See: Street Furniture; Multi-Story Car Parks, Swerving

LIMOUSINES

%%% @

Limousines do not generally come under the same law as Taxis or Motor Coaches. And they *are* rather flashy at the expense of basic safety. Fire is definitely the worst problem within Limousines: affording no chance to get out in an emergency. Also Limousine occupants might be rowdy, drunk, not secured by seat-belt, or simply asleep... especially where that

Limousine is hired for a stag- or hen-Party far away. Altogether: a very unsatisfactory set of circumstances.

See: Taxis; Coaches; Minibuses; Alcohol; Rowdy Passengers

LOADING THE LOAD / UNLOADING THE LOAD
%% @@@

The skills - and attentiveness - needed for Loading/Unloading are very different from everyday navigational & vehicle-control skills: yet many cheapskate employers demand of their Drivers that they fulfill *both* roles. That leaves Truckers in particular exhausted, and on edge, before they even begin to climb the 5 foot necessary to access their cabs. Additionally, should they have a *flat-back* trailer - or an open Skip - their loading skills might fall below an optimum, leading the whole load to shift or scatter, especially bales of hay, pallets and pipes.

See: Tiredness; HGV Safety; Unsafe Load; Shed Load; Low Pay.

LOCALISM
%% @@@@@

Seemingly *a contradiction*: quite a number of serious or fatal Crashes - particularly late-night Collisions involving Teenagers & a Teenaged Driver - happen just three or four miles, maybe less, from home. Logic would dictate further *afield* being the problem. But a lot of Drivers & Riders assume they know their own locality enough to see little or no danger in its traffic patterns. Additionally, the pub or the party or the function just attended is more likely to be near than far.

See: Loss of Concentration; Drink-Driving; Young Drivers; Loud Music; Boy Racers

LONE TREES
%% @

Many students of Suicide have been puzzled: first by the numbers of Drivers in distress who drive straight into Lone Trees; second by the number of Coroners who put such Collisions - usually fatal because of their sheer purposefulness - as *"Misadventure."* Suicidal Drivers are not daft. They search out the Lone Tree.

See: Suicide; Veering Out of Control; Speed; Ditches & Dykes; Anger; Imprisoned in the Vehicle

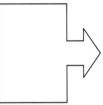

LONG JOURNEY
%% @@@@

Each Long Journey ideally needs an hour of preparation : checking lights, luggage, seat belts, shovel, triangle, fuel level, seat height, windscreen back & front, mirrors, whatever. *Because* Long Journeys demand so much more of the Driver and Relief Driver than the School Run or Market or Club drop-off. And Long Journeys become worse upon encountering Road Works, Diversions, Traffic Jams, Crashes, or false directions. It is estimated one third more Collisions happen to families going on holiday or for custody & access [always stressful in any case] than on time-honoured "routine" shorter excursions; but then very *short* & hurried journeys raise many problems too.

See: Tiredness; Traffic Jam; Time Limits; Deadlines; Arguments: Lack of Exercise; Traffic Jams

LONG LOADS
%%   @

For some decades, the Drivers of very Long Loads, at their longest: 18.65 metres long, used to mark the back of their trailers: "Long Vehicle." That was in order to warn motorists and cycles overtaking them, sometimes recklessly, that they would need a remarkable spurt of speed to overtake the whole length without being surprised or defeated by that length. Many supermarkets in particular have now been allowed to lengthen each vehicle in their fleets. That, of itself, raises the important danger of the rear of these giant Juggernauts mounting on to the Pavement: injuring or frightening Pedestrians [or squashing parked cars!] Nor will a Juggernaut Driver be best-placed to *see* any casualty - be that Pedestrian or Cyclist - beneath his back wheels. With the Pedestrian who has merely fainted, that absence of vision really is a matter of life-&-death. Of note, *very few* long vehicles carry a Co-driver to direct the main Driver in reversing. As if matters could get worse, several branded juggernauts are driven by Agency Drivers not salaried staff.

See: Agency Drivers; Pedestrians from Nowhere; Reversing; HGVs; Motorways; Overtaking

LORRY CABIN HEIGHT   *[too high]*
%%   @@@@

There are numerous inventors able to lower Heavy Goods' Vehicle cabins to street-level with consequent $180°$ vision.

Instead, Lorry Drivers are eight or ten foot above contradiction. Thankfully, this elevation has the effect of reducing Drivers' &

Mates' exposure to road hazard - but reduces, also, any sightline downwards or on the crucial lower nearside. It is estimated at least 10 pedestrians - maybe those 5'5" or less in stature - are killed because, at an authorized crossing, even a Zebra, they stand lower than the Driver's sightline.

See: Cab Comfort; HGVs; Pedestrian from Nowhere; Mirrors

LORRY CABS FAR TOO COSY
%%% @@

Modern Lorry-Cabs have undoubtedly become too cosy. Some are fitted with bed, TV, computers, electronic games, comfy seating, a fridge and effective heaters. That is because the Cab is often that Driver's *home* overnight. Highway Police following up Road Crashes rarely raise the question of the implicated Driver having too much comfort, too many distractions in the Cab, including that gaily-lit Christmas Tree!

See: Sat-Navs; Distractions; Tiredness; Just-in-Time; HGVs; Long Journeys; Dashboard Reflecting

LORRY COLLISIONS WITH CYCLES OR MOTORCYCLES
%%%%% @@

These Collisions rarely lead to any result other than death or life-changing injury: this fate unlikely to overtake the Lorry/Tractor/Trailer Driver himself.

In other words, the Lorry is the more powerful vehicle with the greater propensity for creating spray or a slipstream; greater chance of reaching its destination unharmed. Could the Driver have used mirrors to greater effect? Or was the Cyclist /

Motorcyclist so hidden by Cab Height that the Lorry only learnt later that day that there had been a terrible Collision?
See: Slipstream; Wind-Tunnel; Left Turning; Unseating; Loss of Concentration; HGVs

LOSS OF CONCENTRATION
%%%% @@@@@

Loss of Concentration is both predictable and unpredictable - but its *origins* are better traced: Road-Users tired or preoccupied; arguing, or burdened. Loss of Concentration is the one factor that applies to *nearly every* death or injury or near-miss on the highway. Nor can this condition, this deficit, be remedied in a minute or two. We are not granted that extra minute or two: which cumulatively makes the road more dangerous than owning an assault rifle.
See: Tiredness; Fleet Driving; Time Limits; & most other Entries

LOSS of CONTROL
%%%%% @@@@

Lorries, Cars, Motorcycles, Pedal Cycles, Mobility Scooters, whatever, all rely on someone, somehow, retaining Control. Loss of Control happens from the road or pavement, surface level; from people & obstacles on the Left or Right; from the skies - or even flyovers -above; from catastrophic engine failure; from unresponsive steering; from speeding; from loss of concentration; arguments - or Drink/Drugs. As starters!
The *penalties* for Loss of Control are countless & endless. In the immediate, there will nearly always be Collision, Injury or

Death. Sometimes these Collisions - and consequent injuries - will be multiple. All in those first 2 to 10 seconds.

See: Loss of Concentration; Speed; Escape; Distraction; Swerving; Unseating; & most other Entries

LOUD MUSIC
%%   @@

In-Car Entertainment is now strong enough for its volume alone to shake a vehicle; also for the sound to be clearly heard by both Pedestrians & passing vehicles. Loud Music distracts the Driver: not least when he or she has to switch from one track, or one CD, to another.

See: Boy-Racers; Underage Drivers; Teenage Passengers

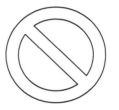

LOW BRIDGES
%%%%   @

Over the years, most Low Bridges are extremely well signed, audibly as well as electronically or visually. Moreover local Low Bridges appear on various maps & websites, even mentioned on sat-navs. Nonetheless, buses occasionally have their roofs sliced off beneath the Low Bridge; whilst Lorries get stuck or simply keel over. Not unusually, traffic becomes single-lane beneath the Low Bridge, sometimes governed by traffic-lights, oft-times not. There are 50+ "Bridge Strikes" every week -= which is totally inexcusable - as well as extremely dangerous.

See: Bridge Strikes; Unfamiliar Route; Sat-Navs

LOW PAY *[awarded Fleet Drivers, Agency Drivers, Bus & Coach Drivers, Taxi-Drivers, Commercial Travellers, Itinerant Carers, Meeters-&-Greeters, Commuters, whoever]*
%%% @@@@

From the very first Rolls-Royce owner's Chauffeur to the modern-day *Uber* Driver: the profession, the highly-skilled profession, of being a Driver by profession has generally been appallingly paid. Most times, if you counted in getting *to* work; getting between workplaces; preparing a vehicle; cleaning a vehicle before & after use; medicals; training; getting kitted-up for work; checking the vehicle's tyres, windscreens, mirrors, door, fuel; fallow hours waiting for next paying Passenger(s); waiting in an almighty traffic-jam; completing & filing all the paperwork; filling up with fuel; appeasing Competitors, Regulators, whatever, Professional Drivers - & those who will later in the day drive one of their Employer's vehicles - are frequently either paid nothing per hour [especially applicable to those whose workplace demands they *own* or purchase a vehicle] - or a pittance.

Gaps between split-shifts & "Marginal" times are recorded & rewarded at a rate far lower than any Minimum Wage - let alone any "Living Wage." Worse, Professional Drivers who have dozens of people's lives, safety & overall wellbeing in their care & keeping, are then paid peanuts while actually "On Duty." Bus Drivers, for instance, might be paid, after 20 years behind the wheel of a huge double-decker, one single pound above the lowest minimum allowed - nor paid anything at all for those 2 dead hours between clocking-off & clocking back on again. This very low status impacts on overall Highway Safety because of recurring low-motivation, acute fatigue, irritability - including a very understandable shirtiness. The lesson to be learnt from this lowliness is that Driver-pay should be *at least 3 times* more than it is, as well as extra to make up for all that marginal time "donated" to skinflint Employer.

See: Tiredness; Taxis; Bus Drivers; Coach Drivers; Time-Limits; Distractions; Low Bridges; Loss of Concentration

MANSLAUGHTER
%%%%% @

Whether by dint of compassion, leniency, plea-swop, or the availability of other charges, very, very few motorists are charged with Manslaughter. Yet *a proper* understanding of the distinction between Murder, Attempted Murder, & Manslaughter would lead to *dozens more* Manslaughter-on-the-Road charges would be brought each year.

Because a death is a death - and it has been long-established that 95% of Collisions are the result of human frailty, *not* the weather; or some mechanical fault; least of all an Act of God. One can only conclude Courts are brimming over with compassion for all *the Offender* has had to go through, nightmares, whatever. Hence the plea-swop.

See: Hit & Run; Death by Dangerous [or Careless] Driving; Speeding; Driving while Disqualified; Dishonest Driving; Lenient Sentencing; Imprisoned within a Vehicle

MAP-READING WHILST DRIVING
%%%% @

Most Drivers or Pedestrians have witnessed the moonlighting Map-Reader at some point. Particularly in an unfamiliar town centre, one can sympathize with the Map-Reader: a task far better suited to a good Sat-Nav or Navigator.

See: Loss of Concentration ; Distractions; Sat-Navs; Cosy Cabin

MARKET-PLACE PARKING
%%% @@@

Although Market-Places are, by definition, reserved for Market Stalls: on other days of the week, car-parking is allowed on the cobbles or both sides of the piazza. In practice, this permission, often bringing in some huge receipts of cash, rarely works. There is too close a mix of shoppers and motorists. Some Market Towns have introduced either 60° or 45° angled parking in preference to 90°: the theory being obtuse angles afford far greater visibility, and more ease of clearance. Other Councils have combined angled-parking with reverse-in-only Market Place parking: much to the despair of Drivers who have never developed the art of reversing in.

See: Reversing; Shopping Streets; Pedestrians from Nowhere; Impatience; Pedestrian Precincts

MINIBUSES
%%%   @

There may only be a few Minibuses around - but when Collision & Disaster does happen, Minibuses have multiple

casualties almost immediately. It could be the Minibus Driver is tired, exhausted even, & fighting against the clock. Or (s)he might be unfamiliar with that vehicle. Or Passengers might be drunk, rowdy or disobedient. Minibuses also get lost. Some Minibuses arrive via *Eurostar*; other Minibuses are overloaded after a Booze-Cruise. More Minibuses for hire or for bringing in Construction Workers would struggle to pass any M.O.T. Test
See: Taxis; Limousines; Coaches; Distractions; Rowdy Passengers; Alcohol; Swerving; Long Journeys; Hire

MINI-ROUNDABOUTS
%%   @@
The reason Mini-Roundabouts lead to so many Collisions is that they look to the uninitiated as permission to drive straight on. Moreover, most lorries & service vehicles cannot possibly turn Right at a Mini-Roundabout except by crossing it from point A to point B. Maybe Mini-Roundabouts are a poor-man's substitute Traffic Lights? Nor are these petite painted circles in the road always isolated from each other!
See: Traffic Lights; Side Roads; Urban Driving; Rat-Runs

MOBILITY SCOOTERS *[powered Invalid Carriages]*
%%%% @@@

Mobility Scooters have undoubtedly given thousands of Adults with a Disability new freedom to roam & to participate in wider Society. But built into the Mobility Scooter's advance are several factors making roads & pavements *far less safe*.

First, and most important, Scooters have no real policing; nor a requirement to take out compulsory third-party Insurance. Second, Scooters can be souped-up to go a lot faster than 8 or 12 miles an hour. Third, Scooter-Drivers might have so incapacitating a disability that they are too frail to manage all the controls; or to take avoiding action prior to Collision.

Fourth, those notionally controlling the Invalid Carriage might never, ever, have been Drivers or Cyclists in the past. Fifth, Pedestrians on the Pavements shared with rampaging Scooters are seriously hurt [or killed] by the unseen or out-of-control Owner; & Sixth, & crucially, hardly any Mobility Driver has ever discovered - let alone *used* - a warning signal, a bell or a hooter; nor at least attempted a shout to alert fellow Road-Users. Is it pride? Is it laziness? Is this lack of any warning *cussedness*? Or is this reticence sheer *stupidity*? If only Pedestrians could hear their silent progress, ingress, behind them, or to the immediate Left, Right or approaching blind "T."

See: Elderly Drivers; Reversing; Pavements; Pedestrians Unseen; Waving; Warning

MOTORCYCLE COLLISIONS WITH CARS OR WHITE VANS
%%%%% @@

These Collisions are absolutely calamitous due to a noxious combination of speed & inattention. Was the Motorcycle involved in a false Middle Lane? Or occupying a blind-spot? Or emerging from behind an on-coming HGV or Coach? Who was the stronger Party? Perhaps there was a Motorcycle Convention nearby? Or a Music Festival? Or the cars or white vans causing or impacted by the Collision might themselves be off on holiday or in holiday mood?

See: Loss of Concentration; Speed; Unseating ; Motorcycles; Mirrors; Three-Lane Carriageways; Right Turns

MOTORCYCLE-MOTORCYCLE COLLISIONS
%%%%% @

Although rare outside the race track: when there *is* a Motor-Cycle/Motor-Cycle Collision it is extremely serious, frequently fatal. Did one Rider misjudge a closing distance? Were both Motorcyclists dazzled? Or did *one* Rider suddenly emerge from behind an oncoming HGV? Or was this *a rear shunt*?

See: Motorcycles; Glancing; Speed; Swerving; Unseated; Swerves; Defective Vision; Loss of Concentration

MOTORWAY SLIPROADS
%%% @@

It's hard to work out which is more dangerous: the Sliproad *onto* a Motorway or the Sliproad for exit. Worst of all is the *truncated* Sliproad: particularly common on Dual Carriageways and A [Motorway-class] Roads: where entry & exit are angled more like 60-80° rather than the far gentler & more generous 15-30°. Some Drivers overtake, or worse swop lanes, upon entry or exit.

The very worst driving behaviour entering is *forcing* entry to the peril of fast-moving traffic already on a Motorway / or Dual Carriageway; or swinging straight from Sliproad to the Fastest Lane of moving traffic. Additional problems arise where the exit Slip-Road unexpectedly has 3 Lanes, not two.

See: Motorways; Mirrors; Speed; Queues; No Signals; Dazzle

MOUNTING THE PAVEMENT
%%%% @

The tantalizing aspect of mounting the Pavement is that it may not be "just" a Pedestrian or, Heaven Forbid, a group or queue of people impacted. The out-of-control vehicle - *or* the under-control vehicle seeking to avert calamity - might then enter a dwelling or de-stabilize that dwelling, in the process injuring the Driver or Rider him- or herself. Very occasionally, a heavy vehicle mounts the Pavement *deliberately*: out of anger; or revenge: as a targeted manoeuvre.

See: Hit-&-Run; Loss of Concentration; Loss of Control; Pavement Parking; Swerving; Dishonest Driving; Dazzle

MOVING A CASUALTY
%%% @

Where a Road Casualty, Injured or Dying, is moved, there is a risk of *greater* injury, especially spinal, head or internal injury; also the risk of choking. Moving a Casualty is an enormous temptation: especially in the event of Fire. But it is hardly ever advisable unless conducted by a trained Paramedic or Police Officer. Additionally, there are problems with obstinate self-removers: those who try to leave the scene of Collision under their own steam.

See: Head-on Collisions; Pedestrian from Nowhere; Steering-Wheel rigidity; Good Samaritans; Windscreens

MULTI-STOREY CAR PARKS
%%% @

Whilever potentially lethal Multi-Storey Car Parks are in operation, there will be prangs and Pedestrians run over. The engineering of these Multi-Storeys is bad enough: lots of steep ramps, sharp corners, confusing signage, and remote pay-machines. Added to that imperfect *design* are clutches of men & women who feel distracted; stressed before or after shopping; in charge of young children; oppressed by the darkness, danger and claustrophobia of the Multi-Storey. Who knows? That Multi-Storey might charge extra for times before or after collecting a ticket? Or to save money, the Car Park Owner might have made all his bays impossibly narrow. This combination of factors leads to lots of misunderstanding, not to say *anger*. Worse, there is a time pressure bearing down on the Driver to clock-in for work or collect a teenager from the Railway Station All sorts of penalties - literally -await anybody even attempting to abandon surface-parking or a public transport alternative.

See: Impatience; Anger; Airports; Road Rage; Car Parks; Commuting; Time Limits; Reversing; Pedestrian from Nowhere; Unfamiliarity; Failure to Stop to Report

MOTOR SCOOTERS [*excluding Mobility Scooters]*
%%   @

When Lambretta & Vespa Scooters were perfected in the late 1950s and early 1960s, it was hoped the Scooter would become the mass transport of Students, Young Drivers & Commuters. Whole Scooter-Parks were built. And then, at least in the UK, interest in these very modern wide platform / small wheel radius Motorbikes waned. But not before the sharp-suited "Mods" clashed with the chain-wielding "Rockers" [Grease-boys or Grebos] in their leathers: real-time period drama, or free entertainment!

There is *still* debate as to whether Scooters have a better or worse safety-record than their brothers: full-sized Motorcycles. *Lambrettas* are not especially fast: 45mph optimum on long journeys - yet their cornering of steep bends always appears odd due to their different centres of gravity. Then there is the Pillion question: *Lambrettas* having the sort of broad seating and generous foot platform to encourage a Pillion to join main Rider. Finally, the headlights & windscreens of mainstream Motor Scooters have caused some anxiety, particularly surrounding the weight of being trapped once unseated.

See: Motorcycles; Banking; Unseated; Skidding; Competing

MUSIC FESTIVALS
%%% @

Driving safely to an open-air Music Festival is a fraught activity. There are often long queues to access either the Site or the appropriate gate. Additionally, many Drivers or Riders are distracted & tired: some having taken time off work to get to the Festival. Cars & vans joining the fray might also be *older* than anything found in normal city traffic.

See: Queueing; Traffic Jams; Loud Music; Loss of Concentration; Crawling Traffic; Pedestrians from Nowhere

NARCOLEPSY
%%%% @

Although this medical condition is relatively rare; and although drivers suffering Narcolepsy are *supposed* to declare their sudden drowsiness to DVLA, many crashes - whether of cars or goods' vehicles - are the direct result of such unexpected sleep. Yet *proving* this cause is extraordinarily difficult, for obvious reasons. For instance was a Collision caused by hot sunshine after a full meal? Or by the sheer length of the journey? Maybe nobody should drive if they've been on an aeroplane in the past 6 hours; landed by Ferry; or had less than 5 hours sleep the night before? And certainly nobody susceptible to undeclared Narcolepsy should drive on a very straight road - or next to concrete barriers - where there is no visual stimulus.

See: Elderly Drivers; Tiredness; Long Journeys; Cosy Cabins; Medical Conditions; Mobility Scooters; Swerving

NARROW LANES
%%% @@@@

Driving on Narrow Lanes raises many challenges: not least who should come to a halt in the event of two vehicles trying to pass each other or overtake Pedestrians? And isn't it strange how the moment of crossing another moving vehicle or bicycle is the very moment a Pedestrian-with-Pram or Pedestrian blackberry-picking enters the equation? Narrow Lanes demand much slower speeds; much more thinking ahead. Also the encountering of tractors or milk-tankers in rural areas makes all the difference.

See: Overtaking; Speed; Unfamiliarity; Pedestrians from Nowhere; Refusal to Give Way

NEAR- MISSES

%%%% @@@@@

Driving would not be driving; Riders would not be riding, without Near-Misses. And by definition, Near-Misses are not the same as Collisions. But, crucially, Near-Misses follow-up and lead into *actual Collisions*. Sometimes a Fleet actually expects a quota of both Near-Misses *and* Collisions. Each Cyclist; each Motorcyclist; each Driver; each Pedestrian is fully aware of where there has been a Near-Miss - but human nature is that the Driver Rider, Pedestrian or Witness most affected, and frightened, simply whispers thanks and puts it all down to experience. *Better* to chalk everything out & work out exactly how the Near-Miss occurred, also how it might have been averted by at least one of the Parties. Some Drivers / or Riders even keep a Diary of Near-Misses!

A final problem with Near Misses is the *fear* they instill in Road-Users, undermining their confidence to face that situation -*any situation*- ever again, however far into the future. And those *causing* the Near-Miss are *the last* to learn from the experience!

See: Speed; Giving Way; Overtaking; Bus-Driving; Roundabouts; Dishonest Driving

NEW DRIVERS
%% @@@

New Drivers struggle to learn everything all at once: being on their own, driving in the dark, motorways, crises. They are participants or casualties in more Collisions because *some of them*, by no means all, are too impetuous, too impatient, & too dependent on loud music from the stereo.

See: Underage Drivers; Inexperience; Pedestrians from Nowhere; Overtaking; Dazzle; Inexperience

NIPPING INTO A ROUNDABOUT
%%% @@

Once Roundabout discipline is established and correctly maintained even a complex Roundabout does its job. The way to know whether a Roundabout is succeeding is each Driver or Rider aware of what traffic is already on that Roundabout and which exit each Road-User is likely or all-too-occasionally signalled to choose. Enter then a rogue vehicle or motorcycle and discipline is turned upside down. The *late* joiner and the nipper-in or the nipper-round makes accurate forecasting, accurate decision-making, impossible. We even have a name for Roundabout misbehaviour: the "zippy" Driver, quite often a man or woman aged 18 to 22.

See: Signalling; Roundabout Exits; Impatience; Speed

NOVICE DRIVERS
%%% @@

Novice Drivers are rarely a problem of themselves. After all, a series of driving lessons followed by the Theory- then the Practical- Driving Test should weed out unfit, totally unprepared, Drivers & Motorcyclists.

Nonetheless, each new Driver or Rider will never have faced as many real-time scenarios on the road as a more experienced Driver or Rider. Nor will he or she have done a lot of Motorway driving or night-time acclimatization: nighttime driving being everso different from daylight, demanding a whole new set of perceptions & reactions on the road.

An added - but thankfully rare - tactic of the complete novice is *impersonation*: where the person taking the Driving Test is not the actual licence-holder. And Foreign Drivers are by their very nature Novices in Britain - where these imported Drivers are certainly not expecting occupation of a Left-Lane.

See: Foreign Drivers; Underage Drivers; Pedestrians Unexpected; Lane Switching; Darkness

NORMALIZATION
%%% @@@@@

Normalization is the process whereby everybody from Police Constables to Statisticians, from Highway Engineers to the Magistracy accept Highway Collisions as *a given*; as a fact of life [more accurately, a fact of injury or death]. Because Car Crash is built into the national consciousness: any expectation of reduction, better still banishment, comes across as pie-in-the-sky thinking. Yet 95% of Collisions are either foreseeable or avoidable by one or more of the Parties impacted. By normalizing Collisions, the public minimizes the devastation Car Crash causes. Collision is then for the "unlucky ones" who just happened to be in the wrong place at the wrong time.

See: Lenient Sentences; Weather Conditions; Lack of Concentration; Coincidence; Lack of Control

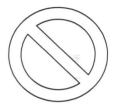

OBJECTS THROWN
%%%% @

Mercifully, very few objects are thrown onto Pavement or Carriageway as "mischief"; but where something *is* thrown, the result is frequently catastrophic. For instance, in anger a man threw the TV out of his Sheffield Tower-Block flat and killed a Pedestrian passing below outright. The same frightening result applies to stones or spanners or bottles thrown from bridges onto Motorways. The first the Driver below knows is when his or her car or lorry goes out of control through shattered windscreen and head injury doubled through the missile itself.

See: Road Rage; Limited Visibility; Vehicle out of Control

OFF-ROAD BIKES & JALOPIES ON THE PUBLIC HIGHWAY
%% @

Off-Road Transport obviously should be Off-Road: either on authorized hillsides, across farm-land or competing at racing circuits. But this traffic has *to get* where it is to be tested-out.

Usually, jalopies & BMX Bikes are carried on purpose-built trailers. But what happens when they aren't?

See: Trailer Safety; Four-by-Fours; Road Rage; Narrow Lanes

OIL & CHEMICALS on THE HIGHWAY
%%%% @

Sometimes a car or lorry has got a leaking fuel-tank. Other times, a vehicle is carrying extra oil in containers. At yet other times, brake-fluid is leaking. Rarely, but still horribly, disgruntled householders have deliberately spilt oil on the carriageway in order to deter night-time traffic, grease-boys, or the exhausts of passing Motorcyclists.

And spilled chemicals present the additional hazard of toxicity. A *helpful* motorist could be severely burned / scarred simply by raising the alarm.

See: Swerving; Front Windscreen; Limited Vision; Animals

OPENING A CAR DOOR in HEAVY TRAFFIC
%%%% @@

Motorists suddenly parking are very likely also to be sudden openers of their offside doors. After all, these Drivers only want *one* newspaper or *one* pint of milk - so they won't be there long. The trouble is this sudden disrupter of an established queue of traffic sees neither another vehicle passing vehicle nor traffic far behind anxious to close in on the newly-created gap. Hence crumpled doors & amputated arms.

See: Opening Door on a Cyclist; Pavement Parking; Impatience

OPENING A CAR DOOR ON A CYCLIST
%%%%% @

This is about as fatal as any piece of careless or criminal road behaviour could be. Tends to happen a lot with Taxis, immediately their Passengers have paid No Cyclist can predict the exact minute of unseating. Nor understand any Driver's negligence either opening the door himself onto the Cyclist or not forbidding his Passenger's untimely exit.

See: Opening Door on Traffic; Hidden Cyclist; Impatience

OPENING A VEHICLE DOOR ON THE NEARSIDE
%%% @@

It is not even safe at the kerb-side to open the door of a car, van or lorry in a hurry. Yet parking restrictions, also double yellow lines, often mean the Commuter, the Passenger or Delivery Driver is in a hurry. Hence Pedestrians & prams or disabled Scooter-Riders suddenly knocked for six.

See: Opening a Door on Moving Traffic; Taxis; Delivery Drivers; White Vans; Pedestrians from Nowhere; Hurry

OVER-FAMILIARITY
%%% @@@@@

During the 4 hours of each day dedicated to commuting or shopping or delivering groceries -or completing the School Run- the *un*familiar Driver, Rider or Pedestrian is absolutely certain to encounter the Over-Familiarity of Road-Users who use that Highway every single day. Nor does Over-Familiarity apply only to one route or one particular stretch of road; Over-Familiarity exists *between* hazards, between Passengers,

117

between loads, between stop-overs, between shopping-malls, between days of the week, between quieter nights, between car-parks, between vehicle-types, between almost everything. Over-Familiarity is at its most dangerous when it does not anticipate the unanticipated. And most road hazards, most Collisions, are unanticipated - though definitely not *unforeseeable*.

See: Tiredness; Boredom; Commuting; the School-Run; Rat-Runs; Nearness to Home; Lack of Concentration; Traffic Jams

OVERNIGHT DRIVING
%%%% @@

Overnight driving - especially heavy haulage - has its own benefits: eg. clearer mind, clearer roads, easier decision-making, looking forward to the Dawn. But there are also many perils: insomnia, tiredness, impatience, narcolepsy: the main debilitating factor being darkness - sometimes accompanied by fog , frost, and snow; the second drawback being lack of rest *prior to shift*: something that impacts heavily on airline pilots. Some Overnight Drivers have to wind down their windows to let fresh air in, or pinch themselves to maintain wakefulness.

A new peril faces motorcar Drivers on their way to the Seaside at the end of July or beginning of August. They have been busy packing and locking-up; then have to pacify, occupy, remonstrate with infants in the back who keep asking: "Are we there yet?" Cornwall is a long way from Durham.

See: Tiredness; HGV Safety; Lack of Concentration; Darkness; Long Journey; Narcolepsy

OVERTAKING
%%% @@@@@

Right from Day One of learner-driving: it is drummed into the Novice that overtaking is a potentially dangerous manoeuvre. Yet overtaking is so *tempting*: especially where a Corporation Bus or dustbin lorry has ground to a halt - or where there's a roundabout a mile ahead that might necessitate Right-hand approach, Right-hand exit.

Another aspect of overtaking is *pride*. It is not very macho for a powerful S.U.V. to be following a *Mini* or *Lada* for mile after mile - especially if that is on a winding country road: destination still 6 miles onward.

Additionally hazardous: overtaking can easily become a Highway *habit. Urgency.* Urgency every day. Every trip out. And the more a driver overtakes "successfully," the greater the temptation to overtake unsuccessfully the next time - when conditions are less favourable; when there is an unexpected traffic movement; when road space runs out; worst of all , when an approaching vehicle is also overtaking in the opposite direction.

As if these scenarios weren't depressing enough, there are added ill consequences for Motorcycles overtaking cars & goods' vehicles. They might be in *everybody*'s blind-spot; more in danger of being unseated by an upcoming driver's switch of intention.

Then there are lorries overtaking other lorries: worse when the "faster" vehicle runs out of steam. Most tantalizing: on a 300 mile excursion, the perpetual over-taker possibly gains only 17 minutes benefit through his or her recklessness. That anomaly arises from new & unforeseen slow-moving traffic once overtaking is accomplished. Perhaps better not to try in any circumstance that does not look safe or straightforward.

See: Speed; Impatience; Long Journey; Head-on; Unseated

PAPERWORK ON THE DASHBOARD
% @

Where the car or lorry is used as Office: map or paperwork dumped on the dashboard will usually reflect its image on the inside of the windscreen.

See: Inside Windscreen; Distractions; Food Deliveries; Loss of Concentration; White Van Man

PARCEL-DELIVERERS
%%% @@@@

Never before has the UK seen so many Parcel Deliverers: most of them outwardly "self-employed," but in reality fully employed by an often ruthless, penny-pinching, and totally unscrupulous employer : a version of modern slavery. Pay - as one might expect - is peanuts, solely by commission. Many Delivery or Despatch Employers insist on Zero-Hours or Not-worth-the-paper-they're-written-on Contracts. And all Parcel-Deliverers are held up in terrible traffic-jams & are working against the clock. Bad enough if the intended Parcel-Recipient can be traced, then got up from bed.

See: Low Pay; Traffic Jams; Tight Deadlines; White Van Man; Commuters; Tiredness; Low Pay; Just-in-Time

PARKING IN BLINDSPOTS
%%   @@@

A national shortage of off-street parking; crowded employer Car Parks; also Illegal Parking where it should never have taken place, result in cars & vans parking in Blindspots. That misbehaviour almost inevitably leads to Collision or risk of Collision. Because *legitimately* reversing vehicles neither see nor anticipate a car or taxi in their Blindspot. More Collisions or near misses happen when Drivers cannot reach or get out of their own drives! And when *fights* break out, they are ugly - and cause additional injury!

See: Rat-Runs; Anger; Reversing; Roadside Parking; Multi-Storey Car Parks; Hurry

PARKING AT JUNCTIONS
%%%   @@@

Parking at a Junction, except in an emergency, is a selfish & thoughtless act. Junctions are complicated enough without Drivers' & Riders' forward or rear vision being obstructed by parked vehicles. In effect, near traffic lights, those parked vehicles form an extra lane to be avoided or squeezed past. Pedestrians also suffer through Junction Parking.

See: T-Junctions, Overtaking; Pedestrians from Nowhere

PAVEMENT PARKING
%%   @@@@@

Pavement Parking is a particular hazard outside of London. Grass Verges and depressed side-walks are especially prone to the scattering or dumping of immobilized cars & vans unable to be garaged... sometimes when the adjacent house has a long drive! Children, Blind or Elderly Pedestrians & prams attempting to *dodge* Pavement-Parkers might well be involved in a worse misadventure than simple eyesore.

What exactly happens if the Pavement Parker actually knocks a child over whilst mounting the verge at speed or in twilight?

See: Pedestrians from Nowhere; Parking; Mounting the Pavement; Hurry

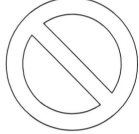

PEDESTRIANS APPEARING FROM UNEXPECTED QUARTERS
%%%%% @@@@@

The "unseen" Pedestrian is as universal as he or she is the *weaker* party on the Highway. There is little or no history of Britain separating Driver/Rider & Pedestrian. Some Pedestrians, especially children, emerge from hidden angles, side-roads or parked vehicles. Other Pedestrians are technically not permitted to be where they are. Yet other Pedestrians are already on authorized Pelican crossings or Zebras - but occupying them too soon or too late. Some of the most common unseen Pedestrians are in darkness, wearing dark clothing, obscured by glare or twilight or shadow; victims of fused lighting or sodium lighting.

See: Careless Pedestrians; Boredom; Over-Familiarity; School Run; Rat-Run; Pavement Parking; Multi-Storeys

PEDESTRIANS NOT USING A REFUGE
%%%% @@@

A Refuge can be Pelican Crossing, Zebra Crossing, Footbridge, Bollard, Grass Verge, Central Reservation ... or a purpose-built island dedicated to Pedestrians. These latter Refuges break up a road: usually halfway across - so making a busy Highway much more crossable where crossing would otherwise have been impossible.

Most reckless: even college lecturers, off-duty Professional Drivers, Bus Drivers finishing their shifts; and normally-sensible shoppers trying to catch up with someone, dash across the carriageway without looking, hoping for the best.

But the best *doesn't* happen. Instead, traffic moves *faster* than expected - *to front as well as to rear* - with the added horror that a *new stream* of traffic emerges from somewhere, nowhere? Perhaps there is a side-turning opposite you didn't see, suddenly frees-up. Or a harmlessly parked car, far down the road, suddenly decides to set off to fill the gap. The advantage of Refuges is that they are safe, or safer, havens in a profoundly unsafe urban environment.

PEDESTRIAN PRECINCTS
% @@

Pedestrian Precincts are often more honoured in the breach than the observance. Everyone : Cash Vans, Security Vans, Police Patrols, Hotel Guests, Shop Owners, Royal Mail - plus loads of late or "lost" delivery drivers: *all* claim to need to be driving through a Pedestrian Precinct during the forbidden hours. If a Town makes too many exceptions to the rule, errant Drivers, lazy Drivers, will run roughshod over the authorities. And what's to say the rampaging Driver in this Pedestrian Area is not a Terrorist intent on *ploughing Pedestrians down*?

See: Anger; Rat Runs; Parcels Delivery; White Van Man; Traffic Police, Pedestrians from Nowhere; Unfamiliarity

PELICAN LIGHT CONFUSION: *[formerly known as PELICON FAILURE]*
%%% @@@@@

As with most Highway inventions, the [1969 inspired] Pelican is not as bad as the misunderstandings / mixed messages it gives rise to. Other names for Pelican-type Crossings are *Puffins* [without the word WAIT written in full], *Toucans* [safer crossing for Cyclists as well as Pedestrians], & *Pegasus'* [safer crossing for Horses in addition to Cyclists & Pedestrians].

Confusion arises when oncoming traffic simply ignores the Pelican; or when the Pedestrian dashes across on flashing Green or flashing Green Man; when a few Pedestrians begin crossing on Red Man, thus setting a bad example for others; & when new streams of traffic constantly enter or clear the Pedestrian space; when the Green Man is sited at the Pedestrian's waist when everybody expects the Green Man to be right *in front of* them; or when a blind Pedestrian expects a beep-beep-beep and no beep-beep-beep happens.

Pelican Confusion leads more often to *Pedestrian* injury as opposed to Driver injury or car-body damage. A further insult to the longsuffering Pedestrian, particularly on a busier road, is the Highway Engineer who deliberately sets the Pedestrian Green on "never" - unless all other traffic *has already* passed!

See: Impatience; Speed; Closing Distance; Pedestrian Unexpected; Jumping Lights; Cycle Safety; Zebras

PARCEL DELIVERY
%%   @@@

One of the newest Industries of the 21st. Century is Parcel Delivery. Internet shopping can perform a lot in the ether - but eventually a Parcel or Package must be sent out to an actual Address or Lock-Up. Parcel Deliverers are notorious for being Self-Employed Commission Slaves. Even if one deliverer completes his round, and a colleague's round, without any traffic jams or hold-ups or aborted deliveries, that deliverer would never, or hardly ever, earn a minimum wage, let alone a *living* wage. There is nowhere for the deliverer to park in most busy city streets; nor is there any guarantee that the deliverer traces the correct address; gains admission to flats; acquires a signature; let alone securing a toilet or a sandwich-break between deliveries. Worse: early in the morning, parcels have to be collected from a distant depôt; then it's pressure, pressure, pressure. And Delivery Driving becomes unsafe, unsafe, all through one Hell of a shift.

See: Tight Deadlines; Food Deliverers; Impatience; Reversing; Tiredness; Rat-Runs; Pavement-Parking

PEDAL-CYCLISTS COLLIDING WITH PEDESTRIANS
%%%% @

Still relatively rare: Cyclists running into, or brushing aside, passing Pedestrians - nevertheless cause life-changing injury. Here, unusually, it is *the Cycle* that is the more powerful party. Admittedly *the Pedestrian* himself or herself might suddenly change direction; Pedestrians are impulsive & keep forgetting road manners - or something they wanted in shops they have already passed; to say nothing of meeting old friends welcoming their re-acquaintance.

See: Pedestrians from Nowhere; Loss of Concentration; Braking; Pedestrian Precincts; Pavements

PEDAL-CYCLE COLLISIONS WITH CARS OR WHITE VANS
%%%%% @@

Calamitous. And here the *more powerful* Vehicle should take a large share of responsibility - even where the rule of 50-50 blame is embedded; even where the Cyclist has wobbled. At best the stuck Cyclist will be thrown onto the verge or the Highway itself - not beneath the wheels of the Car or Van itself.

See: Pedal Cycle-Pedal Cycle Collisions; Unseating; Loss of Concentration; Glancing; Opening Doors; White Van Man

PEDAL-CYCLE -PEDAL CYCLE COLLISIONS
%%%% @

These Collisions are fortunately rare outside the Velodrome: nevertheless terrible *within* the Velodrome. Cycle/Cycle Collisions on a main Highway, even under the auspices of Bike-

Hire or Cycle Club outing, lead to terrible facial, shoulder & leg injuries. Were the Cycles progressing on their journey too near to each other? Or did they all see a new hazard simultaneously? Or did the lead Cyclist sneeze?

See: Loss of Concentration; Cycle Helmets; Unseating; Speed

PIECEMEAL ROAD & TRANSPORT POLICY
%%%   @@@@@

In Post-War years, British Transport Policy has been *disastrously* Piecemeal: a type of happenstance, partial, thoughtless - and totally unco-ordinated. In many post 1997 administrations, there has been a different Minister of Transport every twelve months! Worse, that Ministry has not always enjoyed Cabinet status: merely an offshoot of the Department of the Environment. This all has an impact on Highway Collisions which, in turn, are *normalized.*

One ring-road or by-pass is constructed without an end-plan for what takes place when it rejoins existing carriageways. Two lanes become Three Lanes. Three Lanes then acquire a fourth crawler or Right-turning Lane. A Motorway is laid out from nowhere to nowhere. Essential safety schemes are postponed for 90 years or more! Some bridges are public, some private. Sometimes "Smart" Roads are attempted, then modified: then modified or abandoned altogether.

Worse, some Highways & Trunk Roads are *national* assets, whilst *most* Highways remaining under Local Authority control & suzerainty. Then Airlines start offering £10 flights, so encouraging all that travel to and from Airports. Then railways are run into the ground - or ridiculously overcrowded: again forcing more traffic onto the road. Worse, Offices & Shopping Malls are built to the detriment of home-working and High Street shopping respectively.

To sum up, Road Safety could not be attempted in a more hostile, even chaotic, political climate: had the internal combustion engine never been invented!

See: Bypasses; Airports; Multi-Storey Car Parks; Commuting; HGVs; Fleets; Normalization

PILE-Ups

%%%%% @

Pile-Ups are fortunately relatively rare: but where they *happen* they are fatal both literally and metaphorically. Like the Penalty Shoot-Out in Football, Pile-Ups have been dismissed as *chance* happenings *nobody* can make sense of.

So untrue. Every single Pile-Up results from one vehicle's positioning; one Driver's miscalculation. All the resulting chaos is a direct consequence of that first vehicle's stalling or skewing or rubber-necking. *Up to 150* vehicles can pile into each other "like cocoa-tins." Was it fog? Was it momentary lack of concentration? Or was it irresistible propulsion from behind? Maybe it was Highway *bullying*: never a factor to ignore. But somehow, *one* succeeding vehicle has, with boldness or ingenuity, to succeed in halting the carnage. Or else….

And Police or Highways Agency response should be less "Act of God! Or should be less: "Let's clear it all away!" Or less: "50-50." Or less: "When sea-mist drifted in, it was *bound* to happen." Instead we owe it to all car & lorry occupants that there should be an absolutely meticulous gathering of evidence, shooting of photographs, modeling on computers, interviewing of witnesses. In the wake of the dreaded Pile-Up, no stone should be left unturned.

See: Loss of Concentration; Jack-Knifing; Speed; Fog; Flyovers; Weather Conditions; Sudden Braking

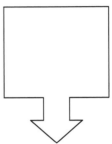

PLOUGHING DOWN
%%%%% @

The ploughing down of Pedestrians; equally - but usually without so many injuries - the ploughing-into of parked vehicles, are atrocities thankfully rare. But this stratagem, this *criminality*, has been greatly enhanced *as a terrorist tactic* by Nice on the French Riviera, Bastille Day: 14th. July, 2016. Once that catastrophe proved "a success," *other* vengeful terrorists copied both the tactic and the manoeuvre. Needless to say, ploughing down is as unpreventable as it is devastating. If a Council erects barriers in one market, one pedestrian zone, or one thoroughfare, the terrorist, or the upset husband, or the religious fanatic will simply choose another *un*protected crowd, another Promenade, another Pavement, another Bridge. Hence the importance of keeping track on suspiciously-hired vans or lorries, at the same time allowing *no* exceptions in daytime within Pedestrian Precincts.

See: Anger; Mounting a Pavement; Pedestrian Flow; Road Rage

POOR DRIVER-BEHAVIOUR
%%% @@@@@

Poor Driver-Behaviour is universal: committed even by otherwise careful or subdued Drivers. And the bracket of Poor Driver-Behaviour includes everything from eating whilst driving, smoking whilst driving, speeding, overtaking recklessly, to road-rage; worse, dangerous driving or manslaughter.

Equally universal are the specious excuses for Poor Driver-Behaviour: "bad weather," "something nobody could foresee," "bad light," or "another fool on the road." In other words, most Drivers & Riders prefer to blame anything, anyone, other than themselves for whatever is going wrong. Colluding with the Bad Driver or the Errant Driver is his Passenger. Passengers are taught, expected, from birth not to criticize whoever is driving. Puzzling?

See: Dangerous Driving; Poor Rider-Behaviour; also most other entries in Part One.

POOR PEDESTRIAN-BEHAVIOUR
%%%% @@@@@

Pedestrian-Behaviour is innate to all Pedestrian Movement. By their very weakness - and Pedestrians *are* the weakest Road-Users - Pedestrians are tempted to behave unpredictably, worse dangerously.

Poor Pedestrian-Behaviour encompasses dawdling, zombie-ing, playing chicken, underestimating speeds, jay-walking, not using refuges, passing immediately behind a reversing vehicle - & *un*learning the Green Man Code. That still doesn't excuse the on-coming Rider of Driver who has failed to factor in Pedestrian oddity, occasional Pedestrian perversity.

See: Poor Driver-Behaviour; Pedestrian Unexpected; Road Rage; Pelican Crossings; Pedestrian-Cycle Collisions; also many other - or seemingly unrelated - entries.

POOR RIDER-BEHAVIOUR
%%% @@@@@

Every aspect of Poor Driver-Behaviour applies to Poor Rider-Behaviour and Poor Motorcyclist-Behaviour: with the added danger - a very real danger - arising from all Riders having only two wheels rather than a tricycle's 3, or a lager vehicle's 4, 6 or 8 . Also Cyclists or Motorcyclists are just as reticent to criticize themselves as Drivers. After all, a seasoned Motorcyclist might have been honing his or her skill since mountain-biking, moto-cross, rallying & advance skateboarding at the age of eight. Additionally, many Riders of sophisticated Bikes, whether pedal- or motor-, have been doctors, teachers & lawyers.

See: Poor Driver Behaviour; Wobbly Cycle; Speeding; Overtaking;   .... *also almost any other entry in Part One.*

POOR MOPED, SCOOTER & MOTORCYCLE LIGHTING
%%%% @@@

Riding a two-wheel vehicle is hazardous enough without a quite inadequate set of lights. Nearly every 4- 6- or 8-wheeled vehicle stopping after a Crash says of a Motorcycle: "I just didn't see it..." Better that even the Biker him- or herself is lit up, as well as fitting state-of-the-art rear & pannier lighting.

See: Lack of Concentration; Unlit Vehicles; High-Visibility

PORTABLE COMPUTERS
%%　　@@@@

Portable Computers come in several formats: from fairly bulky Laptops to tiny "intelligent" wristwatches. Yet *all* Portable Computers have one thing in common: they are a big temptation to look at. Why not glance at the Computer or i-phone at traffic lights set at red? Why not have a look during lengthy roadworks? And what about that completely snarled-up Motorway? Drivers are Drivers in control of their vehicles whether at a standstill or not. And e-mails, apps, web-sites, photograph albums, texts, urls, links, whatever, are all intensely distracting. But is it *really* sinful to have the screen on one's lap, *just in case*…. ?

See: Distractions; Hand-held Telephones; Loss of Concentration; Zombie Pedestrians; Car as Office; Sat-Navs

POST-TRAUMATIC STRESS DISORDER
%%%%　　@@

Post-Traumatic Stress is both a contributor to Collision *and* a result of past Collision. Even the most "minor" Collision has the capacity to leave its imprint both on the mental health of the affected Driver, Passenger, Pedestrian, or Rider and on his or her future confidence on the Highway. Highway memories come into the class of "intrusive memories": sudden, repetitive, unasked-for - as opposed to more common *recovered* memory.

Sometimes the sufferer is inaccurately called "accident-prone," where the truth is: all their natural defences have broken down by persistent and unyielding shock. It could be a Driver's fear of ever facing a White Van again; or a Pedestrian's fear of ever using a Zebra Crossing again. Nor do Motor Insurers always compensate Road-Users sufficiently for PTSD; though any sufferer would willingly trade in any sum of money for regained serenity.

See: Accident-Prone; Rear Collisions; Witnesses; Hire Cars

POTHOLES
%%% @@@@

Potholes get their name from Stoke-on-Trent where amateur potters simply dug clay out from beneath their feet! And the more the UK is in recession; the more roads suffer from too much traffic; or too much frost; also the fewer Central Government grants available to Local Government: the greater the number of Potholes, the greater their width & depth, *the longer their lifetimes.*

Potholes cause vehicles & cycles to veer out of control; additionally tempting erratic driving behaviour; at a minimum, causing irreparable damage to tyres and chassis.

See: Loss of Control; Loss of Concentration; Unseating; Swerving; Unfamiliarity

POWERFUL CARS & MOTORCYLES
[also POWERED MOBILIY SCOOTERS]
%%%% @@

If a vehicle or machine has too much horsepower for its particular job, for commuting or the school run, for popping to the supermarket or an amble through the Lake District: then all that wasted power will make the Driver or Rider frustrated that they are not going at the correct speed. Hence late-night racing - or, more commonly, overtaking anything that moves, with zippy acceleration, sudden braking.

Conversely, where a Mobility Scooter is souped-up, it travels at far greater speed than its 4 or 6 mph expectation. And 1950s BSA or Norton Motorcycles were always hazardous on the Highway before really high-powered racing machines, source in Japan or the USA, doubled *or trebled* that hazard.

See: Motorcycles; Overtaking; Speeding; Impatience; Braking

PROTESTORS

%%   @

Protestors come in many shapes & sizes: single people glued to a railing - or blocking a dangerous crossing-point; gay pride; Trade Unionists; disappointed football fans; tree warriors; animal-rights' campaigners;   marchers;   poll-tax   rebels; students; sitters- ins; squatters; pickets;   kettled ... right through to huge rallies . What holds all these Protestors in common is the strength of their cause; *commitment* to that cause; the hostility toward Police;   Police hostility towards their both the protest & the Protestors; and, crucially, hostility displayed by passing - or bottled-up - or held-up - Drivers. These frustrated Drivers do not hesitate to drive straight through a crowd; to accelerate menacingly near to Protestors; threatening also to run-down - or actually run-over - anybody in their way. Nor will Police be inclined to criticize those whom mistakenly they call "innocent parties." Acts of Protest are usually perfectly legal, *but are treated as illegal*.

See: Pedestrians from Nowhere; U-turns; Reversing; Anger.

PUDDLE-BASHING
%%   @@

Drivers Puddle-Bash either deliberately, as a misguided joke, or thoughtlessly, negligently, carelessly: an appalling driving behaviour. For the Driver & his or her Passengers there's a danger of aquaplaning. For Pedestrians: sheer misery.

See: Speed; Rain; Aquaplaning; Bollard-Bashing; Weather

PURSUIT
%%%%% @@

Pursuit by Police, by deprived owners, or by other injured parties is widely accepted to be worse than Non-Pursuit - although it is impossible to assess the relative outcomes in any tense situation. What makes Pursuit more hazardous is the likelihood of impacting upon "innocent" bystanders. At least 100 such by-standers, as well as countless perpetrators, are killed each year by Pursuit: serious Injury a multiple of this figure. Without collaboration or a sting-mat, the outcome of Pursuit is very rarely happy.

See: Joy-Riding; Emergency Vehicles; Speeding; Driving while Disqualified; Wrong Documentation; TWOC; Boy-Racers

PUSHING IN
%%%   @@@@@

Motorists push in because they can. They desperately hope another road-user will allow them to push in. Because they must. Overdose of pride on the part of the one who pushes in. Dented pride: in place of dented vehicle: the Driver who colludes with the pusher-in. Pushing-in happens most when queue-jumping: that behaviour usually following erection or lighting-up of a "Lane Closed" sign. Pushing in is also quite blatant within Car Parks that have run out of parking-lots.

Yet undoubtedly the most dangerous push-in ever occurs where a careless or reckless over-taker faces an on-coming vehicle. Nor is there a clean or clear way of letting the over-taker know someone has bailed him out.

See: Impatience; Queue-Jumping; Side-Swipes; Road Rage; Competing for Road Space; Crawling Traffic; White Van Man.

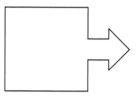

QUAD BIKES
%%   @

Quad Bikes are perhaps an ideal way to get around a farm or a ranch. The difficulty is when they attempt to take to *main* roads. Quad Bikes are not subject to compulsory seat-belts or crash helmets but must still fulfill very strict safety standards & registration when they take to the public road. They also need superb *lighting* in the dark of the countryside.

See: Mobility Scooters; Segways; Electric Scooters; Motocross

QUARTER-GLASS / QUARTER WINDOW
%%   @@@

Car side-windows need, ideally, to be fairly large: single uninterrupted panes without any vents or letter A's. Both Cyclists & Pedestrians disappear when Quarter-Windows are fitted. For such a minor accessory: major Collisions.

See: Hidden Cyclists; Pedestrians from Nowhere

QUEUEING TRAFFIC
%%   @@@@@

Queues of traffic form quite easily wherever there are roadworks or "simple" traffic jams & hold-ups. But in one or two places, the queue *itself* sharply increases the chance of a collision rather than simply slowing everyone down. Generally, the Motorist or Lorry Driver does not expect a queue on a fast Motorway: maybe a queue to exit; but almost worse is the queue on the slip-road. Queues demand a particular sub-genre of driving skill. Ironically the queue for the Seaside leads a few Drivers not to go to that Seaside at all - doing a U-turn instead!
See: U-turns; Rear Collisions ; Crawling Traffic; Loss of Concentration; Pushing-in

QUEUE-JUMPING
%%   @@@

Just as in the Dinner Queue, the Bus Queue, the Check-out Queue or the Post Office Queue, Queue-Jumping on the road is as "successful" as it is prevalent. Some queueing motorists judge that if they overtake *the whole of* the hold-up, the motorist at the front of the queue - or second back - will unwillingly let them back in again. If not, the shameless Jump-er will so place his or her vehicle as to *force* re-entry.
See: Queueing Traffic; Crawling Traffic; Impatience; Competing for Road Space; Pushing-in

RACE MEETINGS
%%   @

Race Meetings matter for road safety not because of whatever happens on or in the environs of the actual Race Track, but the impact Racing has on the audience or attendees. Onlookers & paying customers alike are psyched up - even after Motocross, Jalopy or Dirt-Racing: so the temptation is to ride or drive as your heroes did. Police report lots of casualties in the vicinity of Race Circuits. Also cars might have to queue to get in.
See: Daring; Imitation, Impatience; Speeding

RAIN
%%%   @@@@

Rain does not by itself cause Collisions, except a landslide onto the road or when accompanying a tornado - but Rain *is* a factor in a huge number of Collisions. Windscreen-wipers are tested to their limits; and Drivers and Cyclists and the Riders of Motorcycles soon get tired, irritable, bewildered; wet through to the skin, if they're *not* shielded. Rain also has the property of greatly increasing mist inside & outside a vehicle: testing car often-primitive heating systems to the limit.
See: Weather; Windscreen Wipers; Puddle-Bashing

RAMBLERS RAMBLING
%%%   @

Seasoned Ramblers nearly always prefer footpaths and bridle-ways, or deserted country lanes, to rambling on a main road- or a road with extra hazards like blind-bends or blind hills. From the birth of the motor car to the beginning of this

Century, it was orthodoxy that Ramblers Rambling either on a main road, or on a secondary road, or any road without pavements or wide verges, that Ramblers or Guided Parties should march on the *Right* hand side of a British carriageway, boldly facing *oncoming* traffic. Then, with the invention of Hi-Vis jackets, someone suggested marching could be safer *on the Left* [a suggestion dismissed out-of-hand by old-stagers; also not a few motorists]. When a heavier vehicle *does* plough into clutches or parties of Pedestrians or Ramblers with whom they share the Highway, the results are disastrous: *many* deaths or serious injuries, plus a lot of fright.

See: Dark Clothing; No Pavement; Pedestrians Unexpected; Speeding; Ploughing-into

RAM RAIDING
%%% @

Ram Raiding is a frightening sequence of events where the Car, Lorry or Motorcycle is itself used to break glass & enter premises which might be open or closed. Pedestrians using those convenience shops - & it *is* convenience shops where the temptation to Ram-Raid is greatest - are the first to suffer. By definition a Ram-Raid is also a Collision. You can tell a past Ram-Raid by the footage of plate-glass now boarded up. Sometimes, now, solid posts are erected outside commercial premises to deter Ram-Raiders.

See: Dishonest Driving; Swerving; Vehicle as Weapon: Mounting the Pavement

RAT RUNS   *[SHORT-CUTS or CHICKEN-RUNS]*
%%% @@@@

Every Driver of a small vehicle is proud to boast of his or her best Rat-Run. That Rat-Run then becomes more & more popular! Sceptical or intimidated local residents may *not* be car-owners - & if they are, their houses were not designed with off-street parking. Thus Rat-Runs only benefit the transgressor- & even then, there is the enormous chance, probability, of Collision at the moment of leaving the Rat-Run in order to join or re-join a preferable route. For instance, Drivers have to turn an awkward Right into jammed traffic on the next main road. Meanwhile, for Drivers who've used a Petrol Station to cut off a corner, speed is of the essence: first, so as not to lose the net time advantage; second, not to be spotted or told off by the owner! And as if matters could not get worse, Rat-Runs in school holidays contain lots of wandering children or children at play; also delivery vans delivering.

See: Access Only; Parked Vehicles; Pedestrians from Nowhere

REAR COLLISIONS / REAR SHUNTS
%%%% @@@

Rear Collisions are unusual in that the Law says they shouldn't happen - but what happens when they do? Rear Collisions are nearly always the result of either or both of sudden braking by the front, or lead, vehicle & lack of concentration on the part of the following Driver. Shunts also occur frequently on busy Roundabouts; in slow-moving traffic jams; or after deliberate braking on behalf of the front Driver. Then there is the scenario where a car or van unexpectedly turns Left or Right onto a minor road where there is a parked, or parking, vehicle also unexpected. Fudged or inept kerbside parking is also a factor.

Rear Collisions should *not* be written off by Motor Insurers as 50-50: because the following Driver or Rider *does* retain agency. That accepted, the follower *is* sometimes hapless, particularly in unfamiliar light or an unfamiliar area.

Back-seat Passengers - especially those not belted in - are severely jolted, sometimes thrown onto the highway, by a Rear Shunt at speed.   And in the midst of Pile-Up: everyone impacted is in the middle of a nightmare. One little-recognized side-effect of Rear Collisions is where the following Driver suffers undetected pulmonary injury, not to raise PTSD.

See: Crash for Cash; Pile-Ups; Loss of Concentration; Over-familiarity; Sudden Braking

REMOTE CROSSROADS
%%%% @@@

On country lanes, also unclassified roads, the Crossroad becomes much more problematic - dangerous - because it is so Remote, it is not really anticipated, let alone slowed down for. Yet probability is very high that some other person or vehicle will be crossing when the primary oncoming vehicle is.

See: Crossroads; Speed

RESPONSIBILITY TO LOAD & UNLOAD A CARGO
%%%   @@@

Research would seem to point to a greater safety record for Lorry or Juggernaut Drivers who have not had to do their own loading & unloading. Where the Driver has been left with no alternative but to load at yard or depot then unload at destination, that makes he or she that much more tired and less patient when they actually take to the Highway.

See : HGV Safety; Lorries; Lack of Concentration; Impatience; Low Pay; Long Journeys

REVENGE
%%%%% @@@@@

Road Revenge is another maximum hazard: one, ironically, neither attracting maximum attention nor maximum penalty. This outrage could be as "simple" as a Driver's solo curse, a Pedestrian's solo grunt or irritable wave. That yearning for Revenge soon *amplifies* itself to become shouting or gesturing at other Riders / Cyclists / Drivers / Pedestrians; worse, leaving the security of one's own saloon, one's own bubble, in order to begin or continue - or attempt to subdue - a heightening outage. An incomprehensible outrage in most instances.

Road Revenge has a delayed as well as an immediate impact: making affected, affronted, Motorists, Cyclists or Pedestrians far more anxious or irritated or angry for the rest of the day.

One aspect of Road Revenge attracts *minimum* interest: that is *manufactured* disconsolation. This phenomenon is most associated with "joy-riders" & "boy-racers." They simply wind down their window in order to abuse & unsettle passing Pedestrians who cannot *fathom* what's going or gone wrong. Then these pranksters hoot and hoot with their hooters in order to unsettle a lead Driver to check their boots, tyres or exhausts. One huge "joke" - but *could* it be more serious?

See: Road Rage; Good Samaritans; Anger; Boy-Racers; Horns; Joy-Riding; Loud Music; Post-Traumatic Stress.

142

REVERSING
%%%% @@@@@

Reversing is nearly always a hazard. Nor are Reverse Warnings fitted to vehicles other than Brewer's Drays or Dustbin Lorries. Even [white] Reverse Lights are next-to-useless in crowded areas. That means Reversers reverse regardless of anyone walking behind their reversing vehicle; regardless too of hidden posts, pillars & bollards. An added problem - if additional danger were possible - where the Reverser reverses out of an alley or ten-foot or private drive on to a carriageway, any unwary Pedestrians are completely *unseen*. The same - and more - applies to reversing from a side-road onto a main road; or reversing in or from yards or depots.

Another Reversing problem is traffic build-up, leading the impatient Driver to reverse, do a 3-point turn, then discover an alternative route. Worse: the hastier the decision to reverse, the poorer the result. Also included here: Reverse *Parking*, so difficult for many Drivers that they never attempt it - instead mounting the pavement in order to forward park into a tight space. Not for them *the correct* reverse-parking procedure.

A final reversing problem is maintaining a straight line. This, possibly, can only be successfully achieved by the old-fashioned expedient of putting one's head out of the Driver's window. Far too many people suddenly stopping in narrow streets of terraced housing - including parcel & fast-food deliverers - reverse *at speed,* still aiming at that straight line: a "skill" which nearly always carries greater imprecision and greater fright to passing Pedestrians, playing children too.

See: Impatience; U-turns; Speed; Rat-Runs; Deliverers; Parking; lack of concentration

RING-ROADS
%%% @@

Urban Ring-Roads are a relatively cheap answer to suburban congestion: usually a joining together of formerly minor roads that were *not* heading into the City Centre. The trouble is: Ring-Roads are often *not* truly circular; nor for the most part do they segregate Pedestrian from Motorist. In fact, they have to be crossed, & crossed at frequent intervals, because Underpasses are too expensive; also people's homes straddling Ring-Roads continue to be lived in; & shops continue to trade: most of these buildings long predating the Ring-Road that has been built - or modified - to serve them.

See: Piecemeal Roads' Policy; Pelican Crossings; Footbridges; Underpasses; Hidden Flows of Traffic

ROAD FLOODED
%% @@

Some Drivers are eternal optimists and either ignore *totally* a sign that says "Road Ahead Flooded" - or *do* take note but think the sign is a few hours out-of-date. It is then quite frightening to have one's engine stalled in deep standing water. Pedestrians also behave very differently on roads or pavements that have been submerged.

See: Heavy Rainfall; Speed; Skid; Aquaplaning; Puddle-Bashing

ROAD RAGE
%%%%% @@

It is certainly impossible to underestimate the hazard presented by Road Rage whether deserved or undeserved, invited or suppressed, signalled or hidden, fair or unfair, reasonable or unreasonable. If it comes across as Road Rage then it is Road Rage, and - at its most extreme - it's a killer. Short of *never* flashing, *never* remonstrating with another Road User, there is little any Driver can do to avoid *the other party's* Road Rage. That leaves the *cautious* Driver with no option but to swallow his or her pride; to pray for the angered or aggrieved person; and to hope fervently one's *next* good or kind or generous gesture will balance past hurt.

See: Arguments; Anger; Dishonest Driving; Failure to Stop

ROADWORKS
%%   @@@@@

On the surface : Roadworks should greatly *decrease* Collisions or Near-Misses. After all, these perennial excavations aim to repair the tarmac, add to the lanes available, lay the essential cables, restore damaged Crash-Barriers, improve lighting, clarify signage whatever. A perfect good?

Where it all falls apart is speed & subcontracting: a noxious mixture. Not the speed of the Road Works! Go on hoping. The speed of trench-avoiding traffic is the point at issue. Plus subcontractors who fail to leave their half-completed endeavours properly fenced off; and their "temporary" traffic-lights properly timed.

The end-result: gigantic traffic jams, Driver impatience, motorcycles disappearing in the holes, and nobody understanding who's got right-of-way.

See: Traffic-Lights; Jumping Lights; Traffic Jams; Queueing Traffic; Crawling Traffic; Motorways; Speed; Long journeys

ROLLING FORWARD or BACKWARDS
%%% @

Rolling doesn't only happen on hills and slopes. Private drives are a problem also: with many a householder vainly trying to bring their car to a stop. Rolling also happens in a traffic jam because sensitive clutch-control has failed. A chief occasion for Rolling-Backwards is of course, thick mud, sludge or snow - where a vehicle looks as if it is stuck. Immediately everyone groups together to help the stranded motorist, rolling begins.

See: Hill Starts; Lack of Concentration; Good Samaritans

ROOF-LOADS [UNSAFE]
%%% @

Roof-Loads are most Unsafe when not skillfully & absolutely tied down. Moreover Roof-Loads will nearly always work themselves adrift if not shackled to a roof-rack. How often one encounters someone with a divan, a set of ladders or a wardrobe strung round using the car or van interior as the underpin. And wonderfully-soft divans have a wonderfully rapid chance of getting away from their ropes. Suitcases are also a problem. A few very well-off motorists invest in a purpose-made roof-box, aerodynamically shaped. The correct way to carry Cycles on one's roof is, of course, that they stand upright & facing the way of travel.

See: Unsafe Loads; Emergency Stops; Distractions; Speed; Cycles in Transit; Long Journeys

ROUNDABOUT DISCIPLINE
%%%% @@@@

Roundabout Discipline is frequently a contradiction of terms: where the rule is "every man for himself!" So it is that big Roundabouts nearly always favour *frequent* users: those familiar with most of the hazards, most of the outcomes.

Unfamiliar Drivers are always at a disadvantage, perhaps due to *too much* caution! Additionally, nearly all the Lane Ahead instructions are actually written on the tarmac: tarmac obscured by the traffic standing on it. So anything except the straight-ahead-with-one-stream-joining-from-the-Left-layout spells Danger. It's as if Roundabouts are combative : a test of strength as well as resolve.

See: Roundabouts; Mini-Roundabouts; Changes of Mind; Road Rage; Traffic Forcing Itself In; Swerving

ROWDY PASSENGERS
%%   @@

Raucous, Rowdy - or Drunk - Passengers can indirectly cause numerous Collisions: mainly because they really upset or impair both Driver & that Driver's Roadcraft. This is a problem of such prevalence that some insurance companies, also many parents, *ban* groups of Teenagers travelling in the same vehicle, or in the same vehicle after 5pm. As aggravation, Rowdy Passengers also demand rowdy music!

See: Limousines; Taxis; Boy Racers; Distractions; Loud Music

RUBBER-NECKING
%%%% @@@@@

It shouldn't happen; but what happens when it does? Every single Road-User is a Rubber-Necker. At normal times, that keeps us all safer. But when does such natural curiosity become lethal? At worst, when one carriageway of drivers strain their necks to see what's happening on the opposite carriageway. Or when folk are secretly attracted to blue lights.

On Motorways, in particular, there is ample *time* to look at the sad fate of someone - anyone - else in trouble; then to dwell on it. That amazement *does* reduce the attentiveness of both Driver & Navigator. In consequence, everyone *not* affected by adversity slows down a little to get a better view. Cue for more Collisions impacting on the Rubber-Neck-ers.

See: Loss of Concentration; Loss of Control; Police Patrols

RUNAWAY TYRES
%%%% @

Because HGVs & some SUVs have to carry spare tyres, it is possible these tyres will detach themselves and hurtle at up to 70mph towards any traffic following the unsecured fastening.

Additionally, *whole wheels* sometimes detach themselves & roll or lie, unattended, in the carriageway. It is estimated there are up to 15 deaths a year being struck by - or striking - a loose[d] tyre.

See: Motorways; HGVs; Off-Road Vehicles; Insecure Loads

SAT-NAVs
%%% @@@

In one way, Sat-Navs were intended to make Driving *safer*. On the contrary, these devices have thrown up lots more unforeseen hazards than their inventors could have imagined. First, size: Sat-Navs are getting bigger & bigger. Second, noise : Sat-Navs are getting louder and ever more persistent, its announcer ever strident & far more frustrated. Third - & crucially - *positioning*. Many Sat-Navs are glued or held by suction onto the front Windscreen where they look all-too-much like a miniature TV - whilst blocking out Cyclists & Pedestrians ahead. Finally, Sat-Navs lead directly to more Collisions and mishaps by misguidedly directing a trusting Driver towards a one-way street, a low railway bridge or a farm-track: definitely an invention with question-marks.

See: Distractions; Unfamiliarity; Front Windscreen; Map-read

SCAFFOLDING
%%% @

Scaffolding presents all sorts of challenge for other Road-Users. At its worst, the whole lot will simply collapse causing terrible fright, injury & death. Thankfully, those collapses are relatively rare; but the Scaffolding still has to carried to site on very exposed low-loaders. Then it has to be discharged onto a public pavement. Finally, after partial erection, it needs to be tied securely. Then a week or two later, the framework is dismantled beginning the whole dangerous process in reverse. Scaffolding makes a spine-chilling noise, *especially in deconstruction*; and Pedestrians or passing motorists have every reason to be terrified.

See: Loads Shed; Insecure Loads; Pedestrians from Nowhere; Debris on the Carriageway

[THE] SCHOOL-RUN
%%% @@@

By its very nature, the School-Run is boring and repetitive. Worse the School-Run is *always* subject to personal and time-pressures. Almost nowhere parking in the precincts of a School legal and/or advisable. Distracted & inattentive children appear everywhere & from nowhere. Nor are strangers' children the *only* child hazard. What about the ill, unwell, noisy or irascible child or children actually *inside* the car? Or the so-called friend waving, or frantically signaling, outside the car? If motor insurers did not have to respond to the dire School-Run, they'd have to invent it: a nightmare for every single party involved, whether active or passive. Then comes the Mum or Grand-dad who has to deliver two children to separate Schools. Then comes the Head Teacher having to go outside and beg Drivers not to park on banks, pavements or double-yellow lines. And what if Step-Dad has a dual mission: to actually talk to the Head about his child's health or homework?

See: Commuting; Over-Familiarity; Tiredness; Unruly Passengers; Child-Seats; Boredom; Pedestrians from Nowhere

SEAT HEIGHT *[Incorrect]*

%% @@

See: Cabin too Cosy; Rest Breaks; Underage Drivers

SEAT BACKS *[Incorrect or Uncomfortable]*

% @@

See: Cabin too Cosy; Rest Breaks; Driving with a Disability

SEAT-BELTS *[or Declining / Refusing to Wear One]*

%%% @@@@

Some years ago, in 1983, the Seat-Belt debate was put to bed: fourteen years since they were fitted as standard in UK cars, and with some acknowledgement that, in a small proportion of Collisions, wearing one could lead to more injury or death than compliance with the law. That law itself is all-too-rarely *actively* enforced. Teenagers - also Long-Distance Coach and Taxi Passengers - are renowned for un-learning Jimmy Savile's lesson of "Clunk-Click." Ideally, compliance should be more universal: at the same time taking into account Delivery Drivers and Milkmen who are exempt whilst on active delivery.

See: White Vans; Immediate Braking; Buses; Coaches; Boy-Racers; Rowdy Passengers

SECOND-HAND CARS

%%% @@@@@

The same suspicion that a 14-year old girl has for hand-me-down clothes does not necessarily translate into her suspicion inheriting a Second-Hand Car ten years later. Second-Hand Cars are not, of course, inherently unsafe. They might be owned already by a parent or brother-in-law; or sold by a reputable garage; or else this Second-Hand Car might carry a genuine no-quibble 5-year Guarantee.

The trouble arises from either no-questions-asked Auctions, or, worse, backstreet merchants posing as bereaved widows: the sort of trader who'll willingly solder the front half of one car to the back half of another. Moral: know your seller. If a bargain motor is too good to be true then it *is* too good to be true.

See: Dishonest Driving; Bald Tyres; Unmaintained Vehicles; Documentary Offences

SEGWAYS   *[Human Transporters; Personal Transporters]*
%% @

As with Electric Scooters, Segways are far less common on the streets of London or Brighton than Paris or Marseilles. Undoubtedly, however, they will become more popular, thus need closer regulation. Segways are a very good idea: but *three* of their 4 popular destinations, pavement, gutter, carriageway, or municipal park are inherently unsafe - particularly where Segway collides with Pedestrian.

See: Mobility Scooters; Pedal Cycles; Electric Scooters; Surfing

SHOPPING STREETS
%%%%   @@@@

Not every Shopping Street is also a Pedestrian Precinct: anything but. Especially in rural towns, suburbs, also well-established Market- or County-Towns: there is a tradition of mixing Pedestrians, Shoppers & Motorists along the same stretch of road. Worse, a number of toddlers and school children add to the mix. Then - as if matters could not deteriorate further - *parking* for cars & white-vans is allowed at the kerbside. Gaudily-lit shops with lots of offers, big hoardings, runaway shopping-trolleys, people squatting anywhere or everywhere to consume fast-food - not forgetting those numerous A-boards cluttering the pavement: also distract the already poorly-concentrating Driver trying to find somewhere to stop, or stop & shop.

See: Pedestrian Precincts; Reversing; Pavement Parking; Distractions; Tight Time Limits; Pedestrians from Nowhere

SIDE-SWIPES
%%% @@

Side-Swipes are a particular category of Collision no less to be feared because they cause less death and injury than Rear Collisions or Head-On Collisions. Side-Swipes are the result of Competing for Road Space - or misunderstanding direction ahead. Side-Swipes are far more likely to happen on a busy Roundabout or at a multiple-choice Junction; also where a larger vehicle: Coach or HGV has to take a straight line where other road-users expect a curved line of travel.

A recent increase in Side-Swipe *severity* arises from the amazing popularity of 4x4 Vehicles with their much higher driving-position. Side-Swipes have greater toxicity, also, on a three- or four-lane Motorway. That is because the Motorway is a hostile environment for Side-Swipes. It is almost impossible for the victim or survivor to take down the number-plate of the offender, let alone time enough to drive to a safe place to exchange details. Other Side-Swipes destroy side-mirrors.

See: Competing for Road Space; Motorways; Mirror Positioning; HGVs; Low-Loaders; Lack of Concentration; Head-on Collisions; Rear Collisions or Shunts; Switching Lanes

SKIPS
%% @

Skips are relatively rare - yet when they are delivered, collected, positioned, or emptied, they cause all sorts of trouble. They are rarely lit up properly where a parked car would normally be next to the pavement. Additionally, crane movements are extremely erratic handling them. Finally, Skips on journeys to their dump tend to shed part of their load on to the carriageway.

See: Parked Cars; Cul-de-Sacs; Unsecured Loads; One-Way Streets

SLIPSTREAM
%% @

Slipstream on the nearside or rearside of HGVs or Buses is a real problem for Cycles & Motorcycles in the vicinity: slightly different from a Wind Tunnel and less gusty. Slipstream interrupted is probably worse than a stable Slipstream. The worst outcome is either Unseating or veering into the larger vehicle in the surrounds.

See: Cycle Wobble; Wind Tunnel; Loss Of Control

SLOW LIGHTS *[Slow Pedestrian Crossings]*
%% @@@@

80% of pedestrian-crossing lights, what used to be called Pelicans, are poorly-adjusted. The Green Man is set not to appear till all the oncoming traffic has disappeared - which rather makes nonsense of the whole initiative.

Pedestrians then become impatient - at exactly the same time approaching drivers "jump" in response to the injustice of their being kept waiting when so much other traffic *was* given the go-ahead. So here is the recipe for Pedestrian Collision: all because Pedestrians are rarely, if ever, afforded due priority.

See: Pelican Lights; Jumping Lights; Impatience; Footbridges

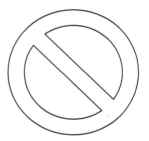

SKIDDING
%%% @

Skids & Skidding happen not just on Black Ice or White Ice. It's quite possible - probable? - to skid on snow or slush or oil - or even during torrential rain. But what do you skid into? Unless one is trained on a skid-pad: the skid - staple of every crime movie - will nearly always be unexpected, and *much more dangerous at speed.* Skids are also far more dangerous mile-by-mile for *Motorcyclists* than for most other Drivers or Riders.

See: Icy Roads; Out-of-Control; Swerving; Motorcycles; Snow; Unseating; Tyres

[THE] SLOWER DRIVER
%% @@@

It is far from apocryphal that several novice Drivers fail their Practical Tests for proceeding *too slowly*. Slowness might arise from old age, failing eyesight, a too powerful car, years of traffic jams, unfamiliarity with the road or the district, listening to a favourite track on the radio, listening too attentively to a Sat-Nav - or being a survivor of a past Crash.

Other Slow Drivers & Riders, plus many Deliverers, are turning their heads first Left, then Right, in search of an intended side-turning, or even an intended house. Another category of Slower Drivers are those following previous advice changing down the gears prior to a hold-up: deliberately dawdling so that the engine is never switched off. Crawling in crawling traffic is a very precise accomplishment. On an unhappier note, Drunk Drivers go very slow for fear of not being in complete control - which, of course, they aren't.

The penalties for Slowness can range from a Police fine - especially on a Motorway - to the sound of Horns, flashing and rear shunts. Maybe a driver in a hurry will not take kindly to his Colleague on the Highway who doesn't budge when a long roadworks eventually shows Green; less when a Hill-Start goes pear-shaped.

See: Slower Pedestrian; Traffic Jam; Crawling Traffic; Impatience; Overtaking; Undertaking; Sat-Navs; Flashing

[THE] SLOWER PEDESTRIAN
%% @@

The Slower Pedestrian is one who moves at far more sluggish a pace than anybody should reasonably expect. To some extent, Pelican Lights are timed to make allowance for the laggard. Even then, one would need to be an Olympic Sprinter to get safely across some Highways. Prams, baby-buggies and reins slow down many parents with children. Also a normally fast Pedestrian might slow because he or she hasn't *seen* a vehicle.

See: Fallen Pedestrian; Pedestrian from Nowhere; Congested Traffic; Pelican Crossings; Distractions; Zombies

SLUSH
%% @

Slush is a hazard for several reasons. First it is relatively uncommon. Second it can easily re-freeze at night into ruts. Third it deprives Cyclists of their gutter. Fourth it allows for more skidding than most other road surfaces. Fifth - & frequently forgotten - Slush deprives Pedestrians of their pavement which will almost certainly be in worse condition than the Highway. Thus it is that skirted Pedestrians directly compete with traffic from front *and* rear.

See: Snow; Weather; Skidding; Pedestrian from Nowhere; Ice

SMART MOTORWAYS
%%%%% @@

As the BBC, also many Motoring Organizations, have discovered: "Smart" Motorways are not nearly so Smart as the Highways' Agency hoped or planned for. Originally there were to have been really frequent lay-bys to replace the permanently removed Hard Shoulder; plus cameras to indicate when & where any vehicle had stalled, stopped or broken down in an active lane. Neither installation happened.

So to stop for any reason in the active lane of a Smart Motorway is to sign one's own death certificate. At best, all following traffic will suddenly swerve out of your way: an act of kindness causing its own deaths & injury. And avoiding, with no notice, a broken-down or wrecked vehicle leads to so many Near-Misses that there are roughly *50 times more* Near-Misses per smartened stretch than on a conventional Motorway.

So it was: Smart Motorways were a bad idea, implemented far too quickly, without forethought, by an Agency that is basically answerable only to itself - having been declared "arms-length."

See: Stalling; Swerving; Near Misses; Hard Shoulders; Sudden Braking; Emergency Vehicles

SMOKING BEHIND THE STEERING WHEEL
%%   @@

Smoking whilst driving, or maneuvering, or braking, or accelerating is not against the law *of itself*; but in some jurisdictions it is banned whilst carrying fostered & / or birth children. Smoking is a complicated procedure: finding the packet, opening the packet, extracting the cigarette, lighting the cigarette, brushing away fallen ash, stubbing it out, whatever: so driving is hardly improved by smoking at the same time. Besides, Smoking might be a sign the Driver is worried or unhappy: not the best mental state for a journey?

See: Eating at the Wheel; Drinking; Distractions; Controls

SOCIAL DISTANCING
%%   @@@@@

Social Distancing on Pavements or on Shopping Streets forces far more Pedestrians - perhaps misguidedly - onto unsafe roads full of moving - or parking - traffic. Moreover, much of this dodging of each other is done "blind."

Social Distancing on public transport has another unfortunate side-effect. Reversing 3 decades of City Mayors' pleading, also established Government Policy, hesitant Drivers are being encouraged to take their sanitized cars into work in preference to travelling into work in maybe un-sanitized buses, trains and trams. If ever this trend takes hold again, much road space will again be occupied by cars instead of people. And where will everybody *park-up* ?

See: Multi-Storey Car Parks; Kerbside Parking; Pedestrians from Nowhere; Traffic Jams; Queueing Traffic

SPEED-BUMPS, SPEED-RAMPS
%%   @@@@

Strange it is that the very Speed-Bumps & Speed-Ramps that are meant to make our roads safer can actually make them un-safer: particularly where an approaching vehicle is speeding - or where somebody has foolishly parked on or opposite the Speed-Bump. Some Ramps are gently & well-profiled; more are built too high & jolt vehicles & cycles unexpectedly in the dark.

Drivers & Riders are taken by surprise - and find themselves too easily swerving off-course. They might even side-swipe a vehicle or cycle coming from the opposite direction.

See: Skidding; Side-Swipes; Swerving; Unseating

SPRAY
%% @@@

In 1 single minute of heavy rain, an HGV can throw up more than 75 gallons of spray. Nor do most Drivers - whatever the size or weight of their vehicle - consider just how much Spray they might be responsible for, particularly when they have fun "puddle-bashing" in order to drench Pedestrians & Cyclists alike.   Then there's the joint problem of windscreen-wipers going too slow and aquaplaning.

See: Torrential Rain; Weather; Puddle-Bashing; Aquaplaning

STARTING THE ENGINE FROM KERBSIDE PARKING
%% @@

Most Pedestrians look Left, look Right, look Left again - or take similar precautions. But *if* a car or van suddenly *ends* its Kerbside Parking, that is a new factor in the Pedestrian's equation. Possibly too late to take into account. An additional hazard, here, for *moving* traffic, is that the "finished" driver is going to *rush* his or her manoeuvre between streams of oncoming traffic from both directions.

See: U-turns; Careless Pedestrian ; Mirrors; Door Opening; Hill-Start; Rolling-Back; Pushing-in

STEERING-WHEEL RIGIDITY
%%%% @@

Traditionally, Steering-Wheels are Rigid - and so plunge into a Driver's abdomen or chest immediately in the event of Collision; the harder the Collision, the more catastrophic the internal injury. Crucially, Steering Wheel Rigidity is also a problem in the event of sideways glance. The impact does not have to be head-on only. Hopefully, as cars being sold or re-sold become more modern, Steering-Wheels will become more collapsible and *more effectively* collapsible; or, if need be, enveloped to a greater degree by the inflated Air-Bag. Of interest: Piaggio was a rare experimenter with introducing cycle handlebars into some of their smaller vans. And some conventional vehicle manufacturers have experimented with getting rid of a Steering-Wheel altogether, replaced by levers: but don't write off the old goat yet!

See: Head-On Collisions; Glances; Air-Bags Defective; Moving a Casualty; Swerving; Rear Collisions & Shunts

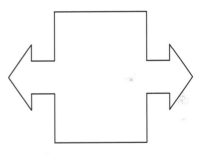

STRAY CARAVANS
%%   @

Most Caravans are securely fastened to their tow vehicle but the few which are *not* cause hazard for other Road-Users. Nor are Caravans very robust when crashing into a crash-barrier. Sleeping or preparing meals in a towed Caravan is forbidden by law - but still happens. As Caravans become longer & heavier, more skill will be needed in their towing. Also Caravans in tow are tricky to overtake! [*partly due to their lower speed limit*]

See: Mirrors; Overtaking; Impatience; Road Rage; Flip-Overs

STREET FURNITURE
%%% @@@@@

Street Furniture covers everything from roadside Benches & Litter-bins to Telephone green-boxes & red Pillar-boxes. Depending on the Town Centre or suburban road, there is a whole array of ill-conceived and readily multiplied Street Furniture forever cluttering up pavements & despoiling the transit experience. It is not unknown for nearly every other shop to have an ugly A-Board outside it; and nearly every "Pedestrian Precinct" boasts a market-trader's wooden stall. And many a Collision, many a sudden loss of vehicle control, would have been far less consequential, far more survivable, but for this proliferation of hard concrete or steel objects.
See: Street-Lamps; Zombie Pedestrians; Swerving; Unseating

SUDDEN BRAKING
%%% @@@@@

By definition, Sudden Braking is also the sudden switch-on of brake-lights. And that surprises any Driver or Rider who happens to be following the sudden-braker. Generally, it is poor road behaviour to drive on one's brakes. Several older Drivers were taught or self-taught rarely if ever to need sudden braking - or much braking at all!

More modern driving technique would suggest rather more braking, if only to tell following Drivers & Riders what's happening. Gone the gentle changing down of the gears!

However awful, sudden braking does retain one advantage above all other: Collisions become fewer than would be the case *without* sudden braking. Many Bus Companies & fleets practise *emergency* braking on a weekly or quarterly basis. Sudden Braking is also - rather artificially - included in the Practical Driving Test.

Please do not sudden-brake for small animals - unless nobody else is around; and unless there is no fear of skid.

See: Brake Lights Malfunction; Animals on the Road; Pedestrians Unexpected; Poor Driver-Behaviour; Skidding

SUICIDE ON THE CARRIAGEWAY
%%%%% @

Suicide on the Carriageway is heavily disguised - therefore less detectable: one hardly ever raised in the Coroner's Court. Maybe a Road-User is depressed; maybe distressed; maybe returning from a funeral; or in the middle of either an argument or a disputed custody-&-access.

At worst, a Suicide parks up - perhaps on a level-crossing - in order to be hit. Or the Suicide stands on the top level of a Multi-Storey Car Park ready to jump, *maybe directly onto an unfortunate Pedestrian below*. Yet, in the absence of "A Note," there is hardly anything to distinguish a "normal" Collision, say with a lone tree, from a suspicious and unsolved "ordinary" road Collision. Coroners almost uniformly prefer the Verdicts of "Open" or "Misadventure" if only to pacify the family.

See: Speeding; Multi-Storeys; Level Crossings; Dangerous Driving; Head-On Collisions; Lone Trees; Ditches & Dykes

SUNLIGHT
%%   @@@@

Sunlight is slightly different from Dazzle. Sunlight actually *saves* very many possible Collisions by making Drivers happier, giving their wipers a rest, allowing good all-round visibility, also showing up particular hazards such as speed bumps, roadworks and gateways. On the other hand, if someone drives 200 or 300 miles South in the middle of Summer, or 100 miles East after Breakfast, or 100 miles West after Tea, Sunlight is an inescapable *enemy*. Furthermore, where there is Sunlight, there is often shadow: with the added hazard that the Sun brings every child or Cyclist for miles out onto the road: *Promenade* Highways presenting a particular hazard.

See: Dazzle; Commuting; School Run;, Loss of Concentration; Inside Windscreen; Weather

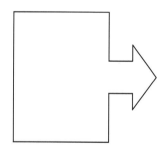

SWERVING
%%%%   @@

Most of the problems of Skidding also apply to Swerving. Other Road-Users don't expect, therefore are slow to respond to, Swerving. But Swerving isn't an Act of God. A Driver, perhaps in haste, has to *decide* to Swerve: thereby either creating or bypassing worse trouble ahead.

See: Skidding; Speeding; Unseating; Motorcycles; Loss of Control; Sideways Collision; Pedestrian from Nowhere; Banking

TAILGATING
%%%% @@@@

All drivers are told *not* to tailgate. Because Tailgating leaves little or no room for error: nowhere to go instead of into the vehicle just in front. There *might* just be an excuse in a heavy & slow-moving traffic jam - with fewer adverse consequences.

But Tailgating at any speed remains a terrible problem: particularly where, perhaps on a Motorway, lorry hugs up to lorry. These HGVs need at least 3 double-decker bus-lengths between them, as do many far lighter vehicles. After all, arrival times do not change a jot through the assistance of Tailgating. So Tailgating is a chimera: a purely manufactured time-saving. With lots of flashing by the following vehicle if a cautious Driver does *not* relent - nor conform to the bunching that is expected of progress. Emergency braking happens whenever & wherever. Should a following driver leave just a few feet or inches of leverage, a rear shunt, worse a disastrous Pile-Up will happen as certainly as night following day. Convoys sometimes bunch up, as well - but at least are served by a Pilot.

See: Sudden Braking; Emergency Braking; Lorry-Lorry Collisions; Lorry-Car Collisions; Pile-Ups; Impatience; Flashing

TAMPERING WITH TACHOGRAPHS
%%%% @

Tachographs are complicated instruments. Where a Tachograph is tampered with, or doctored, it will give an incorrect reading. Also the Driver gains an unfair advantage: many more driving hours or driving days than the permitted maximum. That means the HGV Driver is potentially driving when he is unfit to drive: too tired; no lunch break; no time to stretch his legs; trying to take short cuts; fearing the next traffic jam; too late for a just-in-time delivery; displeasing an oppressive employer…. altogether friable & *exhausted*.

See: Dishonest Driving; HGV Crashes; Exceeding Weight; Lorry-Lorry Crashes; Cyclists Mown Down; Tiredness; Long Journeys

TAKING WITHOUT THE OWNER's CONSENT
%%%%% @

It is impossible to underestimate the danger of Road Hazard & Road Crash resulting from illegitimate ridership of a car, bicycle, Tractor, JCB Digger or service vehicle. Guilt, haste, pursuit - & unfamiliarity with the controls all add to impending disaster.

See: Joy-riding; Pursuit; Boy-Racers; Driving while Disqualified

TANDEM OCCUPANCY OF THE CARRIAGEWAY
%% @

The temptation for a Cyclist / Motorcyclist is to seek virtual - or actual - companionship by Riding Tandem. And this is legal. The trouble is: other Motorists, especially lorries, might understand neither the need for this nor the danger. For Pedal-Cyclists, as road trial or outing might be on the cards.

See: Motorcycles; Overtaking; Concentration; Car-Cycle Crash

TAXIS
[.....as an unusual category of vehicle]
%%% @@@
Taxi-hiring is definitely not a neutral or an automatically safe form of journey. These special factors tend to impact on Driver & Passenger Safety : Taxi unregistered; Taxi poorly maintained; Passenger(s) not secured; Taxi running against a deadline; Taxi speeding ; Taxi-driver distracted by walkie-talkie; Taxi-driver exhausted; No clear route chosen or instructed; No safe place for Taxi to pick-up; No safe place for Taxi to drop-off; Rowdy Passengers; Anger; stuck for hours in a traffic-jam; Open doors.

And because Taxis do far more U-turns and strange manoeuvres ; because they weave in and out of static or slow-moving traffic: these factors alone could bring about Collision.

See: Limousines; Coaches; Speed; Distraction; Rowdy Passengers; Bus lanes; Hand-held Telephones; U-Turns

TEENAGE PASSENGERS
%%% @@
Teenage Passengers are different from other Passengers, even from growing children. They might be moody and disputatious; conversely merry and shouty. Statistically, Teenage Passengers distract some of their Teenage Drivers - perhaps daring them, goading them, singing, wanting sudden change of destination, whatever - to the extent Motor Insurers might reduce premiums for daytime driving and/or a ban on Passengers under the age of 21 or 24.

See: Distractions; Back-Seat Drivers; Loud Music; Boy-Racers

THROWN OBJECTS
%%%% @

Luckily - & it *is* luckily - fewer objects are thrown onto the Highway, deliberately, than one might expect. Even so, the consequences are *devastating* upon impact: shattered windscreens, swerving Motorcyclists, concussed Drivers, whatever.

Motorway bridges & pedestrian walkways above busy dual-carriageways are the chosen location of the brick- and cat-throwers. One can almost predict that a group of lads congregated on open-air bridges are "up to no good."

See: Debris on the Carriageway; Front Windscreen; PTSD

TELEPHONE CALLS   *[Mobile Telephone Use]*
%%% @@@@

Telephone Calls made & received directly cause very many Collisions and not a few deaths. Police used to be reticent to seize a Phone: perhaps assuming it was jolted by the Collision itself. Hands-free telephones are almost as dangerous in a vehicle as hand-held models. That surprising result arises from the sheer degree of *concentration* a Driver needs to absorb complex telephone messages, make financial calculations, also decide when & how to reply. That concentration applies far less when *one-to-one* conversation is started in a vehicle. Everyone relates to telephone cues differently from familiar cues. So prominent a place do telephones have in modern living that *any* law restricting their use is widely disobeyed.

See: Portable Computers; Distractions; Sudden Braking

THREE-LANE TRUNK ROADS
%%%% @

Three-Lane Trunk Roads were an experiment even as far back as in the 1960s with the A38 from Gloucester to Bristol and back. And whereas 3-Lane Motorways make sense because all traffic is heading in the same direction, the logic of the 3-Lane Trunk Road is that both lines of traffic will negotiate as to who should occupy that middle-lane; or who should stay exactly where they are. Hence their very high potential for Head-On Collisions. Some 3-Laners have reverted to being wider two-lane carriageways with periodic bollards & hatching.

See: Motorways; Overtaking; Hurry; Long Journeys; Head-On Collisions

TIGHT DEADLINE[S]
%%% @@@

The trouble with a Tight Deadline is that it is often invisible, therefore unknown, to unrelated road-users; unknown to the Driver him- or herself as far as it is affecting - ruining? - their driving behaviour.

The Deadline might be set by Workplace; or by the commute; by Town Council for the parking space; or by Contract for the delivery; by Factory for just-in-time; or by School for the drop-off; by partner for the return home; or by fiancée in Pub.

And *where* there is Tight Deadline, there will be inevitably increased risk of Collision.

See: Impatience; Commuting; Reversing; Car Parks; Just-in-Time; Speeding; Traffic Jams

TIREDNESS
%%%%% @@@@@

Tiredness is an ally of boredom - and at least as dangerous. Sleep deprivation is not the only cause of driving while tired. *Too much* sleep; too many distractions; too great an information overload; too many non-driving related worries; emotional exhaustion; recent influenza; also work-based anxieties, are just a few of additional causes. Unlike age or illness, tiredness, like boredom, is almost completely invisible.

See: Commuting; Boredom; Motorways; Narcolepsy; Over-familiarity; Rest Breaks; Long Journeys

TOO LITTLE CLEARANCE
%%%% @@@@@

Ever since Adam had to share a pathway with Eve, one Road-User has not left sufficient Clearance for another. Car brushes past Pedestrian & Cyclist; Car crowds Motorcyclist off the road; Lorry brushes past both Cyclist & Motorcyclist: creating unpleasant slip-stream; Mobility Scooter brushes past Pedestrian. So great is the danger of Too Little Clearance, Bus-Drivers have it drummed into them that they must not proceed on their timetabled journeys unless they can pass another Road-User without scare or near-miss.

The other aspect of Too Little Clearance is the residential street or *cul-de-sac* cluttered with parked vehicles. On 90% of roads no way is there enough room for either double parking & double flow of traffic, or nearside parking & double flow. Yet many Drivers have forgotten the Highway Code which states it is the obligation of the first Driver or Rider to encounter obstruction to give way to oncoming traffic before proceeding through the gap oneself. If only!

Fire Engines & Ambulances have a very real difficulty with double-parking resulting in greater torment for whoever is waiting for Fire Crew or Paramedic.

See: Double Parking; Pedestrian from Nowhere; Lack of Concentration; Pavement Parking; Swerving; *Cul-de-Sacs*

TOO UPSET TO DRIVE
%%% @@

Those unfortunate Drivers who are too upset to drive still take to the road tears streaming down their faces; regrets welling up within; deep resentment expressed to all other occupants of the car; anger smoldering in their hearts. It's *wrong* to drive Too Upset to Drive, yet it happens. Then all judgments and driving decisions become distorted: clouded vision & a Collision or Near-Miss a very real possibility.

See: Commuting; School Run; Anger; Road Rage; State of Mind; Tiredness; Telephoning while Driving.

TRAFFIC JAMS
%%% @@@@@

On the surface, Traffic Jams should make the roads *safer*. After all, every vehicle is going so slowly, nothing can go wrong. Not at an intermittent 5mph! But that's the trouble. Weary and wary drivers begin to occupy themselves in other ways: texting, changing music station, admiring passers-by, quietening down children on the back seat, whatever.

Worse, the inside Windscreen begins to smoke up. And what about that Pedestrian emerging "from nowhere" between all those vehicles intentionally and unintentionally "parked-up"?

Later that same Traffic Jam causes further havoc when all those delayed vehicles - *with delayed schedules* - have lost time to be made up for. New tensions. New risks.

See: Crawling Traffic; Queueing Traffic; Roadworks; Rubber-necking; Distractions; Pedestrian from Nowhere

TRAFFIC POLICE SHORTFALL
%%%% @@@@@

The Shortfall in Traffic Police - estimated, depending on Police Authority, to be between 10% & 50% since the Year 2001, Blair's second term, or 2010's Coalition - impacts on nearly every aspect of Roadcraft & Road Hazard & Road Collision. The causes of this Shortfall are first & most important, "lack of money;" second, lack of recruitment; third, lack of ring-fencing for Traffic Management as opposed to Burglary, Disorderly Behaviour or Fraud; & fourth: sending former local Police Force Patrols further afield to do Motorway Patrol. Passengers without Seatbelts; Drivers on the telephone; white-vans without adequate maintenance; Dishonest Drivers, whoever, are among the heaviest sufferers - or beneficiaries! - of Traffic Police cutbacks. Worse, errant Drivers & Riders *know about* these cutbacks - and. in the event of non-injury Collision, there will not be *any* Police Officer in attendance, just an incident number. And as for professional drug-dealers using their cars to distribute produce, also collect debts; as for reports about irresponsible driving not resulting in collision: forget it! Not even telephone 101 will listen. At best, fill in a form! In summary, the nation needs at least double the present contingent of Traffic Police.

See: Lack of Enforcement; Seat-Belts; Underage Drivers; Drink-Driving; Telephone Usage behind the Wheel; Speeding

TRAILERS & LONG LORRIES CLOSING IN ON INSIDE TRAFFIC
%%% @@

Because of the paths chosen by long-loads and articulated juggernauts, it is not unknown for Trailers to creep in, or edge in, to crush or damage any hidden car or bike on the nearside. Paradoxically, this phenomenon, this potential for Collision, is far deadlier whilst the Trucker turns Left, not Right. Oft times, Long-Load lorries also clip the pavements at their furthest extremities. Running out of road space is a frightening place to be. And there's no way of warning the Trailer!

See: Swerving; Lorry Safety; Motorist Unseen; Cyclist Unseen

TRAM TRACKS
%%% @

For most of the period 1945 to 1990, most of the driving or riding populations did not have to think about Trams or Tram Tracks because there weren't any outside of Blackpool. Then Croydon, Sheffield, Nottingham and other Cities joined Greater Manchester to lay - or to reinstate - Rapid Light Transport. That led to four "new" causes of Crash & injury. First, comes the Tram/Car, Tram/Bus, Tram/Taxi or Tram/Lorry Collision or Side-Swipe: partly caused by *shared* road space. Second is the almost inevitable - though rare - running over of an unwary Pedestrian by the Tram. Third, it is well-documented that Cyclists & Motorcyclists can get stuck, in reality *locked*, in forward Tram Tracks: a predicament leading to unseating. Fourth, arises more recent concern, originating in Edinburgh, that road lanes Left or Right might be wrongly *angled* for traffic passing over Tram Tracks. It's easy to dismiss this 4th. danger as anecdotal; but there comes a point where this obvious danger must be disentangled *and* designed out.

See: Bus Lanes Running Out; Motorcycles; Hidden Cycles; Unseating; Skidding; Rain; [Corporate] Manslaughter

TURNING SHARP LEFT
%%%% @@@@

The Left Turn off a highway should be the safer in Britain when compared with perilous Right turns. But there's lots of evidence that vans & lorries turning Left - to some extent cars doing the same- trap injure or kill any Cyclist or Motorcyclist or

174

Pedestrian already on the nearside. Worse, it's not at all clear that the one trapped can see the larger vehicle's Left signal.

The other cause of injury & death associate with Sharp Left is the Pedestrian taking a straight line ahead unaware that the vehicle behind him or her is Turning Sharp Left. That vehicle or cycle might be silent - or too swift to raise the alarm, or too oblivious of the danger to hoot. Yet this hidden Road-User probably imagines the Pedestrian knows they are there. Finally, specific dangers are associated with turning Left at a T-Junction, particularly was the light just set at amber.

See: Pedestrian from Nowhere; Mirrors ; Loss of Concentration

TURNING SHARP RIGHT
%%%% @@@@

In the UK, turning Sharp Right is always perilous because the manoeuvre relies on four essential observations: who is behind? who is in front? who wants to turn Right at exactly the same time; finally, who is turning Left or Right from the chosen destination road on the Right? In these circumstance, for Riders as well as Drivers: *mirrors* are vital; also a fine and correct judgment of on-coming speeds. And hazard of serious injury or death is doubled if there is a second on-coming vehicle currently hidden. This latter coincidence is more pronounced where a saloon car is turning Right *out of* a side-road than into one. This tricky manoeuvre from slow ambience to fast is not as frequently counted as the hazard in the opposite direction. Even turning sharp Right from an ordinary home's ordinary drive is perilous.

See: Mirrors; Loss of Concentration; Closing Distance; Pedestrian from Nowhere; Gaps in the Dual Carriageway

TUNNEL VISION
%%% @@

Tunnel Vision may impact upon a number of Drivers without their being aware of it. The Tunnel is only the road straight ahead. But good driving demands 180° vision, more if possible. Another version of Tunnel Vision is where a Driver is so preoccupied by his load or his mission or his schedule that he *deliberately* does not look to either his Right or his Left.

See: Defective Vision; Pedestrian from Nowhere; Junctions

TWILIGHT
%% @@

Twilight is a particularly hazardous time of day - exacerbated by a fierce low Sunset, fog, light rain - or a recent change of the clocks. Pedestrians, like Drivers, are more tired than in the morning. Nor do ineptly parked vehicles or dark clothing help.

See: Tiredness; Careless Pedestrians; Darkness; Hidden Cycles

TYRES: WRONG PRESSURE
%%% @@

Where Tyres are inaccurately or incorrectly inflated - or where they're subject to a slow puncture - the whole vehicle cannot keep its correct balance or direction. Many Drivers who cannot really afford to drive try to get more miles from their existing ill-aligned tyres which then bald, shard or worse, blow up at speed: result calamity.

See: Worn-Out Tyres; Swerving; Poorly Maintained Vehicles

U-TURNS
%%%% @@@

The trouble with U-turns is that they're rarely permitted, so have to be executed in a hurry; worse, executed without 360° vision at all times. That 360°vision is absolutely essential as driver-held-up-in-traffic-jam, driver-changing-his-mind, taxi-driver, or driver-wanting-to-avoid-longer-drive-to-big-roundabout faces peril on Left & Right, front & behind. Except on a quiet stretch of road early in a morning, the carriageway will rarely be clear enough for U-Turns, even where theoretically they are allowed. Then there is the problem of cars and Pedestrians appearing from nowhere. Unlike the measured 3-point turn of the Driving Test, in congested traffic there is not enough time to do most U-turns safely. They are an impetuous manoeuvre, taking much longer than impulsive Drivers imagine will be the case - and taking up more *road space* than any Driver anticipates. The problem starts *straightway* in a traffic-jam or crawl. And, by definition, in a jam there is no good rear vision.

See: Hurry; Poor Driver Behaviour; Young Drivers; Impatience

UNCLEAR VISIBILITY
%%%%% @@@@@

Unclear Visibility has a strict definition of inability to see other Road-Users 100 metres ahead without impairment. Obfuscation might arise from fog, snow, driving-rain, time of day - or even dazzle.

However, Unclear Visibility surrounds the unexpected Pedestrian; the Pedestrian in shadow; the Pedestrian in dark clothing made worse by a Driver's own failing eyesight; by each Town Centre's oddities; or simply by too much traffic swirling around. In other words, it is every Road-User's responsibility - every Pedestrian's life-&death consideration - to think about *Unclear* Visibility. Tantalizing indeed - because what might be one Road-User's ambient visibility is an on-coming Road-User's invisibility.

See: Unlit Vehicles; Fog; Pedestrians Unexpected; Upkeep

UNDERAGE DRIVERS
%%%% @

Anyone can drive a car or motorbike or tractor: provided they have the keys or borrow the keys or steal the keys. Underage Drivers do have some skill born of watching other people - but disaster is only just round the corner: literally. Some Underage Drivers are so small they cannot see out of the front windscreen. And, of course, there's no minimum age for Pedal-Cyclists.

See: New Drivers; Inexperienced Drivers; TWOC; Police Chase; Front Seat Height; Insurance

UNDERTAKING
%%% @@

Undertaking : passing a UK vehicle on the Left or Nearside, is not strictly against the law. Occasionally, as when traffic control on a busy Motorway dictates that one lane can progress whilst a "faster" lane cannot, Undertaking is the correct option. The same applies to Right-turns by filter.

However, in built-up areas, or away from hold-ups on the Right, Undertaking is usually the wrong choice. For instance, what would happen if the driver ahead suddenly realized they were in the wrong lane, or heading out of a Roundabout the wrong way? Or what would happen if a Driver successfully negotiated a Roundabout all the way round without notice or vision of a vehicle creeping up to rear nearside passenger? Undertaking and blind-spots are unhappy bedfellows.

See: Impatience; Overtaking; Flashing; Sudden Switch of Lane; Roundabouts; Blind Spots

UNLIT ROADS & MOTORWAYS
%%   @@@

Lit Roads cause difficulty through Light Pollution, glare, & false apparitions. But *Unlit* Roads are possibly worse due to the Wilderness Effect. The Wilderness Effect is the total aloneness the Driver or Rider faces when unable, now unwilling, to complete a journey because of the absence of cues or orientation. *Most* Motorways are actually lit, nowadays.

See: Defective Lights; Speed; Stalling; Darkness; Skips; Lay-Bys

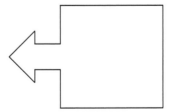

UNLIT VEHICLES
%%%% @@

Totally Unlit Vehicles always spell trouble in remote regions. By definition, cars & white vans parked up *in urban areas* remain unlit, due to carefully positioned lamp standards. Skips, brick deliveries, trailers & caravans unexpectedly parked-up should usually be either lamped or coned. So what are the dangers of vehicles - particularly HGVs - parked up, unlit, in Lay-Bys - or stalled; or dropping off groceries or fast-food Lorries; also unlit vehicles not lit because their Drivers or Riders "forgot" to switch on the lights, in the middle of nowhere? Potentially catastrophic. On dark & narrow country roads in the night, few drivers are concentrating enough to detect suddenly unlit vehicles or unlit vehicles or bicycles encountered suddenly: *even if* those vehicles or cycles are actually moving.

Lighting laws are quite strict - but the greyest area is a suggestion that in Britain *everyone* should maintain dipped headlights whatever the time of day; whatever the weather condition. This is not a legal requirement for older vehicles bought & sold, although this law changes overseas.

What *is* a legal requirement is that every single driver be lit - & not just with side-lights - each and every time visibility is reduced 100 metres ahead : which covers dusk, dawn, snow, hale, fog & driving rain. By some drivers' behaviour, one would imagine they are afraid of being sent an electricity bill at the end of each driving month!

An unlit vehicle can, in theory, be *un*intentional - where the light or lights simply aren't working: but then it is *still* the driver's absolute duty to ensure that this is not the case. Extra hazards befall a Cyclist or Motorcyclist riding unlit.

See: Unclear Visibility; Fog; Pedestrians Unexpected; Maintenance; Unlit Roads; Loss of Concentration

UNMAINTAINED VEHICLES *[especially PSVs & HGVs]*
%%%%   @@

Better to save money by not putting vehicles in for servicing and repair? That way the vehicle is actually out on the Highway many more days. So brake pads wear out, tyres bald, harmful emissions are facilitated, smashed mirrors remain un-replaced, nuts come loose.

In the big scheme of Collisions, relatively few are directly attributable to lack of maintenance - but where that *is* a factor: the result is death rather than life, calamity rather than incident. And certain lorry or coach firms are known for cutting corners - as are the owners of cars & white vans that should have been scrapped already. In the end, the remedy is possibly a 3-way plan: 1) More "routine" roadside checks; 2) More subsidiary checks when a vehicle or machine has been stopped for another reason, eg. Paperwork, Seatbelts; & More unannounced raids on lorry yards and bus depôts.

See: Dishonest Driving; Tyres; Lights

UNSAFE ROADS
%%%%% @@

In this context, the use of the word "Unsafe" needs to be severely qualified, or disqualified altogether, because, in a very real way, one cannot have Unsafe Roads, only *unsafe Drivers*, Unsafe Riders, Unsafe Road Signs or Unsafe Pedestrians. Or any combination of these factors spelling unsafety.

That said, *Unsafe Roads* do actually exist anecdotally - & even statistically. In the Peak District alone: the *"Cat-&-Fiddle"* from Buxton to Macclesfield; the *Via Gellia* from Wirksworth towards Hartington; the *Snake Pass* from *Ladybower* to Glossop; the Woodhead Pass from Sheffield to Manchester; & the A515 Buxton to Ashbourne road would all rank amongst the most dangerous roads in England.

In each & every County, and not least North of the Scottish Border, this list can be greatly expanded: leaving the Newbury Bypass behind, avoiding the notorious Preston Bypass, heading to Edinburgh on the A68 via Hexham & Jedburgh.

Additionally, some Drivers & Fleets would call *all* Motorways Dangerous, especially those "Smart Motorways" so recently discredited. That is because speed doesn't sit happily alongside safety. One needs sacrificing to assist the other.

And, of course, it is possible for a "Dangerous" road to be more dangerous for one cadre of road-user than another. Back in the Peak District, the *"Cat-&-Fiddle"* & the *Snake Pass* present specific challenges for Motorcyclists. Fast Motorcyclists on winding roads have the opportunity to mimic the tactics and skills required of *Donington Park*, *Brands Hatch* or the Isle of Man. By way of contrast: long straight roads have other drawbacks: not least the need to turn from fast main Highway to dawdling side-road; dawdling side-road onto main Highway.

Finally on the subject of Unsafe Roads, there is a dreadful temptation for both Transport Ministry & Highways' Agency to chalk up fatalities & life-changing injuries until the tally warrants widening or hatching; also the eventual *prohibition* of Right Hand or U-turns.

See: Death by Dangerous Driving; Death by Careless Driving; Loss of Concentration; Banking; Racing Circuit; Speed; Hairpins

UNSEEN ROAD LANE-MARKINGS
%%% @@@

Road planners tend to put Lane-Markings in 3 places: Advance Direction Sign[s], Gantries [rare] or painted on the actual carriageway.

Those arrows & road numbers [road intended] are absolutely useless for new Drivers or Riders in the area; or when vehicles - especially HGVs- are parked, or stalled, over them.

The Road User new to the area then has to decide on one of 3 options: to stay in an existing lane and hope for the best; to switch lanes half way through a Junction or Roundabout in order to achieve the right destination; or to go down a deliberately "wrong" exit in the hope of then doing a U-turn to get back onto the Junction & so have another go. With uncertain hand on the steering-wheel combined with confused mindset: all 3 of these options lead to Collision, in particular Side-Swipe.

See: Impatience, Flows from all directions; Lane switching;

UNRESPONSIVE PEDESTRIAN LIGHTS
%%%%% @@@

Pedestrian Lights only succeed if , with some frequency, they allow Pedestrians to cross in safety! Too often, these Lights, especially those positioned on Trunk Roads, are totally unresponsive. Speeding traffic then comes to expect that they will not be operative. And impatient Pedestrians start running across the carriageway too early, too hesitantly, or well after the intermittent Green Man has disappeared.

See: Pelican Lights; Impatience; Speeding; Flows of Traffic

UNSEATING
%%%%% @

Unseating - being thrown off your seat or saddle - affects Riders, Cyclists & Motorcyclists in a majority of cases, but can also happen *within* cars, minibuses & coaches. The result is massive injury to the body, internally & externally - but an almost greater danger is being immediately confronted by a vehicle that has not seen, less prepared for, the original unseating. That sequence increases motorcycle fatalities more than any other, but also kills, or seriously injures, fallen Pedestrians & Pedal-Cyclists.

See: Motorcycles; Horses; Cycle Safety; Sharp Turning Left; Potholes; Blind-spots; Loss of Control; Side Swipes

VERY HIGH MILEAGE
%%% @@

Not for nothing do Motor Insurers ask about *annual* mileage. "Normal" is unofficially taken to be 8000 miles in any one year. If that sounds low, very many Pensioners in particular only drive about one thousand miles just to and from market!

But it anybody drives twice as many miles as even a Professional Driver's already sky-high mileage, the risk of Collision is that much higher. Tiredness, exhaustion, boredom, tight schedules, whatever, all come into play - & with greater potential for disaster. This danger can be reduced by more frequent & longer comfort breaks; also by 52 set-aside *non-driving* days every year.

See: Tiredness; Boredom; Over-Familiarity; Commuting; Long Journeys; Rest; Tachographs; Narcolepsy

VIGILANTE ACTIVITY
%%%% @

At best Vigilantes merely hold up a placard for oncoming Drivers to read - or home-made speed-detectors. Or go down to Peak District village car-park and complain that thoughtless long-distance hikers are taking up all the available 2-hour bays. But, at worst, Vigilantes will take the law into their own hands by erecting blockades; spilling fuel, scattering tacks, onto the carriageway; chasing alleged sex-offenders; erecting razor-wire across cycle-paths; or pursuing errant Drivers on foot. Some of the most unpleasant and parasitic Vigilantes are the supposed "owners" of supposed "private land" - or gangs of youth at night wishing to keep their "patch" clear of Mods or supporters of Leyton Orient. Very quickly what started as a cut-up cyclist lightly tapping the roof of a passing saloon grows into full-throated, calamitous, Road Rage.

See: Road Rage; Hidden Cyclists; Waving; Impatience; Anger; Dishonest Driving; Boy Racers; Good Samaritans

WAVING   *[In Recognition]*
%   @@@@

The trouble with Waving in Recognition is that it can mean so many things - including a resulting loss of concentration. Is this person waving to a past friend?   neighbour? colleague? business associate? church congregant? Who is it? And *why* the waving? Has the person waving perhaps not got to the bus stop in time? Or has the person waving seen a danger or a dead cat? Has the person waving just come away from a

Collision or perennial roadworks? Or is a Constable or Parking Attendant on his rounds? Wild waving could even mean : " My car's broken down; please take me to the Garage!" - or more simply: "I'm a hitch-hiker needing to get to the next Town..."

Waving in recognition is made more puzzling because it is far easier for the Driver or front Passenger to see the Pedestrian / or other Road-User through a front windscreen than it is for the person being waved-at to see the Driver or front-seat Passenger back through that same windscreen! The result: more confusion, not less. Then a near-miss or a collision.

See: Waving-On; Parked Vehicles; Near Misses; Pedestrians from Nowhere; Hidden Cyclists; Good Samaritans

WAVING-ON
%%% @@

Waving-On is only "safe" if done by a genuine Police Officer. Every single Waving-On by *anyone else* is inherently dangerous. That applies to well-meaning Gas-Fitters; well-meaning road-diggers; well-meaning Pedestrians; well-meaning relatives saying "Goodbye;" well-meaning wives saying "Reverse a little bit more;" well-meaning Survivors of Collision or Prang; well-meaning work colleagues; *or* ill-intent pranksters; ill-intent fraudsters; ill-intent individuals causing the original hold-up or traffic-jam. Unauthorized - and soon totally *unwelcome* - Waving-On has no legitimacy whatsoever in law or in any Motor Insurance claim. The Driver or Rider or Pedestrian should only use *their own* cautious judgment, their own careful weighing-up of the situation: far preferable to a relative or stranger's frequently misguided judgment.

See: Waving in Recognition; Traffic Jams; Roadworks; Roadside Parking; Anger; Vigilantes; Boy-Racers; Good Samaritans

[THE] WEATHER
%%% @@@@@

The Weather is, not surprisingly, blamed *directly* for a large percentage of Collisions on the Highway - where Weather is far more frequently *a prompt* to the human error that in 19 out of every 20 Collisions is the principal cause. Ice, fog, rain, burning heat, whatever, can, of course, always alter or modify Driver-Behaviour. Instead, most Drivers continue as if Weather hadn't happened. They have a timetable firmly based on *better* Weather! And they don't even want a blanket in the boot.

Snow is undoubtedly trickiest - because it is the most visible - and frightening of all Weather Events after freezing rain; also slowest to be cleared. And with global warming, there will be fewer snowfalls in Winter. A brand new Driver, therefore, could never have faced Snow blanketing the Highway, falling heavily from the sky - as opposed to commoner frosts, sleet, hale, thunder. The obvious answer to heavy snowfall is, simply: abandon journey. Yet many Road Users feel constrained not to do this: their plans too set in stone.

See: Torrential Rain; Ice; Igloo Driving; Skidding; Braking

WHATABOUTERY
%%   @@@@

The mindset of too many a Driver or Rider is "Whataboutery" as default position: "What about *that* car?"; "What about *that* person not wearing his seatbelt?"; " What about that Minicab sat outside the Night Club hoping to be hailed down?"; " What about that speed-merchant who wasn't clocked?"

The trouble with "Whataboutery" as standard response to *every other* Road-User is that it always deflects the issue of bad driving *away from* the person saying - or thinking - "What about....?" So it si the Highway World is divided into Saints & Sinners. Of interest: those Drivers Riders concentrating solely on their own performance often avert far more crashes than those they might condemn.

See: Irritation; Commuting; Bad Road-Behaviour; Road Rage

WHITE VAN MAN
%% @@@@@

You can buy any small works' van.... as long as it's white. "White Van Man" does actually *exist,* unlike Essex Girl, Mondeo Man or Warrington Waverer [marginal voter].

The trouble with White Van Man is he [and it usually is a He, self-employed] always seems to be in a mighty hurry - too many jobs to fit in; too much equipment to drop off; too many mobile calls to return;, too many materials to buy; too many quotes to send out; too many worries on his mind. This potentially makes White Van Man's driving erratic, even thoughtless. Yet White Van Man is perfectly positioned on the Highway: immediately identifiable & half way between Saloon

& HGV. Also by being self-employed, he might be extremely discombobulated by a Collision - though so often he appears to be heading in that direction.

See: Trailer in tow; Commuting; Over-familiarity; Hurry; Tiredness; Insecure Load; Paperwork on Dashboard

WIDE LOADS
%%   @

By their nature, very Wide Loads : defined as over 2.9 metres in width, are almost safer than normal lorry-loads. Wide Loads are very visible & frequently accompanied by a Pilot or an out-rider. What is much less safe is the Wide Load *unseen*: such as a tipping-lorry or construction truck with machinery sticking out; swinging, pirouetting at one particular point. Cranes, for instance, tend to move in transit - unless doubly secured. And trailers for 5 motorcycles are also deceptively narrow. Then follows the car that takes a punt to swerve round the Wide Load, its Driver believing he is holding everyone up. Yet there might not be enough road to do this overtake.

See: Abnormal Loads; Insecure Loads; Overtaking; Trailers

WIPERS NOT WORKING
%%%   @@

Good Wipers, in superb condition, are set at one of four speeds, depending on the weather: None / Intermittent / Normal / Very Fast. And these Wipers do not even need to be plural. Some modern vehicles have just one Wiper. But too few Drivers accurately judge whether <<Fast>> is better than <<Normal>> or <<Normal>> better than <<Intermittent>>. Yet clear vision *front & rear* is essential for safety. Those Rear Wipers might be employed so occasionally, a Driver may not know how to set them going. Also the best Wiper in the world cannot compensate for grimy or foggy *interior* windows.

See: Front Windscreen Obscured; Heavy Rain; Snow; Fog; Pedestrians from Nowhere; Jumping the Lights; Igloo Driving

WORN-OUT TYRES
%%%% @@

Worn-Out Tyres are a Collision or Swerving off the carriageway waiting to happen: terribly dangerous. Yet so many impecunious Drivers want a few extra miles for their money.

See: Poorly Maintained Vehicles ; Wrong Tyre Pressures; Swerving; Vehicle Out of Control; Second-Hand Cars

WRONG SIDE OF THE ROAD DRIVING & RIDING
%%%%% @

Driving or Riding on the Wrong Side can happen for a variety of reasons : Roadworks, passing a Collision, contraflow, signalled Right Turn, overtaking - or simply being accustomed to driving on the opposite side due to Driver-training overseas; being stationed overseas; or cycling or caravanning overseas. So it is, it takes a long time to adjust to the Left Side in Britain - which, even then, persistent overtakers are not interested in, Some of the worst, cruelest, harshest Head-On Collisions happen on that Wrong Side of the Road, including that category of Driver: impeccably safe in Britain, forgetful abroad.

See: Foreign Drivers; Driving Abroad; Overtaking; Unfamiliarity; Sharp Turn Right; Sharp Left Turn; Hidden Cyclists; Mirrors

WRONG STATE OF MIND
%%%%   @@@@

If anyone drives in the "Wrong State of Mind," it's a bit like driving on the wrong side of the road. Because driving is all about Roadcraft - and Roadcraft is all determined by state-of-mind. In some situations, like sunbathing, or clothes washing, or attending the conveyor belt, the wrong state of mind is not relevant. But behind the steering-wheel of a car, or seated on a fast Motorcycle, state-of-mind is massive. Crashes happen in the flash of a second and that second is the epi-centre of distraction or diversion. Moreover, the Driver or Rider with the wrong state-of-mind is more likely to put on a CD or worse: pick up the telephone. Of interest, nearly all British Law is not determined *by result* but by what is happening in the mind. Illogical but true; & grossly insulting to relatives who've lost a loved-one on the Highway where *death* cannot even be mentioned in Magistrates' Court because proceedings are all about the degree of a Driver's intent: "due care & attention."

See: Commuting; Too Upset to Drive; Anger; Loss of Concentration; Alcohol; School Run; Impaired Judgment

YOUNG DRIVERS & MOTORCYCLISTS
%%%   @@@

Not all Young Drivers are worse Drivers. Many Teenagers are far safer on the Highway than their grand-dads. On the other hand, Drivers & Riders under the age of 21 are between 2.5 & 3.5 times at risk of causing death & injury to themselves, or to other Road-Users, than those aged 22 or over, mile-for-mile. Maybe Young Drivers are more impulsive & less experienced dealing with hazard? Or maybe too little variety of time-of-day or traffic congestion was incorporated into their learning? Also certain Young Drivers & Riders are distracted by noise.

See: Novice Drivers; P-Plates; Impatience; Rowdy passengers; Loud Music; Loss of Concentration

Z-BENDS
%%%% @@

Any rural road with a succession of Z-Bends is full of Collision opportunities. Sometimes one Z follows only 100yards from the past Z. Where is the hidden Pedestrian? Walking on the Left or walking on the Right? Perched on a verge? Or totally unaware? In the gutter? Or in the middle of the road? Listening to headphones? Or *fully* aware you are there? Z-bends then tempt the impatient Driver or Rider to cut out the Z by taking a *middle* course.   Scary!   All Z-bends are best approached with much reduced speed.

See: Speed; Hairpin Bends; Cutting Corners; Pedestrian from Nowhere; White Van Man; Speeding; Emergency Braking

ZOMBIE PEDESTRIANS
%%% @@

So called Zombies are heavily engaged on their i-phones or smart-phones - or listening to their Walkman. That makes them inattentive or impervious when faced with any new hazard: reversing car, lamp-post, on-coming cyclist, man-hole, whatever. We are getting to the point where we perhaps should *actively* expect the Zombie Pedestrian - as keenly as we now [reluctantly] make allowance for the Zombie Driver totally immersed in his telephone-call.

See: Pedestrian from Nowhere; Loss of Concentration; Distractions; Telephoning; Roadworks; Z-bends; Social Distancing; Iced Roads

****

High above the Estuary.... like all Collisions, unexpected....

TANGLED   WRECKAGE :

AN   ENCYCLOPAEDIA   OF

COLLISIONS   ON   THE   PUBLIC

HIGHWAY :

PART TWO :

an   A to Z of

ADDRESS & PREVENTION

*** nearly 400 entries ;

*** many more cross-references ;

*** an award of up to 5 # # # # #

for *potential to save lives & minimize injury*;
but also up to 5   X X X X X for *standing in the
way of avoiding Collision; backtracking.*

ABOLITION of the TAX DISC
[this Government Policy, dated 2014, allegedly to save £7 million a year but in fact costing the Treasury £300 million over their first 6 years of disappearance. Now absolutely impossible to detect who has paid their Road Tax and who hasn't - except with specialist equipment]

X X X

ACCESS-ONLY ZONES
[these very useful near football-ground or on rat-runs. Access only for local residents or deliveries to those residents. Take a lot of Policing]

# # #

ACCIDENT BLACK-SPOT NOTIFICATION
[these Notices now much less common - because they could provide Drivers & Riders with a false sense of security where not fitted]

# #

ADDITIONAL ZEBRA CROSSING
[this after local protests, but nearly always refused]

# # # #

ADVANCE[D] BOOKING ONLY HIRECARS
[this essential for safety and to prevent cowboy or unlicensed Private Hire; also deterring non-black cabs from queueing outside venues for instant hire]

# # #

ADVANCE TESTING for HGV DRIVERS

[these Voluntary - or Compulsory for certain Fleet-Drivers - laid on to iron out bad habits]

# # # #

ADVANCED DRIVING TEST [VOLUNTARY]

[this membership of the Institute of Advanced Motorists, for instance: laying on paid courses & tests aimed at fostering better, more considerate, Road Use.... quite a tough qualification]

# # # # #

ADVERTISEMENT MONITORING in the LOCAL NEWSPAPER

[this aimed at catching any back-street fraudster posing as a Widow sadly having to part with her late husband's treasured motor]

# # # # #

ADVISORY SPEED ALERT SIGNS TELLING YOU EXACT SPEED DONE

[this not intended for prosecution purposes; more for reminder... Very prominent, giving immediate feedback, & often mistaken for Gatso]

# # # #

AIRBAGS

[these fitted to newer cars with dashboard confirmation that they are ready: yet sometimes faulty; sometimes giving Drivers false sense of security in the event of Head-On Collision]

# # #

ALL-CAR LOCKING

[this fitted standard to some vehicles ; might be helpful in the event of Robbery or Road Rage. But difficult to disengage]

X X X

ALLOWING A VEHICLE TO PROCEED PENDING DOCUMENTATION

[this allowance coming after a routine roadside check; after a breathalyzer that has shown no excess of alcohol; or after a minor Collision - in the case of a foreign Driver, risking he or she removing themselves immediately from the chance of any follow-up]

X X X

THE ALTERNATIVE CHARGE of DEATH BY CARELESS DRIVING

[this used in Plea-Bargaining instead of a charge of Death by Dangerous *Driving]*

# # #

AMBITION TO DRIVE

[this a great rite of passage to show a Teenager he or she can now move from the Passenger Seat of a Parent's motorcar to the Driver's Seat. Modern University education, High Insurance Premiums & postponed marriage are factors in delaying this ambition : a privilege many Teenagers are not quite so ready, mentally, to inherit]

X X

ANONYMITY for DRIVERS & RIDERS
UNDER THE AGE of 18 or 19

[this to ensure that young people, also young offenders, aren't named & shamed - but given a second chance, out of the glare of local or prejudicial publicity]

X X X

ANTI-SLIP or ANTI-SKID ROAD SURFACES

[these asphalts very much of experimental status : an engineering triumph when they work; an alternative to concrete roads which some observers blame for icing up more quickly. Anti-Slip Footbridges, Pavements & Cycleways commoner than long Anti-Slip Highways]

# # #

APPEALS for ANONYMOUS INFORMATION REGARDING DRIVING PERFORMANCE

[these placed on the back of vans & lorries or in the local press]

# #

ARBITRATION

[This on offer to both Parties, or all Parties, after a Collision: to work through what happened and to point ways forward towards settlement. Very much a collegiate approach, in contrast with a harshly adversarial approach adopted by most injured Parties, most Insurers, most Police Forces, most Magistrates' & Crown Courts in England & Wales.]

# # # #

ARROWS WRITTEN ON THE ROAD

[these very helpful if Drivers or Riders are unsure whether they are allowed to occupy road-space or not. Often these arrows are accompanied by lots of Road Numbers: eg. B6050/ B6057]

# #

AUDIBLE REVERSING WARNINGS

[these usually fitted to dust-carts & to HGVs... but still very uncommon for white vans or ordinary saloons]

# # # # #

AUDIBLE PEDESTRIAN CROSSING

[these an occasional option offered, especially where 2 or more Pedestrian Crossings are adjacent]

# # #

AUDIBLE SPEEDOMETERS
[these a marvellous invention indicating with a bleep or siren whenever the vehicle in question is driven or ridden above the stated speed-limit for that particular stretch of road. Too many bleeps in a car for too many contrasting purposes can however be as distracting as they are muddled].

# # #

AUTHORIZED PHOTOGRAPHY AFTER A COLLISION
[this photography by one of the Parties or by Police only]

# # #

AUTOMATIC ENGINE CUT-OUT
[this facility, allegedly a fuel-saving mechanism - certainly a cleaner-air enabler - is very new in UK Buses, Coaches & certain saloon cars. Whenever traffic comes to a standstill, so does the engine. It has the brilliant side-effect of making Drivers really think about their re-starting the engine: the how and the when to do that best]

# #

AUTOMATIC LOCKING of ALL CAR DOORS
[this extremely useful where there are bandits, people demanding money, or demanding directions to create a distraction; or wishing to settle a score. Disadvantage: getting locked in during a fire or after a life-threatening crash]

# #

AUTOMATIC LOCKING of PEDESTRIAN GATES BESIDE RAILWAY LINES
[this enabled a minute or two before a train arrives]
# # # #

BACKWARD-FACING PASSENGER SEATS or CHILD-SEATS
[these compulsory for any baby under the age of 15 months... but also provided for Teenagers in some Buses & Taxis, also some people-carriers; recommendation still for children to travel forward-facing on the middle set of seats where there are three rows - in case of rear Collision]
# # #

BENCH-SEATS
[these fitted to the front of saloon cars, sometimes in the back of S.U.V.s too, to ease entering or exiting the Driver-seat. They also have a side-effect of not making the Driver too comfortable. Their greatest advantage is no more need for "Car Dooring": opening an offside door straight onto Cyclists or Pedestrians]
# #

BIG NOTICES : <<KEEP YOUR DISTANCE>>
[these to remind Drivers & Riders not to tailgate- but like so many permanent notices: easy to push to the back of the mind]
# # #

BLACK-BOXES
[these fitted compulsorily to all vehicles after 2022 - sometimes already - not to track where the Driver is - but how he or she is driving, including speeds attained. Especially useful to Insurers]
# # # #

BLANKETS
[these a very simple addition to routine cargo; but absolutely invaluable in the event of ice, snow, snowdrift, traffic-jam or Collision]
# #

BOARDS TO ASK FARMERS, TRACTOR-DRIVERS & LAND ROVERS TO RING A SIGNAL-BOX BEFORE CROSSING A REMOTE RAILWAY
[these offering an alternative to slow vehicles proceeding without explicit permission]
# # #

BOARDS TO WARN PEDESTRIANS THEY HAVE COME ACROSS AN ISOLATED - but SILL ACTIVE - RAILWAY LINE
[these asking Pedestrians to look & listen before attempting a crossing]
# #

BOLLARDS
[these erected to ensure traffic only passes to the immediate Right or Left of them ; often positioned on an Island or a Roundabout]
# #

BOOSTER-SEATS

[these compulsory for children & teenagers until they reach either the age of 12 or the height of 135 cm.: whichever comes first]

# # # #

<<BRAKE>> CAMPAIGNS, DVDs & AWARDS

[this Charity : Brake being established in 1995: possibly the most influential - & versatile - & inventive - Road Safety Charity, intent on educating everyone from teenagers to lorry drivers; also counseling those surviving or seriously injured in Collisions]

# # # # #

BREAKDOWN FIRMS OFFERING TO INSPECT NEWLY-PURCHASED SECONDHAND VEHICLES BEFORE FINAL PAYMENT

[this is usually a charged service.. but is independent enough to re-assess, to challenge, & to override, a vendor's own inspection]

# # # # #

BREAKDOWN VEHICLE AMBER LIGHTS FLASHING

[these switched on immediately an AA or RAC Rescue Crew arrives at a breakdown or begins diagnostic/recovery work]

# #

THE BREATHALYSER

[this introduced decades ago to act as a deterrent to drink-driving]

# # # #

BROADENING THE NATIONAL CURRICULUM

[this broadening would definitely include both Water Safety & Road Safety, also the language & lore of Supermarkets! Hope on... because Hazards scholars face daily, and several times each day, are cruelly excluded from nine out of ten Timetables]

# # #

BUMPERS

[these shock-absorbers now totally out-of-fashion - which is ridiculous because old-fashioned rigid rubber or steel bumpers used to save any follow-up damage to very minor Collisions]

# # #

BUSES & COACHES TESTING EMERGENCY BRAKING, SUDDEN STOPS

[this usually conducted early-morning & on little-used roads]

# # # #

BUS LANES

[these greatly helping some Buses, also some Taxis, get to their destination quicker - but prevailing dangers to be kept in mind: often too narrow; also passing traffic might be going a lot faster than expected]

 # #

BUS LANE PROSECUTIONS

[these after a prohibited vehicle joins a Bus Lane in the wrong place... but with a vast majority of Driver Appeals being successful: indicating a degree of over-punishment]

# #

BUS STATIONS INSTEAD OF INDIVIDUAL BUS STOPS
[these -plus special Bus Crescents for Buses only - to greatly reduce the number of kerbside Bus Stops]

# # #

BYPASSES
[these greatly reducing - but not in all cases - Town Centre & Market-Town traffic; but because of speed & the sheer number of Roundabouts involved: often causing directly or indirectly more Collisions]

X X

CAMERA WARNING BLEEPS
[these fitted in many saloon cars to warn the Driver when they will encounter a Speed Camera ahead. Not foolproof as the Camera might be hand-held or not switched on that particular day. Surprisingly a legal accessory]

X X

CAR REAR-VIEW CAMERAS
[these to detect the lie of the land, other vehicles & Pedestrians to the immediate rear of the car about]

# # # #

CAR-SHARING
[this sharing of fleets or lifts taking an enormous number of cars off the Highway: most effective for the daily commute - or where 4 business-leaders are all heading to the same Convention or Exhibition]

##

CAT's EYES

[these invented, ingeniously, in 1934: an extremely complex piece of engineering in order to delineate clearly the middle of any Highway; in different colours, the edge of some. Fabulous in fog or heavy rain]

# # #

CAUTIONING DRIVERS for MINOR OFFENCES

[this as a direct alternative to spot fines or Court Proceedings]

X X X

CHANGING DOWN GEAR STEADILY

[this a driving technique   perfected far more by older, more experienced, Drivers than nowadays. A slower gear-change is totally invisible - so some braking, instead, might actually prove safer.]

X

CHANGING THE LINE OF A HIGHWAY *[eliminating some bends]*

[this expensive to do - but where tried, reduces previous Collisions by up to 95%. Still problems of Speed & Complacency]

# # #

[THE] CHARGE OF MANSLAUGHTER for DANGEROUS DRIVING

[this hardly ever imposed - but if entered - would save lots of lives through deterrence and public example]

# # # # #

CHILD CAR-SEATS

[these very controversial. Their design has been questioned - hopefully re-designed - many, many times. Better never to fit them if they're worn or second-hand]

# # #

CHILD-PROOF LOCKS
[these fitted to help a Driver secure the 2 or more back doors]
# # #

CHILDREN's CARTS
[these ingenious trailers to a pedal-cycle hold up to 6 infants, with some measure of safety, to School or out for the day. Take cars off the road]
# #

CHURCH SEREVICES TO REMEMBER VICTIMS OF THE ROAD
[these held in several towns across the land; also in several Minsters & Cathedrals: aiming to comfort families & make those who've died or been seriously injured on the Highway more than a statistic]
# # #

CLOSED CIRCUIT TELEVISION IMAGES of DRIVER BEHAVIOUR
[these being difficult for an errant Driver or Rider to detect; these also valid evidence in Court Proceedings & the imposition of fines]
# # # # #

CLOSING A MOTORWAY STRETCH ALTOGETHER
[this essential diversion following a complicated Collision - or series of Collisions - but failing to help Drivers already committed to a journey along that stretch ; reduces rubbernecking]
# #

COACH-DRIVER HOLIDAYS
[this provision for Bus & Coach Drivers, UK: 45-hours off - unbroken - every week or a pattern of 45-24-45-24 hours in consecutive weeks; these days off not able to be accumulated to take all at once; & and calculation must start immediately after past day off]   # # # #

CO-DRIVER(S)

[these assisting enormously every Driver or even Rider: useful most on very long journeys. Alternating responsibility]

# # #

COLLAPSIBLE STEERING-COLUMNS

[these not yet standard in UK saloon-cars, but can be purchased. Said to be an asset in the event of a head-on Collision, but still need some rigidity so that they do not collapse in ordinary driving]

# # #

COLLISION INVESTIGATION BUREAU : ABSENCE OF

[this Bureau desperately needed to analyse every single Collision on the Highway - & to draw up recommendations. A Bureau exists for Air Crash & Rail Crash, also for Near-Misses in the air or on the Railway Track - but nothing for Roads]

X X X

COLLISION WAIVERS for COURTESY CARS & HIRE-CARS

[these available for payment of an additional Premium]

X X

COLOURED PAVING-SLABS IN THE MIDDLE OF THE ROAD

[these to break up the urban environment to make it look as if there is no road ahead: particularly useful in Town Centres]

# # #

COMPULSORY<< STOP>> WRITTEN ON or BESIDE A ROAD

[this being an Order not a Recommendation]

# # # # #

COMPUTER-MODELLING of COLLISIONS BEFORE COLLISION
[this data invaluable for preventing future Collisions... NB: this Analysis neutralized if Highways' Agency does not transport these Scenarios to Market Place, County Shows & Village Fêtes]
# # # # #

COMPUTERIZED RECONSTRUCTIONS of A PAST COLLISION
[these feeding in all the known factors, measurements & witness-statements - also known mechanical failures; but nullified if the Highways' Agency puts pressure on to Police for re-opening a road]
# # # # #

CONES
[these often least employed when most needed: a cheaper form of traffic control than Stewarding or mobile Police Patrol]
#

CONFISCATION of a VEHICLE
[this after a roadside check or Road-Tax evasion check or Police intelligence - or after a fatal crash; required more frequently]
# # # #

CONTRAFLOW
[this re-arrangement of priorities to allow fast-moving Motorway traffic to keep clear of Roadworks]
X X X

CRASH BARRIERS ALONG THE CENTRAL RESERVATION of DUAL CARRIAGEWAYS
[these unfairly fitted after the required number of Cross-overs, deaths & injuries has been reached : should have been fundamental]
# # # #

CRASH HELMETS

[these currently compulsory only for the Riders of Mopeds & Motorcycles. Would be brilliant if worn by ALL Cyclists - and even ALL Drivers - & all front-seat Passengers - though there would be resistance for comfort, also cosmetic, reasons]

# # # # #

COMPULSORY CYCLE INSURANCE   *[Pedal Cycles]*

[this not yet introduced - but there are compelling arguments in its favour: particularly third-party insurance.. as cycling gains popularity after Covid-19]

# #

COMPULSORY MOBILITY-SCOOTER PROFICIENCY TESTS

[these not obligatory at present. A very few Scooter-owners are taken out before final purchase. But a half-hour Road Test would be invaluable - & must include Pavement Safety]

# # # #

CONTINUOUS CONVERSATION BETWEEN BUS DRIVER & BUS DEPÔT or HEAD OFFICE

[this system sold as a means for a Bus-Driver to alert his or her employer about anything going wrong on board; also allowing the employer to reciprocate by alerting the Bus-Driver if there is a hold-up, or snow, or a diversion, or a suspicious Passenger, ahead; this system failing when a Driver worries more about the Intercom than his or her own journey]

X X

CONTOURED CAR & LORRY DRIVER's SEATS

[these assisting safety in making the Driver comfortable; also in the best position to control a Vehicle without sliding or straining. On the other hand, many of these Seats are just too comfortable!]

# #

CONGESTION CHARGE

[this introduced to London & one or two other Cities in the hope of discouraging motor journeys actually within or across a particular Zone. Essential to reduce unnecessary saloon traffic-flows in favour of Public Transport]

# # #

CURFEWS

[these imposed by Magistrates, by Judges, by Parole Boards, by Police or by Health Secretaries: restricting when a single person or family can leave home without good reason or an electronic tag. Vital for people who have driven recklessly in the past. Some Curfews develop into "Lockdowns" or shutdowns for the wider population- in which case fewer vehicles out & about leads to greater safety]

# # #

CYCLE BELLS

[these simple alerts now fitted standard on new bicycles - but can be dismantled straightway. Still thought rather cissy, Non-U: so forgotten in real-life riding]

# # # #

CYCLE LANES PAINTED ON A CARRIAGEWAY WHERE CARS CAN PARK IN THAT LANE

[these in Suburbs or along Main Roads where Car Ownership is high - therefore giving priority to Parked Cars & Vans]

X X X

CYCLE LANES PAINTED BETWEEN
TWO FLOWS OF FORWARD TRAFFIC

[these deathtraps popular at major junctions; also on bridges & flyovers]

X X X X X

CYCLE LANES DEDICATED

[these running alongside a main road, but looking like a separate road]

# # # #

CYCLE LANES PAINTED BUT STILL FOR CYCLES ONLY

[these usually on the Left of a Carriageway - with suitable reservations just before Lights]

# #

CYCLE LANES PAINTED IN THE MIDDLE OF A BROAD PAVEMENT

[these usually immediately next to a painted lane for Pedestrians only... therefore barely distinguishable] **X X**

CYCLING PROFICIENCY TESTS

[these all too rarely offered to boys & girls aged 10 to 14 about to embark on a Pedal-Cycling career. Sometimes conducted in school-grounds or disused airfields ; at other times, with tight stewarding, on quiet suburban roads]

# # #

[THE] D.V.L.A. COUNTER FRAUD & INTELLIGENCE TEAM

[this Department addressing those acquiring vehicles or licences to which they're not entitled.. & many other crimes making up "Dishonest Driving." Of course, before savage cuts, Police used to be far more interested in this endeavour]

# # # #

DASH-CAMS

[these fitted to the dashboards of very modern vehicles to record what is actually happening prior to a Collision or a Near-Miss...N.B. definitely not infallible]

# # #

DEAD-MAN's HANDLES

[these fitted so that if a Driver relaxes his or her grip on the Steering Wheel, they having dozed off, the vehicle will be guided to safe standstill; need fitting to a computer within the car or cab & in conjunction with an extra pedal or lever to be held down at all times. More likely to be found in Trams or Trains crossing a public Highway than in less powerful vehicles]

# # # #

DEFENSIVE DRIVING

[this a Roadcraft technique where all the emphasis is on early-indication & self-recognition of imminent hazards or manoeuvres ; driving & riding daily, hourly, almost entirely risk-averse; imagining the worst at all times]

# # # # #

213

DENTING & DIMPLING THE PAVEMENT
TO INDICATE A SUITABLE - OR THE BEST - PLACE TO CROSS

[this re-surfacing has been wildly popular this past decade: costing millions of pounds. Almost every possible, or suggested, crossing-place is depressed, so deemed suitable for Pedestrians with little or no vision. Unfortunately, dimpling does not mean safety, even where the unwary Pedestrian frequently imagines safety was a factor in their siting.]

X X

DIPLOMATIC IMMUNITY

[this granted freely - and without question - to any foreign Diplomat, or Secret Agent, including any known relation of said Diplomat or Agent : ensuring none will ever be held account for, or fined, let alone prosecuted, for offences ranging from parking ticket right through to Causing Death by Dangerous Driving]

X X X X X

DIPPED HEADLAMPS

[these recommended, but not compulsory in the UK, while driving or riding in poor daylight, fog, and falling rain]

# # #

DISQUALIFICATION FROM DRIVING

[this effective if for a lengthy period - and not softened by undue leniency; must be enforced once imposed]

# # # # #

DIVERSIONS OFF MOTORWAYS

[these when a section of the Motorway has had to be closed completely, maybe after a crash or during bridge demolition]

#

DIVERSIONS in TOWN & CITY CENTRES to BYPASS ROADWORKS

[these sometimes of limited use to Drivers & Riders unfamiliar with alternative road layouts; also when these Diversion signs peter out]

X X

DOUBLE SLIPROADS

[these staggering the joining of a Motorway by allowing two lanes of traffic to merge at more or less the same time]

# # #

DOUBLE WHITE LINES

[these painted in the middle of particularly awkward, winding, stretches of country or outer-suburban Highway. Usually meaning no traversing whatsoever]

# # # #

DOUBLE YELLOW LINES

[these supposedly to prohibit street parking at any time; an exception sometimes made for disabled Drivers]

# # #

DOUBTFUL OFFICIAL CASUALTY FIGURES

[this doubt essential when considering the two categories : Serious Injuries & Minor Injuries - both possibly under-reported by 66% : this because Police who supply the statistics are not so much on top of lasting - or unknown - injury as they are dealing with Deaths]

X X X

DRIVER & VEHICLE STANDARDS' AGENCY RAIDS ON BUS DEPOTS

[these visits must be unannounced in order to get true results]

# # # #

DRIVER & VEHICLE STANDARDS' AGENCY RAIDS ON LORRY YARDS

[these must be unannounced & ruthless to get true results]

# # # # #

DRIVER IMPROVEMENT CLINICS

[these a fairly new innovation : computer-rooms where those who passed their Test a few years ago can replicate the Driving Theory Test - or look at similar simulations to assess just how quick their reactions would be]

# # #

DRIVER'S WINDOW : A SINGLE PANE OF GLASS

[this instead of quarter-lights & vents ; a single pane of glass more likely to identify unexpected Cyclists & Pedestrians]

# # #

DRIVERLESS CARS   [eventually,   DRIVERLESS VANS & LORRIES]

[these probably only feasible on guided tracks or tram-lines. Not suitable for the Highway - however sophisticated their "shutdown" in the event of hazard]   X X X X

DRIVING TEST RE-TAKEN, BY ORDER of THE COURT

[these Tests in concert with Plea Bargaining & Disqualification]

# # # #

DRUG-DRIVING ROADSIDE TESTS

[these equivalent to the Breathalyser, but looking for illegal drugs]

# # # # #

[THE] DUTCH HOLD / DUTCH GRIP/ DUTCH HOLD

[this training of Car & Van Passengers always to open their exit door with Left hand, not Right. This builds in a few extra seconds to consider other Road Users parallel to, or catching up with, a newly parked or stopping vehicle]

# # #

ELECTRIC BICYCLES

[these being a very sensible alternative to pedal-cycling in hilly areas - or actual car or motorcycle ownership]

# # #

EMERGENCY REPLACEMENT TYRES

[these rather flimsy & much cheaper to supply than a sturdy 5th. Wheel ready to act as full & perfect replacement]

X X

EMPATHY

[this state-of-mind, in Highway terms, means imagining what that road might be like to another person : a scholar in a hurry; a Pedestrian surrounded by extremely wet puddle; a wobbly Pedal-Cyclist, whoever ... because, in any one day, we might have 3 or 4 different rôles on the road. Nor is it easy in the insulation of a saloon or the cab of a lorry to appreciate life on the other side]

# # #

ENGINEERING OUT POTENTIAL DEATHS & INJURIES

[this a belief that brilliant & finely-targeted Road Design alone can iron out possible Collisions or misunderstandings]

# #

ENTRAPMENT

[this a controversial Police tactic allegedly employed to get Motorists or other Road-Users into trouble - but not on a spot-check or arbitrary basis. For instance, Police might meet a "Booze Cruise" - or wait just round the corner from a Pub turning out. Or infiltrate a Motorcycle Coven]

# # # #

EMPLOYER CAR-PARKING   [*FREE of CHARGE*]

[this provided by an employer either as a perk, or as an employee convenience, or in remote locations, an employee necessity, or as a Site where an employee might transfer from private to fleet vehicle - but with the big disadvantage of bringing far more private transport onto already congested commuter routes]

X X X

ERECTING HUGE SCREENS AT BUSY ROUNDABOUT APPROACHES

[these   aimed at depriving Drivers & Riders of early Right-hand vision, in effect forcing everyone to a halt before entering a Roundabout]

X X X X

ERECTING RAILINGS on the CENTRAL RESERVATION OF A DUAL CARRIAGEWAY

[these effectively barring Pedestrians crossing - without their vaulting; also invaluable impeding cross-overs]

# # # #

ERECTING RAILINGS on the ROUND CORNERS OF ROADS

[these effectively barring Pedestrians crossing at the point of most danger - but risking those Pedestrians taking to the road itself]

# # #

EXEMPLARY PRISON SENTENCES for ERRANT DRIVERS & RIDERS

[these imposed as much as a deterrent to future careless or dangerous driving as punishment deserved by an errant Road User]

# # #

FIFTY-FIFTY SETTLEMENTS

[these when a Motor Insurer decides that a Collision or Incident was 6 of one & half-a-dozen of the other - even where blame really does lie elsewhere; the prospect of such settlements making a few Drivers much, much, more cautious; others less careful because they will not have to shoulder all the blame...]

X X

FIFTY MILES PER HOUR RESTRICIONS ON COUNTRY ROADS

[these positioned where 40-mph would be too low, 60mph too high]

# # #

FILMS of the HIGHWAY in SCOOL & COLLEGE CLASSROOMS

[these intensely informative - as well as shocking. Many pupils or students will not have seen - Heaven Forbid, been involved in - a life-threatening Crash. Films chosen age-appropriate can really stick in young people's conscious & subconscious]

# # #

FILTER LANES

[these clearly marked only for Right-Hand turners: confusing, indeed, where the Filter Lane can additionally be used for Straight Ahead]

# # #

FILTER LIGHTS

[these Traffic Lights having a green arrow specifically for Left- or Right-turners : sometimes this being a Rush-Hour Light only]

# # # #

FIVE-YEARLY TEST RECALLS

[this would involve granting a Driving Licence for 5 years only - after which there would be the option to renew. The Cost of 5-year Re-tests would be considerable, but this could be passed on to the Candidate]

# # # #

FLASHING MATRIX SIGNS

[these often sited on Gantries; apart from advisory speeds or low bridge warnings, these more often seen on major Trunk Roads or Motorways. The flash is the attention-grabber - but grossly misused for silly information like <<33 miles in 33 minutes>>]

# # #

FLEET RULES

[these usually applying to one Fleet only: dictating uniform, alcohol intake, extra rest, whether smoking or eating is permitted in transit; finally listing the penalties for poor or deteriorating roadcraft]

# # # #

FLEXIBLE MIRRORS

[these mirrors adjustable to & fro: either for parking-up or passing people & parked cars on the Nearside. Necessarily, these Mirrors are wind-proof. Slight force: initially backwards is needed to re-position them]

# # #

FOG-LAMPS

[these very bright, best put on in pea-soup fogs... but tending to be left on too long after all mist has lifted]

# #

FORENSIC SCENE-of-CRIME INVESTIGATION

[this where a Police Officer or Police Force refuses to close a Collision File - putting it all down to chance; where investigations proceed without fear or favour. Quite time-consuming.]

# # #

FREE CAR-PARKING

[in Towns & Cities, also along Residential Streets]

[this good for local trade - but generally brings far more Traffic than with Charging. Road Space is limited - giving a powerful logic to rationing: rationing impacted through cost]

X X

FULLY COMPUTERIZED DASHBOARDS

[these immensely complicated: by definition, wresting much of a vehicle's control from Driver or Pilot to inbuilt setting, screaming alerts as necessary. Many disadvantages surrounding complexity & an encouragement of learned helplessness]

X X X

FORTY MILES PER HOUR RESTRICTIONS on SEMI-URBAN ROADS

[these positioned where 30mph is too low, 50 or 60 mph too high]

# # # #

FREE MOTORCYCLE SAFETY SESSIONS by POLICE MOTORCYCLISTS

[these offered in country areas with a high number of Z-bends... or for Motorcyclists congregating in one Destination: eg. Matlock Bath]

# # # #

FRONT-WHEEL DRIVE

[this an invention that owes itself- like so many other innovations- to Formula One technology. The idea is to place the engine above the front-wheels to actively power & direct those wheels - as opposed to either rear engines or Rear-Wheel Drive]

# # #

GAMBLING MACHINES at MOTORWAY SERVICE STATIONS

[these initially installed to make these Stations attractive as destinations - and to give Drivers & Riders far longer rest-breaks. But by increasing safety, marginally, the patrons of these machines then slip into other problem areas]

#

GATSO SPEEDCAMERAS

[these yellow- box Speed-cameras, sometimes active, profit Police Forces most when partially obscured by foliage, or fitted just after big Roundabouts where least expected. Vandalized in Campaigns]

# #

GIFTED CARS

[these most often given by parent or grandparent immediately after completion of 6th-form or University, or to reward a recently-employed 17- or 18-year old. Gifted Cars not only discourage Public Transport - but encourage motoring at too young an age]

X X

GONGS or LOUD-SOUNDING PIPES

[these strung across the carriageway to deter a Double-Decker Bus or pantechnicon, or a high-sided HGV, attempting to negotiate a low railway bridge immediately ahead]

# # #

GREEN MAN FACING PEDESTRIAN

[this man telling a Pedestrian when it might be safe to cross a busy road. Occasionally, replaced with the word WAIT]

# # #

GREEN MAN AT WAIST LEVEL

[this instead of a man or a man-plus-bike straight ahead of a waiting Pedestrian]

X X

GREEN MAN SHIELDED AGAINST SUNLIGHT OR GLARE

[this lit-man shuttered so effectively that he becomes invisible to Pedestrians waiting to cross on a fine day]

X X

HANDS-FREE TELEPHONE   *[with built-in microphone]*

[these perhaps thought to be "safer" than the hand-held phone or i-pad; but in practice almost as dangerous in that the Driver's attention is fully taken up on a complicated series of calls which might demand of him or her urgency or a degree of mental arithmetic plus lots of instant decision-making]

X X X X

HATCHING A PEDESTRIAN REFUGE

[this being much cheaper & quicker than providing a proper Raised Refuge for Pedestrians: one that would definitely *deter a motorist or Rider from colliding with it]*

X X X

HATCHING THE CARRIAGEWAY

[this happening when traffic engineers realize they have built too much *road space : eg. an old dual-carriageway where overtaking fast-moving traffic is now too dangerous to leave that 2nd lane as an option; some hatching to allow special categories of Driver easier sight of where they might park]*

# #

HAZARD WARNING-LIGHTS FOR CARS

[these making an Internal Sound but outside no sound: Left & Right Indicators coming on simultaneously; these more employed, these days, when traffic flow is suddenly slowing unbeknown to driver[s] following]

# # # #

HEIGHT OF LORRY CABS

[these traditionally very high up to afford maximum forward vision, maximum Driver-Safety; but Pedestrian & ordinary car & bike safety would be greatly enhanced by these cabs being at, or just above, floor-level.]

X X

HIGH-VISIBILITY JACKETS or TABARDS

[these most usefully worn by Breakdown Gangs, by Pedestrians at night; by Walk Leaders; & crucially by Pedal-Cyclists]

# # # #

HIGHWAY [CODE] WARNING SIGNS

[these mostly triangular Signs: eg. hump-back bridge, staggered junction... too many to list separately. Characteristic of these Signs is startlingly pictorial or art-deco self-explanatory design: only the word STOP or its Welsh equivalent appearing as Text]

# # #

HOOTER or HORN

[this a very useful for warning a Pedestrian or Driver who has not seen you. NOT to be used in anger; nor in built-up areas from 11-30 pm to 7am]

# # #

IMPOUNDING VEHICLES ON THE SPOT

[this done routinely for illegally or illicitly parked vehicles - or for cars that have fallen behind with road tax ; also very occasionally after a roadside check; but absent for foreign lorries that can quickly get back to port without making the necessary improvements, or report back to Police Station]

# # # #

IN-CAR DE-MISTERS

[these added to car heating & car cooling systems : intended more for dispersing interior misting up than exterior]

# # #

INDICATORS

[these so time-honoured and so routine they are no longer appreciated as life-savers. But indicators do need to be switched on so that all other Drivers, Riders & Pedestrians know the main Driver's intentions. Too often not used at Roundabouts]

# # #

L.E.D. STREET LIGHTING

[this an alternative to helium, sodium, gas or naphtha street lighting. A different quality of beam & scope]

# # #

L-PLATES

[these essential to identify - & make allowance for - Learner Drivers, but easy to remove, or simply not to put on, for under-age or dishonest driving]

# # #

LANE-CHOICE CLEARLY PAINTED ON THE ROAD

[this very cheap & popular before complex road junctions & major Roundabouts; but practically useless for newcomers]

X X X

LIT-UP JACKETS

[these very new for Cyclists & Motorcyclists: the back of the Jacket having flashing lights]

# # # #

LOLLIPOP LADY / LOLLIPOP MAN

[these appointed to stand at busy Zebra - or other -Crossings: especially near Primary Schools. A threatened species]

# # #

LONG-TERM ACHIEVEMENT AWARDS

[these would be given at a Town-Hall or City-Hall ceremony to recognize those who had achieved 10 years without avoidable Collision [Silver] then 20 years [Gold] together with special awards for 25-year old Drivers with blameless records]

# #

LOOSE CHIPPINGS
[these being a far cheaper & quicker way to treat a deteriorating road surface than proper tarmacadam pressed down by a hefty Steamroller]

X X X X

LORRY-DRIVER DAYS OFF
[these in the UK: 45 hours off every week or a pattern of 45-24-45-24 in successive weeks. Must be unbroken periods. Cannot be accumulated then taken all at once. Beware of Drivers for more than one Agency, or tired Drivers just arrived after crossing Europe]

# # # #

LORRY REAR-VIEW CAMERAS
[these a very recent innovation due to fitted mirrors, previously, only showing Lorry & Tractor Drivers their own vehicle's dimensions]

# # # #

LORRY SIDE-MIRRORS DOWNWARD FACING, BLIND-SPOT MIRRORS
[these governed by 2007 EU Regulation - to detect bicycles and Pedestrians close-up to Left or Right sides of the juggernaut]

# # # # #

LAYBYS ON SMART MOTORWAYS
[these for anybody who has stalled or has no fuel or has had a Collision... very strung out, maybe full already]

#

LIGHTING UP MOTORWAY STRETCHES

[this so that Drivers are not solely dependent on headlamps: but light pollution is the penalty]

# #

LIMITED ACCESS to SOME CLASSES of VEHICLE or ROAD-USER

[these very popular at Motorway entrances; also narrow country lanes unsuitable for HGVs]

# # #

LOCAL AUTHORITY ROAD SAFETY TEAMS

[these Employees are immensely valuable, but subject to austerity cuts. Sometimes Teams also take over a local Shop for their Road Safety campaigning]

# # # #

LOCAL AUTHORITY WEIGHBRIDGES

[these a wonderful idea - but now so rare]

# # #

LOCAL NEWSPAPER REPORTING of ROAD CASUALTIES

[this astonishingly influential: provided each Collision is reported twice: 1st. after happening; 2nd. after an ensuing Inquest or Court Proceeding]

# # #

LORRY SPRAY-GUARDS

[these governed by a 2011 law in Great Britain: must be fitted to trailers as well as fixed lorries]

# # #

LORRY UNDER-RIDERS

[these girders to prevent a car being wedged &/or flattened by or beneath a rampaging Lorry or HGV]

# # # #

LOWERED SPEED LIMITS

[this a conscious decision with determined implementation where traffic is not conforming safely within existing speed limits. Lowering might initially be "experimental" - backed up as it happens by research showing overall journey-times are not greatly lengthened by a change from 50 to 40 mph., or 40 to 30mph in outer-urban areas]

# # # #

MAKING THE ENVIRONS OF A SCHOOL
<< NO WAITING AT ANY TIME >>   or
<< NO PICKING-UP or DROPPING DOWN AT ANY TIME>>

[this to reduce the mêlée of Parents & Grandparents coming earlier & earlier to drop children off - or collect them: parking anywhere & everywhere, including on pavements and grassy verges]

# # # #

MANDATORY 50 mph SPEED LIMITS ROUND ROADWORKS

[this at its best with totally unseen *enforcement... usually strict]*

# # # #

MANUFACTURER's CRASH TESTING

[these tests on new & existing motorcars : what would happen in the event of a Head-On Collision at 70,60,50,40mph? + during side & rear Collisions?]

# # # #

MATRIX SIGNS <<FOG>>

[this used to be the longest word available! Fog warning quite reliable & up-to-date]

# # # #

MATRIX SIGNS on MOTORWAYS :<[LUTON] 35 miles,35minutes>

[this a false[?] and over-optimistic [?] way of calculating how long it will take to get there]

X X

MATRIX SIGNS on MOTORWAY
TO TELL DRIVERS THEY ARE SPEEDING

[these a sort of name & shame - as the number-plate is displayed for every other motorist or rider to see]

# #

MEDITATION

[this quarter-hour to prepare a Driver or Rider mentally for the long journey ahead; easily combined with self-massage & other relaxation techniques]

# # #

MOBILE SPEED-GUNS or SPEED-DETECTORS

[these usually totally unprepared-for: eg. beginning of a 40mph. Zone, or from behind a hedge - or, in some countries, embedded in a passing hay-waggon]

# # #

MOTORAIL

[this a once-popular expedient in the UK, now all but abandoned except Folkestone - Calais. The idea was to let a railway train carry cars and lorries for the longest single span of their intended journeys. Reinstating Motorail to destinations like Edinburgh, Ayr, Penzance, St. Ives, Holyhead & Fishguard would be invaluable]

# #

MOTORCYLE MAINTENANCE for YOUNG ADULTS 14-18

[this course progressing from simple mechanics to complex Motorcycle Roadcraft]

# # # #

MOTORCYCLE MENTORS

[these on duty either at Motorcycle Conventions or at Resorts popular with Motorcyclists - like Clacton or Matlock Bath. Mentors mingle with Bikers offering useful tips regarding clothing, protection, safety and Roadcraft]

# # #

THE MOTORING PRACTICAL TEST

[this compulsory for about 85 years and constantly upgraded in difficulty and cost : failure rate about 55%]

# # # #

THE MOTORING THEORY TEST

[this compulsory since June 1996 and constantly upgraded in difficulty - now using CGI - with only a 50% pass-rate; but beware of impersonation]

# # # # #

MOTORWAY GANTRIES
to INFORM ROAD-USERS NO HARD SHOULDER AVAILABLE
[these usually provided in association with "Smart Motorway Ahead"]
X X X X X

MYSTERY SHOPPER "PURCHASE" of SECOND-HAND VEHICLE
[this mystery invaluable wiping off the market back-street dealers & spivs selling clocked, lethal, stolen or illegally welded-together cars, also un-roadworthy motorcycles]
# # # #

NARRATIVE & STORY-TELLING
[this a tried, tested & trusted technique where Cyclist, Driver or Rider maintains a constant narrative - talking to self - as if the whole of a journey about to be undertaken is a Story: which of course it is - but not always a Story with happy ending]
# # #

NAVIGATORS
[these rather overtaken by Sat-Nav - but a trusted human being frequently does the job far better, especially when accompanying a novice Driver: interpreting road conditions, also signage, with a far greater degree of subtlety & explanation. Even so, the Navigator is not the actual Driver]
# # #

NEAR-MISS DIARIES

[these voluntarily kept by Drivers, Motorcyclists, & Truckers to record not Collisions but where Collisions were narrowly averted. Diaries get fairly full fairly quickly - & are valuable to look back on]

# # #

NEIGHBOURHOOD WATCH SPEED GUNS / SPEED VIDEOS

[these being legal provided no fines, no naming & shaming]

# # #

NIGHT WATCHMEN

[these essential where a truck or delivery-driver needs to reverse in a crowded or cramped place ; or where a disabled Driver is reversing - or where the desired parking lot is narrow; the Night Watchman himself or herself sometimes risking being run over]

or X X

NO-CLAIMS BONUSES

[these originally meant to reward a record of no Collisions at all, no other Claims ... but increasingly granted upon payment of a supplement]

# #

NO PAVEMENTS AT ALL

[this being a bold experiment to make every other Road User look out for Pedestrians]

#

NO LEFT TURN

[this prohibition seemingly illogical because Left turns are normally safer than Right Turns. A later alternative Left usually provided]

# #

NO RIGHT TURN

[this prohibition astonishingly successful almost wherever tried]

# # # # #

NO ROAD SIGNS OR LIGHTS AT ALL

[this being a bold experiment to make every single Driver, every single Rider, every single Pedestrian, look out for each other]

# # #

NOTICES ADVISING PASSENGERS TO STAY IN THEIR SEATS UNTIL A BUS HAS COME TO A COMPLETE HALT

[these aimed at preventing Passengers stumbling on stair-cases or shooting from back to front of downstairs' aisle... but more honoured in the breach than in the observance]

# #

NOTICES SAYING: <<DO NOT SPEAK TO THE DRIVER WHILE THIS BUS IS IN MOTION>>

[these quite common in Driver-Only Buses & Coaches]

# #

NUMBER-PLATE ARCHIVE

[this currently available only to Police, authorized individuals & cowboy Car Park operators. Arguably should be available to anybody who has suffered through the bad driving or riding of others]

# #

NUMBER-PLATE MANUFACTURE

[this technically the preserve of licensed garages or craftspeople - but in reality subject to backstreet forgery - or simply theft]

X X

NUMBER-PLATE RECOGNITION

[this being used everywhere from petrol-station exits to beginnings of a congestion-charging zone. The real difficulty comes with False Number-Plates: a means of evading nearly every penalty every day for every nefarious purpose]

# #

ONE-WAY RETAIL-PARK & SUPERSTORE ROUTING OF TRAFFIC

[this in place of free-for-all: a very strict set of One-Way arrows]

# # #

ONE-WAY STREETS

[these being one of the oldest & most tested & trusted means of reducing road casualties ; must be subject to strict enforcement]

# # # #

ORGANIZING A WALKING-BUS / WALKING TRAIN

[these ingenious alternatives with approved parents or volunteers grouping children into 2 x 2s and pretending they are a moving Bus: 4 x 4 imitating a moving train : children with or without tabards, to walk to/from School safely without needing the School Run or a real coach]

# # # # #

OUT-OF-COURT SETTLEMENTS

[these sometimes more generous: more often, less generous, than those settlements imposed inside a Court. Settlements often driven by expediency, saving Court time. With Penalties kept out of Court: very many £100 & £200 Spot- Fines are not imposed by Magistrates but extra-judicially. All leads to some feelings of injustice & letdown]
X X X

P-PLATES

[these optional, but advisable, for any New Driver who has only just passed his or her Test. A good clue for other Road-Users]
# #

P.S.V. BADGES

[these worn by Bus & Coach Drivers during refreshment breaks, also between shifts. These badges save Drivers being kept in a long queue or offered alcohol]
# #

PAINTING <<LOOK LEFT>> or <<LOOK RIGHT>> AT A CROSSING

[this especially at crucial Pedestrian Crossings where it's not at all apparent where traffic is coming from]
# # #

PAINTING ON MOTORWAYS
RECOMMENDED DISTANCES FROM VEHICLE AHEAD

[this an experiment on only one or two Motorways, and then on only one or two sections of those Motorways: to ensure Drivers always keep so many double-deck buses from the Driver ahead]
# # #

PAINTING <<TRAFFIC FROM LEFT AND RIGHT>> AT A CROSSING
[this especially useful in Town Centres - where only some categories of traffic like Buses or Taxis allowed to swing into your path or where priorities are confused]
# # #

PANORAMIC MIRRORS
[these very inexpensive to fit over existing rear-view mirrors: giving a far wider perspective on following traffic]
# # #

PARAMEDICS PARKED-UP
[these Paramedics on call - but not answering an actual Collision at the time they are parked-up ready for a Collision. Cannot prevent serious injury - but can save resulting fatalities]
# # #

PARK-&-RIDE
[this tried with considerable success on the approach-roads to major cities or large towns: but needs expanding to conurbations where it hasn't yet been tried; also to every approach-road where only East or West, North or South has been tried already]
# # #

PARTIES EXCHANGING NOTES AFTER A COLLISION
[this not much use except for garnering of mere names & addresses; soon becomes confrontational - or admissions very soon retracted]
# #

PASS-PLUS DRIVER TRAINING
[this optional for a new Driver - but can dramatically reduce a 1st. or 2nd. Insurance Premium]
# # # #

PASSING PLACES PROVIDED

[these on single-track roads: allaying both head-on crashes and dangerous manoeuvres onto verges & banks]

# # #

PAVEMENTS ENTIRELY BOXED IN BY STEEL RAILINGS

[this a very popular concession to Drivers as they are 90% sure Pedestrians will have to use Underpasses - or a Footbridge; railings erected particularly at major intersections]

# # # #

PAY-PER-MILE ROAD-CHARGING

[this a proposed Government initiative to replace the Annual Road Tax with an elaborate scheme whereby Motorists & Riders would be charged only for the miles they've actually covered. Very complex]

# #

"PEDESTRIAN-FRIENDLY" CAR BONNETS

[these shaped to throw a struck Pedestrian sideways not under : but should come with a warning that NO oncoming vehicle is "Pedestrian Friendly"]   # # #

PENALTY POINTS on DRIVING LICENCES

[these aimed at building to a total of 12 - & then a possibility of disqualification; feared therefore particularly by those whose driving is their living]

# # # #

PETROL TAX / FUEL DUTY FROZEN

[this a well-received measure, for the 11th. year in a row, with 2 purposes : to take the UK off a fuel-escalator of cost of living plus - a type of green tax; and to keep the costs of motoring down for essential users; also those who live in remote rural areas where there is little public transport. Result: more cars owned ; more miles driven]

X X X

PICTORIAL ROADS SIGNS

[these very modern, also supposedly easily understood by Drivers & Riders whatever their ability to read. Problems with ambiguity: eg. Motorcycle over a Car: Flyover? Roadworks ahead: you'll need an umbrella !]

# # #

PILOT VEHICLES

[these most useful where a road is dug up for essential repairs or for re-surfacing over a stretch of more than half-a-mile; the Pilot dictating both speed and chosen lane]

# # #

PINCH-POINTS : SIGNS SAYING <<GIVE WAY TO TRAFFIC COMING IN THE OPPOSITE DIRECTION >>

[these popular on roads of only one-&-a-half car's width; & established in conjunction with a raised and heavily indented pavement at the start of the scheme & sometimes with the priority changing every quarter-of-a-mile or less]

# #

PLAIN-CLOTHES POLICE POSITIONED NEAR PUBS AT CLOSING TIME
[this trap must be disguised in order to catch those unfit to drive before they actually turn their car keys]

  # # #

PLAIN-CLOTHES' , UNMARKED, ROAD or MOTORWAY PATROLS
[these not impossible to detect, but generally extremely diligent- with the Co-Driver doing the Filming and/or Telephoning]

# # # # #

PLAY STREETS
[these useful in inner-city areas to give children permission to play uninterrupted by traffic either for certain hours of the day or week... or, where there is suitable garaging, all the time]

# # # #

PLEA-BARGAINING by PROSECUTORS
[this now standard practice in order to get a Guilty Plea... of interest: always bargained lower not higher]

X X X X

POLICE ACTING AS STEWARDS
[this stewarding to supplement rather than replace amateur stewarding. Very rarely are Police routinely used on the ground except after a big Crash or Spillage. Gone are the days Bobbies on the Beat showing non-Festival, non-Race, Motorists where to go]

# #

POLICE CHASES
[these aimed at reducing taking without owner's consent & reckless driving behaviour; also following robberies needing solving]

X X X X

POLICE PATROLS : DRINK-DRIVING

[these unfortunately greatly reduced in recent years - yet needed]

# # # #

POLICE PATROLS : MOTORWAY DRIVING BEHAVIOUR & LIGHTS

[these, again, greatly reduced in recent years - yet so needed]

# # #

POLICE PATROLS : SEATBELT ENFORCEMENT

[this varies force to force : usually issuing a warning or a fine]

# # #

POLICE PATROLS : USE of HAND-HELD TELEPHONES AT THE WHEEL

[these wherever they happen, usually result in a stern warning or a strict fine +penalty points on licence. Many, many, more of these Patrols are needed]

# # # # #

POLICE SIRENS

[these switched on in order to move traffic out of the way; or to gain ground on a criminal or suspected criminal; or to persuade an errant or drink-drunk Driver to move over for questioning... NB. these Sirens can on occasion cause Collisions]

X X

POSTER CAMPAIGNS

[these extremely useful where there has been a "new" invention like Seatbelts; or a revived danger like people forgetting not to drink and then drive]

# # #

POLICE NOTICE AT SIDE of ROAD APPEALING for WITNESSES
[this often erected where all investigations have proved fruitless; also as a warning to others that they're not immune]
# # #

POLICE WAVING MOTORISTS PAST A ROAD CRASH
[this to reduce rubber necking; also to establish priority]
# # #

PREAMBLE
[this to imitate how travellers are greeted in an aeroplane before it takes to the sky. How Car & Lorry Drivers, also their Passengers, need such a Preamble illustrated as an Appendix below]
# #

PROTECTIVE CLOTHING for MOTORCYCLISTS
[this very expensive: £250 + apart from state-of-the-art Crash Helmet - but amazingly effective in the event of unseating or worse, Collision.   2nd. Hand Army Combat Uniform a cheaper alternative]
# # #

PUBLIC LISTINGS of "THE SAFEST CAR" IN THE EVENT OF COLLISION
[these typically naming the XJ ELEPHANTUS as safest; the MOTOWN TIGERLILY as hatchback most crumpled in testing]
# #

Q CARS
[these unidentified Police Patrols aimed at schoolchildren congregating with malicious intent on bridges & verges]
# # #

RAIDS on BOOZE-CRUISE COACHES & MINIBUSES

[these frequently discovering masses of heavyweight bottles & cans - also impacting on minibus maintenance or overcrowding]

# # #

RAIDS - UNANNOUNCED - on BUS or LORRY DEPOTS

[these all too few - but incredibly effective in taking off the road, instantly, HGVs & PSVs that have not been kept roadworthy, maybe because of cash constraints]

# # # #

RAILINGS ERECTED AT SCHOOL GATES or NEAR TO SCHOOL GATES

[these to prevent excited children rushing out of School without looking]

# # # #

RAILWAY TRAIN HOOTERS as the TRAIN APPROACHES A MAJOR or A *MINOR* ROAD CROSSING POINT

[this sound in case a Pedestrian or Vehicle has not heeded warnings regarding getting stuck, unawares, on the actual railway track]

# #

RAISING BELISHA BEACONS HIGH IN THE AIR

[this to make them more visible to traffic following HGVs]

# #

RAISING THE BRAKE LIGHTS of a CAR TO SHINE IN REAR-WINDOW

[this very good & relatively inexpensive; especially useful in crawling traffic & in long traffic-jams]

# # # #

RAISING THE MINIMUM DRIVING AGE

[this now leaving only moped Riders & Cyclists able to be on the Highway at age 16]

# # # #

RAISING THE HEIGHT of BRIDGE PARAPETS above BUSY TRAFFIC:

[this in order to discourage stone-throwing & suicides]

# #

REAR-WINDOW HEATERS & WIPERS

[these so helpful in maintaining the efficacy of the Driver's central mirror - but no use at all on a modern Coach that might board up its Rear Window]

# #

RETROSPECTIVE ANALYSIS by a FLEET AFTER EVERY SINGLE COLLISION or NEAR-MISS

[this Analysis determining whether an HGV or box-van Driver should remain in that Fleet's employment... best done consensually]

# # # # #

[THE] ROAD RESEARCH LABORATORY [latterly known as the [privatized] TRANSPORT RESEARCH LABORATORY

[this being a well-respected institution, dating from 1933, fundamental to our understanding on the part Roads themselves play in Road Safety] # # #

ROAD SAFETY MINISTER

[this in the UK normally a Junior Minister with a Roads' brief. Fair to say that most of these new appointments have Road Safety on their radar - depreciated by rapid turnover of office-holder] # #

ROAD SAFETY TARGETS

[these often framed as "Give Hellshire 20% fewer Road Deaths" - but ignoring the truth that the only logical Target for deaths & serious injuries is ZERO]

\#

ROAD SAFETY WEEKS

[these held by all sorts of driving bodies to encourage a reform of Driver or Rider behaviour]

\# \#

ROAD TAX FROZEN

[this at a time of austerity when there would be possible protests at it going up. Result: far more vehicle ownership, more miles driven]

X X

ROAD TRAFFIC ACCIDENTS   [R.T.A.s]

[these being Police shorthand for "yet more Minor Collisions" so not treated as worth full Detection - or lengthy Cross-Questioning]

X X X X

ROAD SAFETY AMBASSADORS

[these are being trialled in certain villages where young people help monitor the speed of passing traffic; also where they stand outside a School at 8-30 am & 3-15 pm with badges, his-vis bands, leaflets & advice]

\# \# \#

ROADSIDE CHECKS

[these amazingly productive wherever Traffic Police have the time or skill to conduct them. Can catch one type of offender whilst checking up on another. Useful also for correct documentation]

# # # #

ROADSIDE MEMORIALS

[these consisting of bunches of flowers, football scarves, toys and cards where somebody has recently died at one particular location. Must be maintained carefully - and updated. Best changed into a single memorial stone after about 3 or 4 weeks]

# # # #

ROADSIDE NOTICES : << TIREDNESS KILLS >>

[these positioned half-a-mile before Motorway Service Stations; also on trunk roads in South-West of England during School Holidays]

# # # #

ROLL-BARS

[these sometimes called Anti-Roll Bars : popular in jalopy-racing, also rally-driving; to some extent fixed within SUVs - without being too obvious]

# # # #

ROUNDABOUTS   *[as opposed to linear Junctions]*

[these able to save up to 60% of the preceding number of Collisions. Demand a lot of thought in the negotiation and siting]

 # # #

ROUNDABOUT APPROACH SCREENS
[these to screen out Traffic approaching from the Right: as a deterrent to entering the Roundabout itself, at speed]

X X X

"ROUTINE" BREATH-TESTS at the ROADSIDE
[these typically conducted late evening, & on Saturday nights, on the edge of conurbations - but with the provision the Driver or Rider stopped must have already committed an error, or driven zig-zag, or not used the right lights]

# # # #

RUMBLE-STRIPS on APPROACH to a ROUNDABOUT
[these white or yellow diagonal lines are slightly raised to jolt a complacent Driver: to prepare for a major Roundabout ahead; useful reminders on a long journey]

# # #

SAFE GAP CHEVRONS
[these painted on a motorway to discourage tailgating by showing how many double-decker bus lengths might be needed to come to a halt. Certainly experimented with on one or two stretches of the M1 North - but not widely repeated on the whole network]

# # #

SALTING A ROAD
[this just before, during, or after heavy white frost, black ice, snow or sludge: making a Highway more negotiable, or more-safely negotiable, particularly at speed. Extremely labour-intensive]

# # #

SCHOOL- or GREYHOUND- or YELLOW BUSES

[these Buses taking up to 52 separate cars off the Highway - also saving much wear & tear, also frustration, on the Highway]

# # #

SCHOOL TEACHING ON ROAD SAFETY

[this absolutely essential and for all ages 4-17: divided into Driver, Passenger & Pedestrian Lessons;, later Motorcycle Safety too. Must be part of an established Curriculum. Much neglected]

# # # #

SCREENS ERECTED ROUND SCENE of DEATH or DERIOUS INJURY

[these Screens to deter Rubber-Necking, also the taking of authorized photographs]

# #

SEGREGATION OF DIFFERENT ROAD-USERS

[this most notable in modern Bus & Coach Stations; also attempted on busy Highways where no surface crossing is permitted; sometimes attempted with segregated Cycle Lanes & some sections only of inner-city tramways]   # # # #

SELF-DRIVING CARS   *[sometimes called DRIVERLESS CARS]*

[these currently undergoing   on- & off-road testing. Consistently these automaton robots undermine rather than promoting Road Safety - and are very unlikely to be able to predict more than the simplest of hazards - without some controller Intervention]

X X X X

SELF-TESTING BREATH-TESTS
[these to assist drivers or Riders who might already have consumed Alcohol. Main disadvantage: any *intake of Alcohol before driving can delay reaction to perceived hazard]*
# #

[A] SERIES of MINI-ROUNDABOUTS
[these in suburbs - or near to Town Centres - to control choice of nearly every side-road intersecting with a B-Road; but often ignored]
# #

SEVENTY-MILE-AN-HOUR ABSOLUTE SPEED LIMIT on MOTORWAYS
[this almost as old as Motorways themselves; but honoured in the breach - where the new 70 becomes the 80]
# #

SHARED VEHICLE INCENTIVES
[these provided by employer, or popular venue, or by some local authorities, some Bus Lanes, so that people will fill their cars rather than commuting with one Driver only in position. Some temptation to create a front-seat Dummy!]
# # #

SHATTERPROOF SIDE WINDOWS
[these laminated and a great help when another Road User is trying to enter the vehicle or threaten or distract or steal from the Driver; rather more expensive than conventional side-windows]
# #

SIGNS INDICATING SCHOOL CHILDREN or ELDERLY PERSONS AHEAD
[these erected near Schools & Elderly Persons' Homes]   #

SIGNS SAYING : << DANGER ! NO PAVEMENTS AHEAD ! >>

[these mattering a lot when leaving villages ; also alongside strung-out ribbon housing]

# # #

SIGNS SAYING - or INDICATING - << FROST & ICE AHEAD >>

[this usually a small triangle with a snowflake in the middle]

# # #

SIGNS SAYING: << NO U-TURNS >>

[these popular in City Centres & on heavily-used Dual Carriageways]

# # # #

SIGNS SAYING: <<PLEASE DRIVE SAFELY IN BESTBOROUGH>>

[these usually positioned at the very beginning of urban environment]

# #

SIGNS SAYING << POLICE INCIDENT AHEAD >>

[these Blue in Colour with prominent white writing... often accompanied by a <<ROAD AHEAD CLOSED>> Sign.... & sometimes tempting rubber-necking]   # # #

SIGNS SAYING << THANKYOU FOR DRIVING SAFELY >>

[these usually positioned at the petering out of an urban environment with a sign saying << Please Visit Bestborough Again>>]

#

SKID-PANS

[these specially designed for Police Training - but available for lay-persons, too, as part of voluntary Roadcraft Training]   # # #

SKULL-&-CROSSBONES
[this sign erected where there is a near 90°hairpin bend ahead: to arrest a Driver or a Rider's attention]

# #

SKY-HIGH INSURANCE PREMIUMS
[these set to deter boy-racers & high-risk teenagers - & repeat offenders - getting behind the wheel of any vehicle]

# # #

"SLOW" WRITTEN on the ROAD   [ARAF in Wales]
[this instruction far more effective if very rarely written ; writing on road better where it's unlikely the wording isn't lost beneath halted vehicles]

# #

SPEED AWARENESS COURSES
[these offered as a direct alternative to prosecution - or indeed Court + Fine + Points on Licence. Courses actually cost nearly £100 and may not always be on offer nearer home. Feedback from Courses a mixture of Positive, Surprise, & complete Resignation]   # # #

SPEED CAMERAS [GATSO]
[these popular in areas where Police Forces can acquire much Revenue - not always loaded, but more likely to be loaded where Driver concentration at its least]

# # #

SPEED HUMPS FLATTENED OUT
[this an experiment in some Suburbs & along known short-cuts] ##

SPEED HUMPS STEEPER

[this profile popular in the Suburbs of Towns & Cities; also on rat-runs; harming suspension of some vehicles]

X X X

SPEED-LIMTERS

[these fitted in some saloons; but in most HGVs & long-distance Coaches … often set at about 56 mph]

# # #

SPOT CHECKS on LORRIES ENTERING UK PORTS

[these must be sudden & ruthless, in order to be effective… in search, also, of Stowaways, Counterfeits & Contraband]

# # # # #

SPOT-FINES

[these imposed for a great number of "minor" traffic offences - usually where there has been no serious injury; used especially for low tyres, no functioning lights, non-wearing of seatbelts, use of a hand-held telephone]

# # # #

SPOT-TESTING of DRIVERS' 4, 6, or 8 TYRES

[this usually roadside & without notice - but very rarely instituted] **#**
# # # #

STAGGERED JUNCTIONS

[these, maybe deliberately, designed so that 2 decisions are needed to cross a major Highway, or leave that Highway, instead of 1]

# # # #

STAGGERED PEDESTRIAN CROSSINGS

[this on a dual carriageway or where there's a purpose-built Refuge half way]

##

STAGGERING the BEGINNINGS & END OF SCHOOL DAY

[this so that half the pupils stay in classroom a few minutes longer]

# #

STEWARDING of GARDEN-PARTIES, WEDDINGS or GYMKHANAS

[this routine in several National Trust Properties; at the entrance to all the big Music Festivals, Flower- or County-Shows; also where a popular Church can only offer a few marked bays]

# # # #

STICKERS ON LORRIES INDICATING HAZARDOUS CONTENT

[these being little use in the event of fire or an explosion]

#

STICKERS ON REAR WINDSCREEN SAYING <<BABY ON BOARD>>

[these not entirely convincing when the baby is aged 7!] # #

STING-MATS

[these to bring a suspected stolen or drug-driving vehicle to a standstill without death or injury] # # # #

253

STREET ANGELS

[These Angels go under other names in certain Cities - but their Mission is the same: to talk to Pedestrians in distress through shock, robbery, alcohol, rejection, whatever : then ensure these young men & women get safely back to their homes, without resorting to a long walk in the dark - or an unlicensed hire car]

# # #

STREET-LIGHTS

[these probably assisting Road Safety more than lessening it. All sorts of gases or electricity have been used to power these. L.E.D. is now the preference for many Authorities. But beware of dark clothing still "merging" with the tarmac, at twilight or at night]

# # #

SUICIDE NETS & RAILINGS

[these not nearly widespread enough. Who can know how many Suicides there will be? Nevertheless, these practical rather than emotional deterrents are extremely useful preventing human bodies dropping onto Pedestrians , also between fast-moving vehicles, below]

# # #

SUNGLASSES

[these reducing, even minimizing, glare in Summer; also in dazzle months like September, December & February when strong sun is very low in the sky. Many Sunglasses are illegal for Drivers where they keep out too much available light]

# #

SUSPENDED PRISON SENTENCES

[these imposed after extremely serious motoring prosecutions: eg. Death by Dangerous Driving, Death by Careless Driving]

X X X

SWORD-TOOTH CONSTRUCTION of [ANGLED] BUS STATIONS

[this design now widely adopted in new Bus Stations & Transport Interchanges throughout the land. The angle of Buses entering or reversing is 45°; nowadays hardly ever 90°; and construction absolutely has to incorporate a total prohibition of Pedestrians anywhere - except at sliding glass-doors in the Concourse - for the sole purpose of paying the Driver & finding a seat].

# #

TAXI LICENSING

[this conducted by Local Authorities, & needing very rigid enforcement: taxi-licensing [identification] plates & no permission for removable Private-Hire or Black Cab door signage. Far more restriction needed on Uber Cabs, Limousines & Works' Minibuses]

# # #

TACHOGRAPHS

[these compulsory in new lorries since 2006; complicated devices to record speed , distance, & the number & duration of rest breaks; but can be interfered with before official Inspection]

# # # # #

TAKINGS-INTO-CONSIDERATION

[these being charges added by the Prosecution to an already-full charge-sheet in order to deal with all infringements of good Driver/Rider behaviour / documentation - at 1 Hearing]   **X X X**

TALKING CARS
[these very new on the road : Cars that can communicate direct with each other using 4G or 5G. Very useful warning of hazard] # #

TEACHING CHILDREN & STUDENTS PEDALCYCLE PROFICIENCY
[this conducted usually in school grounds or on side-roads.. to get a Certificate in recognition of good handling & safer road manners] # # # #

TEACHING CHILDREN THE GREEN-CROSS CODE
[this an old-fashioned exercise aimed at good Pedestrian manners; perhaps better updated with the Wooden Cross Code in Appendix] # # #

TEACHING CHILDREN THE WOODEN-CROSS CODE
[this far more realistic: expecting to be run down at any moment…. The whole Wooden Cross Code is actually printed as Appendix 2 below] # # # #

TELEVIZED POOR OR SHOCKING ROADCRAFT
[these Programmes really arresting - in more than one sense! The format is usually one particular Police Force showing off its Patrols - particularly outwitting Motorway Patrols; real-life film footage, also real-life follow-up , but with the proviso no Road-User with evidence they might be innocent should be named or shamed] # # # #

TELEVIZED ROAD SAFETY CAMPAIGNS
[these needing to be conducted very professionally - and not for months on end. Slight risk some of these Campaigns might be a bit too frightening , resulting in an obscuring or shunning of the message] # # #

TEMPORARY ROAD SIGNS

[these erected during a flood or for a very temporary speed-limit or diversion. Research surprisingly shows Drivers & Riders pay far more attention to temporary Signs than their permanent equivalents - because they are not expecting a Sign they didn't see yesterday - or during the week before]

# #

TEMPORARY TRAFFIC LIGHTS

[these installed at short-term or long-term roadworks to make sure only one lane of traffic passes those roadworks at a time. Unfortunately, these Lights often break down, are mistimed - or have to be abandoned in favour of a roadmender manually controlling a Lollipop alternating STOP/GO]

# #

THIRD-PARTY ONLY INSURANCE

[this to reduce the Insurance Premium significantly. Sometimes provided for an unnamed Co-Driver within an otherwise Comprehensive Insurance Policy]

X

THIRTY-ONE DAY ABSOLUTE GUARANTEE
on SECOND-HAND VEHICLE SALES

[this one of the most valuable inducements to go ahead with a purchase; but suffers when a major fault develops after 31 days]

# # # #

TIMING A SET OF PEDESTRIAN LIGHTS to GIVE PRIORITY TO MOVING TRAFFIC

[this set on the assumption that too many vehicles screeching to a halt might be to Pedestrians' detriment; allowing Pedestrians to congregate into bunches before granting permission to cross]

X X

TOILETS IN LAYBYS & PETROL-STATIONS

[these all too rare. Generally the more toilets the better: both to make Drivers, Riders & Passengers more comfortable - and to give Drivers a much-needed rest]

# # #

TOUCH-SCREEN INSTRUMENTS ON THE DASHBOARD

[these rising in complexity in line with the rise in complexity of a vehicle's computer. Unfortunately, these screens take a Driver's eyes off the road for far longer than easier to locate knobs or switches on the dashboard]

X X X

TOUGH LEGISLATION

[this more popular in many other Countries than Great Britain - where the tradition is very much more softly-softly; keeping the Public on board, & on the Police's side? Undoubtedly halving the permitted alcohol limit, or doubling the Fine for Tailgating, does have a direct impact on Collisions]

# # # #

TRADITIONAL ZEBRA CROSSINGS

[these now rather out of favour: therefore unfamiliar to some less seasoned drivers; actually a remarkable idea] # # # #

TRAFFIC LIGHTS *[controlling vehicles as well as Pedestrians]*

[these an alternative to the previous free-for-all; occasionally an alternative to a Roundabout removed ; increasingly an addition to an existing Roundabout whose choices were previously voluntary / or negotiated between competing Drivers or Riders]

# # #

TRAINED SUICIDE NEGOTIATORS

[these needed on Highways because Highways are a natural theatre for men & women "wishing" to take their own lives. Negotiators stand next to a desperate person coaxing them - occasionally pulling them - away from nemesis]

# # # #

TRANSPORT for LONDON

[this a body gaining in importance now it answers to the Mayor of London. A rare example of co-ordinated Transport Policy - which, in turn, has the potential to push Bus, Taxi, Motorcar and Cycle Safety higher up the agenda]

# #

TRIANGLES

[these advance warnings of vehicle breakdown compulsory in some other countries, but not in the UK]

# #

TWENTY MILES PER HOUR LIT-UP SIGNS

[these popular near to Schools and/or applying to certain hours in the day, certain days in the week]

# # # #

UNAUTHORIZED PHOTOGRAPHY of a CRASH SCENE
[this hobby often pursued on smart-phone; inevitably leading to ghoul-like intervention and / or Rubber-Necking; impeding also the emergency services]

X X X

VARIABLE INSURANCE PREMIUMS
[these imposed- or offered - after cross-questioning concerning nearly every variable which could make Motor Insurance viable]

# # #

VARIABLE SPEED LIMITS ON MOTORWAYS
[these allowed & allowed to prosper due to modern technology]

# # #

[THE] VEHICLE INSPECTION SERVICE
[this being an extremely reputable commercial outfit that will do thorough paid inspections to make sure a lorry is road-worthy]

# # # #

VERY HIGH PARKING CHARGES
[these part of rationing both of both on-road & off-road space; also Shopping Mall space ; also Business Park Space ; in some towns, a rationing - or discouragement of employer parking space too. Serve to reduce overall volume of commuting or retail traffic]

# #

VICTIM STATEMENTS IN COURT
[these a wonderful, though necessarily painful, counterbalance to the blandness / or coolth of several Court proceedings. Giving minimum - in a few cases maximum - awareness of impact: that impact all-too-rarely reflected in actual Sentencing]   **# # #**

VICTIM SURCHARGE TO A FINE IMPOSED BY THE COURT

[this a fairly recent idea; earth-shattering if it comes out as £15 for a death resulting from driving without due care & attention - although newspapers do not always make it clear the Surcharge is for all *victims or survivors - not the one in focus that day]*

# #

VOLUNTARY <<GIVE WAY>> SIGN

[this not a very good at stopping a Collision - but its moment of pause at an awkward junction can help delay a Collision if both Parties are alert to a danger]

# # #

VOLUNTARY LISTING of AILMENTS & IMPAIRMENTS over 70

[this requirement being a condition of renewing a Driving Licence - but cannot at present be entered by a GP or family-member]

X X X

WARNING LIGHTS or NOISES TO DECTECT SLIGHTLY-OPEN DOORS or SEAT-BELT NOT WORN

[these covering a wide-range of in-car issues, including freezing temperatures outdoors; tend now to be far too many flickering lights & noises]

# #

WARNING SIGNS : FALLING ROCKS

[these in gorges or next to precipices or on Marine Parades:must not replace actually seeing *the rocks if landslip has already happened!]*

# #

WARNING SIGN : NARROW BRIDGE /
or HUMP-BACKED BRIDGE AHEAD
[these standard pictorial signs found in the Highway Code... everso important for advance warning]
# #

WAYSIDE SIGNS GIVING NUMBERS RECENTLY KILLED or INJURED
[these quite common on busy dual carriageways - & updated; make a bit impact on passing Drivers & Riders]
##

WAYSIDE WRECKED CAR ON VERGE
[this to show passing Riders & Motorcycles what can happen in the event of negligence - or, worse, dangerous or drunken driving]
# # #

WEEKLY ANNOUNCEMENT of CRASH STATISTICS
[this to alert the general public to enormous loss of lives or life-chances. Necessarily must be a week in arrears. Better if issued with huge fanfare and spoken by a Celebrity] # #

WHITE LINES ALL THE WAY ALONG
THE NEARSIDE EDGE OF THE ROAD
[these white lines very helpful at night & on rural carriageways where it is not at all clear where the verge is; the white clearly contrasted with black Tarmac] # # # #

WIDER PARKING BAYS

[these already provided for disabled drivers and families with young children - but desperately needed elsewhere in order to make parking simpler & quicker; better all-round vision to spot wandering Pedestrians]

# # #

WITNESS APPEALS

[these often posted beside a past crash site - usually indicating either or both extreme seriousness & absence of survivors; many witness appeals also appearing in local newspapers - with a sometimes unhappy side-effect of minimizing the tragedy: " If you were passing this double fatality, please quote ref. NH3641"]

# #

WITNESS STATEMENTS

[these not always welcome at the scene of a Collision: as if the Witness is a busybody milking the scene. So Witnesses are often brushed to one side. Their testimony might add hours to detection.
Yet Witnesses can perform a real ministry of comfort & clarification]

# # #

WITNESS SUITES

[these so needed, both at Police Stations but also at Court. Witnesses need cherishing & pampering. Their testimony - frequently at cost to themselves - might make all the difference]

# # #

WORKING FROM HOME / WORKING AT HOME

[this never tried as much as during the 2020 Pandemic. Home-Working removes hundreds & thousands of vehicles from the Highway; in many cases from ownership. Fewer vehicles mean fewer Casualties; also a far less stressful road experience]

# # #

YELLOW-BOX JUNCTIONS

[these popular in congested cities or suburbs where there might be a stacking up of traffic just before, then just after, the lights change at a busy junction. Nobody is supposed to enter till they can clearly see an exit. Frequently ignored.]   # # #

ZEBRA CROSSINGS

[these probably the oldest type of pedestrian crossing in the UK: many more needed now - when Pelican lights cost so much to install]

# # # #

ZIGZAG [PAINTED LINES] OUTSIDE SCHOOLS
& AT OTHER DANGEROUS PLACES

[these being painted just before & after Zebra Crossings]

# #

+++++++++++

SPECIAL NOTE: In Part II of this Encyclopaedia
[above] several common Road Signs have been
left out deliberately ; also several crash-saving measures:
accidentally. *Page 304* has been left Blank for these omissions

TANGLED WRECKAGE :

AN ENCYCLOPAEDIA OF

COLLISIONS ON

THE PUBLIC HIGHWAY :

PART THREE :

TWENTY QUESTIONS

SURROUNDING

THE SEEMING

INEVITABILITY

of DEATH

& INJURY

on U.K. ROADS

& THOSE OF OTHER COUNTRIES

QUESTION ONE :
WHY ARE COLLISIONS CALLED
<< ACCIDENTS >> ?

How unfair, how ridiculous, it is that, with a whole variety of better and more accurate words at our disposal, we call Collisions on the Public Highway: "Accidents."

Worse, Police say they have just come away from an R.T.A.: a Road Traffic Accident. And if the situation could deteriorate further, Radio Stations like BBC's Radio 2 & Radio 5 Live routinely give traffic reports about hold-ups & diversions due to "an Accident" blocking one road or another.

Essentially, the word "Accident" is very comforting & reassuring. It tells the whole population that something has happened in their midst out of the blue, therefore outside anybody's control: like a tornado or avalanche - whereas Collisions on the highway are 95% in *somebody*'s control - what we bracket as "human error" - with the other 5% being far more sudden & arbitrary in impact, though still technically avoidable by somebody.

Therefore a revised definition of a car or motorcycle "Accident" should be an event not *foreseeable* by at least one of the parties involved; nor *preventable* by one or more of the Parties in that event or Collision.

And the advantage of this definition is that it does concede one of the parties in a crash is "innocent": the recipient of a horrible misjudgment by another Road User. Even then the purist would say that the innocent party might have been able to decelerate the pace of calamity.

Foresee, prevent; foresee, prevent: then there is no place for "Accident" now applying more to the sharp knife that slides off a shiny onion; the toast that falls off a plate, butter down, onto the carpet; or the electrical fire started by a short.

So keep to the words: Crash, Collision, Head-on, Smash, Tragedy, Calamity... whatever.... not *Accident.*

✶✶✶✶✶✶✶✶✶✶✶✶

QUESTION TWO :
WHY IS << CAR CRASH >>
USED AS A WORD PICTURE ?

Every hour of every day we use word pictures or metaphors: eg. " I slept like an elephant. Now I'm as hungry as a horse - though this cereal tastes like chaff. Later I'll step into the deep, crowd onto the Tube - where I'll be squashed like a sardine before giving an Army Major's instructions to the work-force ."

And we *mix* metaphors: "It's a pea-souper today, a wilderness out there." But how did the word-picture "Car Crash" enter our language in the early 2000s? "A Car Crash of a job interview;" followed by "a Car Crash of a dinner-party," ending with "a car crash of an argument with Annie over her coming in at Midnight."

Unkindest of all is using the word picture: "Car Crash" when meeting with someone who is a Survivor of car crash, or, Heaven Forbid, the named "cause" of the car crash that killed her best friend and injured two of her three children.

QUESTION THREE :
WHAT HAPPENED ON THE FIRST
FATAL COLLISION KNOWN IN BRITAIN ?

History doesn't record the first motor Collision - but undoubtedly it happened before the first *fatal* Collision.

That awful day was August 17th., 1896, when 44-year old Bridget Driscoll crossed Dolphin Terrace in the grounds of Crystal Palace, accompanied by her 16-year old daughter May & May's friend: intending to go to a Catholic Fête. But a different fate awaited this humble married woman: to be run over by a Roger-Benz horseless carriage that had featured in a recent motoring exhibition.

Arthur James Edsall of Norwood was behind the wheel. He said he rang a bell and shouted out. But Mrs. Driscoll was mesmerized by a vehicle she had not seen before- and was run over. A witness thought Edsall was racing faster than a fire engine: more than 8 mph. [the law had just been changed raising the speed limit from its original 2mph: town, 4mph: countryside to 14mph - but Edsall was sure his true speed was nearer 4 mph.

The Inquest, lasting no less than 6 hours, entered a verdict of "Accidental Death" - with the Coroner expressing the hope there would never be another life forfeited on the Highway. Little did he know Bridget Driscoll's sacrifice would be repeated on British roads at least 550,000 times: 550,000+ teenage daughters weeping - just as May Driscoll did.

****

QUESTION FOUR :
WHAT WERE THE WORST YEARS
IN BRITAIN FOR DEATH & INJURY
ON THE PUBLIC HIGHWAY ?

In 1926, there was but a trickle of transport on the road as compared with 90 years later - yet 4886 people were killed in an horrific 124,000 crashes.

The highest Wartime toll was 1941 - blackout and only a few motorists tested - with 9169 fatalities. And the highest Peacetime toll was 1966: 7,985 deaths in the so-called Golden Age of car ownership.

1990's figures show that with increased total mileage, also much less safety-consciousness: 60,000 people were seriously injured [600 every day], 275,000 people slightly injured [750 every day].

By 1987, and belatedly, the Government lost patience with too wide an acceptance of "inevitability" and set a bold target that those Killed or Seriously Injured [KSI] had to be 33% lower by Year 2000.

****

QUESTION FIVE :

WHAT WERE << THE BEST >> YEARS

IN BRITAIN FOR DEATH & INJURY ?

"Best years" should always come with a qualification that the best possible figure would be 0-0-0, no deaths, no serious injuries, no minor injuries.

That noted, there were to be 40% fewer deaths & serious injuries in Year 2010 than the average for the 5 years 1994-98 [50% less involving children] & 10% fewer minor injuries: this latter aim made more complicated by the fact that if drivers drove more cautiously - as hoped for - each crash that might have caused life-changing or life-threatening injury might be aborted, still too late, to the point of *minor* injury.

And by Year 2009, that first "low" target was exceeded by an extra 4% [4% *downward*] children by an extra 11% [11% *downward*] minor injuries a lot fewer 27% lower than target.

That prepared the nation for Year 2013: the lowest number of people killed on the roads since the birth of motoring [arrival of the "horseless carriage" from which we get the word "car"].

In the 7 succeeding years there have been fluctuations: some years cycling deaths & injuries rising by 10% - with the growing popularity of commuting by bicycle.

In 2008, when detailed figures were first kept for the *types of road* where there might be death & injury, results were somewhat surprising. Motorways thought to be least safe accounted for "only"

158 deaths, 6% of the total + 3% of all serious injuries, 5% of all minor injuries. Meanwhile: Urban roads accounted for 1057 deaths [42% of the total] + an enormous 65% of all serious injuries; an equally high 70% of all minor injuries : all sorts of built-up hazard. That left Country roads, including straggling & village roads: far more deadly at 1323 deaths in 2008 - because where there was Collision it was far less expected - thus far less subject to prevention - by the different Parties. On the other hand, Country Roads accounted for "only" 32% of serious injuries, 25% of minor injuries.

Year 2019, quite recently, won no records: in fact quite a lot of *backsliding* - due to Drivers & Pedestrians wrongly imagining a great *diminishing* of danger - with 1870 deaths [1870 too many]; 27,820 serious injuries; 129, 820 minor injuries [328 a day].

But - and it's a very big but - only the deaths' figure can be taken as accurate. Police are very competent recording deaths on the road: Coroners also in their convening of Inquests. Injuries however are lost in the system - or in the Hospital. Many minor injuries never come to the notice of anybody but Parent, Chemist, G.P or A&E. in all instances not really recorded *nationally*.

✳✳✳✳✳✳✳✳✳✳✳

QUESTION SIX :

WHAT HAVE BEEN THE GREATEST ENGINEERING TRIUMPHS TO LESSEN DEATH & INJURY ON THE HIGHWAY ?

This is a difficult question to answer : because driving instructors have traditionally said it's all about "the nut behind the wheel" : ie. human error.

Notwithstanding, Traffic Engineers boast about their enormous strides reducing death & injuries on the Public Highway - whilst Mechanical Engineers have boasted that *theirs* is the greater contribution! The truth lies somewhere in between.

Traffic Engineers claim their top priority is keeping people safe - whereas the motoring lobby - backed to the hilt by Town Planners - are breathing down their necks with 3 words only : "Keep Traffic Moving!"

Therefore a good half of all Pedestrian Lights have now been timed to favour of traffic streams to the disadvantage of patient or impatient Pedestrians. It is even rumoured that some City Councils set their most popular lights never to change until there is no traffic approaching *in either direction*! Worse, where a Pedestrian has to cross a Trunk Road dual carriageway, he or she might be waiting 4 minutes at both kerbside and on the central reservation.

Yet Traffic Engineers protest the lights *will* come on when pressed once. [These the same Traffic Engineers who got rid of the Green or Red Man straight in front of the Pedestrian, replaced by an obscure instruction at the Pedestrian's Right-hand waist. Equal insensitivity surrounds the digging of smelly, filthy & unsafe Subways beneath shopping streets that should rightly belong to Pedestrians, not Motorists. Or a needless proliferation of street signs & street furniture: a street-scene as cluttered as it is overwhelming.

More worrying - if that is possible - is letting certain Traffic Engineers loose in the Suburbs & the Countryside. Vast Retail Parks & covered Shopping Malls are isolated in arid deserts of land used formerly for mining or manufacture. These hideous - carbon-copy - destinations often cannot be accessed safely by foot or pedal-bike! Instead Cars & Lorries are awarded utmost superiority.

Or when Market Towns are about 10 or 15 miles apart on Trunk Roads: again this is frequently a hostile environment for Pedestrian & Pedal-Cyclist alike: great stretches of speeding carriageway where even Cars are only given a precious few dozen yards to join from villages Left, hamlets Right. All proving that you cannot "engineer out" death & injury except by sticking-plaster after sticking-plaster, hoping for the best but often opting for the worst.

Those other Engineers intent upon reducing needless death or injury on the Public Highway are *Motor* Engineers: design teams in or near Car & Van factories conducting Research & Development. And these Engineers often draw inspiration from Formula One Mechanics: on the assumption that if something works on the race-track, it will work on an ordinary street.

Motor Engineers don't get it right 1st. time or even 2nd. time. Purchasers are breathing down the necks of manufacturers begging them not to put in so many gizmos that the price will rise beyond affordability. Then there has been the European Union these past 5 decades *ordering* Motor Manufacturers to put in Seatbelts, Airbags, Childproof Locks, whatever, as standard; with all sorts of new tyre-strengths, mirror positions and correct headlamp beams.

Without hesitation: I would champion rollover bars, articulated steering-wheels, triplex windscreens, and rigid-steel girders within car doors as 4 of the greatest safety promoters within saloon cars. Plus radial tyres, windscreen heaters and profiled bonnets. Yet for every advance, there is also a backsliding: bull-bars, over-efficient heating, removal of bumpers and installation of remote-controlled side windows; plus over-complicated, multi-choice, in-car entertainment. Not forgetting hands-free telephones which turn out to be almost as dangerous - and just as distracting - as hand-held devices.

Ideally, Traffic Engineers, Motor Engineers & the Ministry of Transport working in concert would indeed have engineered out fatalities and frightful injury on the Highway. But it's that Nut behind the Wheel...

****

QUESTION SEVEN :

WHAT IS THE GREATEST CHANGE TO

THE HIGHWAY *REDUCING* DEATH & INJURY ?

Arguably it is the Roundabout that has contributed most to overall road safety and Collision reduction: not the Mini-Roundabout but the *full-sized* one, so big that the circular middle holds everything from advertisements to daffodils, from concrete cows to single wire or brass sculptures. Some local industries or car showrooms "adopt" one such Roundabout.

The beauty of the Roundabout used to be *its simplicity*: Left Lane for Left Turn or Straight On, Right Lane for Straight On or Right Turn. And although it's not remiss to use a Roundabout for a $180°$ or even a $360°$ re-think, that is not a priority late joiners on a Roundabout fully expect or appreciate.

The real trouble with Roundabouts are the add-ons over the years: full-time traffic lights, rush-hour traffic lights, huge gantries, writing on the road, also a multiplicity of approach lanes: as many as 5! These add-ons have not only led Motorists to come to a sudden stop but also forced them to *switch lane* halfway round: a mirror-only manoeuvre that is extremely hazardous at speed.

In summary, huge suburban Roundabouts, and those at the end of Motorway slip-roads, consistently favour Motorists familiar with them. Unfamiliar Motorists or Motorcycle Riders, also very nervous and hesitant Drivers, are discriminated against. Not for nothing have Crash-for-Cash merchants chosen the Roundabout as the best place to perform their bangers' emergency stops.

The second most important road safety invention is the Crash Barrier, especially that installed on the central reservation of a Motorway or Dual Carriageway. Deadly cross-overs are reduced, not eliminated, by a Crash Barrier easily surmounted by a Heavy Goods' Vehicle. The first Crash Barriers in Britain arrived in the 1970s: too late for the golden age of Motorway-driving a decade before.

At first it was thought central barriers would simply throw a vehicle back across all the three lanes it had just traversed. Then Engineers experimented with cushioning - sometimes cable-cushioning - to absorb colossal impacts, eg. 100mph: leading stricken vehicles to straddle the barrier rather than being catapulted away from it. Other countries, meanwhile, experimented with worn tyres and sand-filled wooden barrels instead of the linear guardrails that in Britain also protect Drivers from culverts, streams, rivers, direction-signs, drops and bridge abutments.

Latterly in this country, the Highways' Agency has made a massive step *backwards* by installing apex-shaped concrete barriers on Motorways which nobody can see through - yet it was *the breaking-up* of the reservation contour that allowed approaching Drivers to differentiate the total Highway layout.   That is *terrible* news for those suffering tiredness, sleeplessness, drowsiness or narcolepsy: no gap - no gap whatsoever in the big white divider.

So those 2 inventions: Roundabouts first experimented down Broadway in Letchworth New Town, 1906 ; and the Crash Barrier have, arguably, done more than anything else to separate traffic and head it in the right direction.

****

QUESTION EIGHT :

HOW WAS IT THIRD-PARTY INSURANCE BECAME COMPULSORY ?

As soon as Collisions began to happen - not necessarily *fatal* Collisions - *very soon* after the invention of the horseless carriage, it was recognized each Motorist or machine-owner would need to take out Insurance. That is not the same as the imperfect notion of 50-50.

Most Collisions can be averted by one of the Parties implicated which really does leave at least one of the other Parties "innocent."

Nobody can *force* someone in Britain to insure their vehicle *Comprehensively,* for all eventualities. And hundreds of responsible Road Users have come to grief at the hands & wheels of totally uninsured Drivers or uninsured Motorcycle Riders; but there really did have to be - on paper at least - Third-Party Insurance.

In fact, it is not normally possible to re-tax a vehicle without that Insurance in place. But still that does nothing to help those poor souls encountering a 13-year old bad-lad or the older Motorist who cares not a whit about *any paperwork at all.*

It was our *Road Traffic Act* of 1930 that first made Insurance compulsory - when there were more cars on the road, each going faster. Of interest, Insurance has never been compulsory for Pedal Cycles, for negligent Pedestrians - nor for the Riders of Mobility Scooters. So much the loss of anybody encountering them! Additionally, the Court fine for being without Insurance is often less than the Insurance Policy itself!

****

QUESTION NINE :
HOW DID *DRIVER-TRAINING*
IMPACT ON DEATH & INJURY ?

Compulsory Tests for driving competence have undoubtedly had a radical impact on driving proficiency: therefore on deaths, serious & minor injuries averted through skills duly acquired for most people after their 17th. Birthday - though there has never been a ban on learning to drive on a farm or on a strictly private land.

The 1903 legislation that brought in Driving Licences contained no provision for testing. This came in a later Act, passed in 1930, so that all newly disabled Drivers could take a test. Finally the 1934 *Road Traffic Act* introduced Tests for everyone: for that 1st year *voluntary*, in order to prevent an almighty rush; then from June 1st., 1935, mandatory for anyone who started to drive after 1st. April, 1934.

These Tests were at 1st. conducted by Police or members of the Forces; later - except for suspensions during World War 2, also the Suez Crisis - conducted by a specialist set of very bold Examiners: bold because they have little or no say in the competency of those put forward by their Driving Schools for the Test.

For over 60 years, a few *theory* questions were added to the end of the Practical Test; but since July 1996, a written Theory Test [revised in format from Year 2000, and subsequently] has had to be passed before any Practical Test on real roads, still a Test excluding Motorways or night-time driving.

Tests do not bring a safe driving environment for *everyone*. Here are a few exceptions : those who pass, then forget what they learnt; those who pass then deliberately flout that which they learnt; criminals & drug addicts; those who knowingly - or recklessly - exceed the permitted level of alcohol in their bloodstreams; those who "passed" their tests through impersonation; those Drivers disqualified from driving; those committing terrible crimes on the Highway but not yet forced to undergo the more difficult Test before re-joining the Highway; also newly ill, elderly or disabled Drivers who do not inform DVLA regarding their change of circumstance.

Occasionally, there are calls for Tests - both Theory & Practical - to be made so strict - also so wide-ranging - that they could better separate the wheat from the chaff. That would bring about a 25% pass rate compared with roughly 50% of all intending Drivers now.

****

QUESTION TEN :

WHAT DO INQUESTS TELL US

ABOUT DEATHS ON THE HIGHWAY ?

Inquests tell us very little - far too little? - about deaths on the Highway. First, Inquests cannot attribute guilt or responsibility. That leads to endless postponements pending Police enquiries.

Second, Inquests generally only listen to *stronger* Parties, not the weaker Parties most likely to be a dead person's family or friends.

Third, Inquests tend to be biased towards an "Act of God" perspective in preference to a belief that Collisions *really are* avoidable - and, indeed, *should have* been avoided.

Fourth, Inquests are generally nervous of "Suicide" verdicts: preferring by far "Misadventure" or an "Open" verdict. This masks the reality that men in general, bereaved or divorcing men in particular, skillfully use their motors to end their own lives - and if possible, the lives of those people, including birth children whom they do not wish to live after their own lives have ended.

Fifth, and critically, Inquests are about closing down deaths, not opening them up again. And because Coroners are themselves drivers, they express rarely refer to safety improvements required on the Highway - also in car manufacture . And some extremely sensitive Inquests are *never* held: for instance where a member of the Armed Forces or MI5 is implicated. *So room for improvement.*

★★★★★★★★★★★★

QUESTION ELEVEN :

HOW DO WE KNOW WHETHER

A DEATH HIDES UNDERLYING FACTORS ?

In the absence of a specific Suicide note, no Coroner is going to advance the Suicide argument in a serious Highway Collision. Here Coroners - also Police - need to be *far more* inquisitive: in particular single-tree deaths, brick wall deaths, "deliberate" Head-on Collision deaths, deliberate U-turn deaths, recently separated or divorced deaths; also self-immolations.

Apart for Suicides, the rest of Society should be alert to Road Collision as part of a criminal network. Was a road death disguising getaway after an earlier crime? Was the dead person a lookout for a criminal accessory? Did the dead person dread being followed? Was the dead person dependent on illicit drugs *or dealing in* drugs? Finally: were *the Police* implicated in a Collision - not only in a car or motorcycle pursuit; *or themselves part of the criminal fraternity*?

Next: Coroners should always be alert to *common factors*: far easier said than done when there is no efficient way of collating relevant data nationally. Common factors include the manufacture of defective tyres; the manufacture and fitting of defective airbags; the obstructed vision afforded by Sat-navs stuck onto front windscreen or dashboard. Also relevant : the contribution of *tiredness* to car crash common to one profession: eg doctors on night-shift, students doing their finals, people going on holiday at the end of July or beginning of August.

Never is commonality more important than lorry, van or HGV safety. Many Inquests never face up to the sheer, unbridled, power and deadly force of this one class of vehicle : Goods in Transit. All other Road Users suffer at the hands & beneath the wheels of Juggernauts.

In summary, both Police and Coroners should be far *more* inquisitive: asking awkward questions outside the box; and disregarding special pleading. The immediate response: "Please Sir? It wasn't *me* Sir?

✱✱✱✱✱✱✱✱✱✱✱

QUESTION TWELVE :

DO SPOT-FINES EVER WORK ?

or PROMOTE OVERALL ROAD SAFETY ?

The term : Spot-Fines is shorthand for "On-the-spot Fines" - because it is relatively unlikely any individual stopped on the Highway or about to join the Highway has the requisite £50, £100, £200 or £300 fine *actually on their person*; nor be willing to part with that amount without further details of the offence or offences they have allegedly committed.

Nor are Police FPNs : "Fixed Penalty Notices" always free of penalty points on one's Licence. Many £50s, and a few £100s. like cycling on a pavement; stopping on a hard shoulder without good reason;

driving along the hard shoulder; slight speeding; using a hooter at night; or not wearing that seatbelt, are indeed non-endorsable offences - but for anything more serious, freedom from penalty points is not an option.

What *is* an option is choice to go before a Magistrates' Bench - but that is highly precarious as an initial "trivial" fine could be magnified to as much as *£2000* therein. Nonetheless, it is surprising how much money + points can be imposed on the roadside: especially the hand-held telephone from March 2017, complete with a whacking half of all allowable penalty points before exceeding 12: ie. six.

Here a distinction should be made between FPNs and the PCNs: Penalty Charge Notices issued to errant Motorists by local authority Parking Patrols; also the non-contestable fines issued by the owners of "Private" land for parking thereon. PCNs *can* be appealed, with quite a success rate. Again the extra penalty for *not* paying on time is a likely doubling of the stated amount.

Prime Minister Tony Blair used to boast that Police under his command might march a recalcitrant to the nearest ATM to draw out their fine straightway! Similar powers are actually used by Revenue Enforcement Officers inside railway trains.

To sum up, on-the-spot fines are an important weapon in any Traffic Police Officer's armoury: achieving instant justice, if not fairness. A very little-mentioned factor in the imposition of such fines is that they are regressive. As with litter dropped or dogs misbehaving, poor people pay exactly the same as rich people.

****

QUESTION THIRTEEN :

DO MAGISTRATES' COURT APPEARANCES

WORK TO ENHANCE HIGHWAY SAFETY ?

In the UK, Magistrates' Courts hear over 90% of cases where there is to be a prosecution. And very rarely are these Magistrates stipendiary; rarer still do offences on the Highway move up the ladder to Crown Court.

That is because Magistrates' Courts can sometimes impose unlimited fines. They can certainly disqualify a Motorist or Rider from the highway. Also, they can resort to a sentence of up to six-months' imprisonment: which tends to amount to 3 or 4 months in practice.

Where Magistrates' Courts fail is their widespread acceptance of "Road Traffic Accidents" as a fact of life. Were Magistrates - *themselves* Drivers or Cyclists - to rage against road crime, to express absolute outrage, the climate might change. If only...

If only errant lorry-drivers or motorists could be compelled to attend Magistrates' Court. There should never, ever, be an allowance for somebody to plead guilty by post. That plea effectively denies aggrieved Parties their day in Court.

Also denied their Day in Court are friends, relatives & survivors at the blunt end of Pleas Bargaining. It is a constant source of amazement just how bad a road crime needs to be before it is *not* downgraded in the interests of saving Police or Court time - or indeed, dealt with solely on the roadside.

Gone are forensic Police enquiries: months of painstaking gathering of evidence, lengthy interviews, and computer reconstructions.

QUESTION FOURTEEN :

DOES IMPRISONMENT EVER WORK

TO ENHANCE HIGHWAY SAFETY ?

The simple answer to this question is "Rarely!" Prison Sentences cannot work if they are too short and / or not accompanied by a fierce and ongoing programme of Driver / Rider Safety; nor followed by very lengthy periods of disqualification because of the severity of the initial offence.

That said, a Driver or Rider is only ever likely to get to prison for causing death by dangerous driving, causing death by careless driving - or driving 6 times above the alcohol limit, 4 times above the speed limit; or driving while disqualified.

Looking at numbers: in Year 2016, there were 168,000 offences of speeding; 133,000 convictions motor-insurance related; 78,000 motorists refusing to identify themselves - and 24,000 offences for careless driving or worse. For these still serious offences, imprisonment came through at approximately a 00.006% chance. And even among this handful of Prisoners, 7 out of 10 will be on their 7th.successive offence, a huge 5 out of 10 having already committed 15 successive offences.

Not a few men - & it normally is men - imprisoned for death on the Highway spend the rest of their lives protesting their innocence. In recent years : the man who reached onto the back seat of his car for a humbug; and the man who committed easily the UK's most expensive motoring crime, Great Heck: neither man ever, or knowingly, repented.

So prepare to rule out imprisonment for motorists or Lorry-Drivers. Much to the grief of Survivors, it is unlikely to happen; and if it does happen, is very unlikely to lead to reform; to bring about born-again cautious motoring or riding.

****

QUESTION FIFTEEN :

WHY ARE COURT SENTENCES

[DRIVING & MOTORING] SO LENIENT ?

Every Police Force; every Crime Commissioner; every Minister of Transport; every Public Prosecutor - whomever one asks - will vigorously deny that Motoring-related sentences are too lenient. Conversely, nearly every Survivor, nearly every family-member suddenly bereaved through the Highway, nearly every impartial by-stander or witness to a Collision would say motoring Sentences are far too lenient!

For instance, if a Truck Driver kills 8 people in a Minibus the fine might be two hundred pounds: twenty-five pounds per life. Or if an Agency Driver ploughs into 5 Cyclists, killing all 5, the Sentence handed down might be £50 plus costs for having one thin tyre. Following a conviction of Death by Dangerous Driving or Death by Careless Driving, the tariff is roughly a quarter for killing-by-car compared with a far heavier Sentence for killing with knife or gun.

This is all because Society in general, and the judiciary in particular, use the invocation: "There but for the Grace of God go I..." : in other words: motor transport is here to stay therefore let's excuse, or listen to heartfelt mitigation from, an errant Motorist or Rider. Therein lies the bias towards leniency or extreme leniency. Admittedly, it is occasionally possible to write to the Attorney General and request a revised Sentence - but in nearly every instance, this request will be turned down.

And dead people cannot appeal.

The problem here seems to be: "What was *in the mind of* the Rider or Driver at the moment of impact?" Now that question will nearly always be answered with "Good Intent." Only in case of drink-driving, parking in a disability bay without a disability badge, excessive speeding without an excuse - or road rage - will there be proven & substantiated evidence that there was *ill* Intent on the part of the Driver; when anything goes "well" in Court.

So it is, clever Defence Counsel can nearly always prove that a Collision came about at random: simply through the combination, or accumulation, of "unavoidable" circumstances. And Magistrates are very easily convinced. Because it is everso difficult to prove an offender is lying. For instance: "a sudden sneeze," or "strong sunshine," or "momentary lack of concentration," go down a treat in Court. Some Courts are not even allowed to hear that there was a death upon impact, or later in hospital - because such a casualty, such a revelation, is not thought to be "relevant."

Hence that degree of leniency. Almost never, & then perhaps only for telephoning before killing, will 10 years + in jail be imposed.

****

QUESTION SIXTEEN :

WHY DO VICTIMS & SURVIVORS

HAVE SO LITTLE INPUT INTO THE COURTS ?

A quick answer to this important question is: Victims are dead or have sustained life-changing injury; while Survivors are mostly *un*welcome in Court. Any Survivor plucking up courage & composure sufficient to appear in person is very soon going to find that Justice & Fairness remain firmly seated in the Usher's Waiting-Room.

There are grim tales of Survivors being left alone outside both criminal Courts & Inquests: sometimes facing the alleged perpetrator; denied even a cup of tea; or any privacy to meet their legal representation, *or just to weep.*

And when they take a seat in the public gallery, they find the devastation a Driver [or Rider] has caused is underplayed. It's as if there had *been* no other Party, no injured Party, no Party deceased. Proceedings are rushed and perfunctory: more intent on establishing identity & "the facts" - rather than feelings. Many of the accused cannot even bother to turn up: preferring rather to avoid all the hassle and take the fine & any points by remote control.

In England & Wales "Victim Personal Statements" have only been permitted as a formality since 2001 - & half of all Survivors can never recall being told about them. They have to be direct & personal, not on behalf of somebody else - unless a person is unable to provide their own testimony: cases of death, loss of sight, illiteracy etc. To some extent, Prosecuting Counsel have always found a means of alluding to a Survivor's devastation: even if by teasing this hurt out, by astute cross-questioning of witnesses , rescuers & other Survivors of the scene.

Needless to say, Judges & Magistrates are generally embarrassed by emotions; they do not do emoting. They do not want to get too tied up with unquantifiable deficits - and sleepless night, fear of ever driving again, haunting nightmares and days of despair as a newly single parent are all unquantifiable in monetary or judicial settlement. So a lot goes unsaid - if only because of a Survivor's horror, reluctance, at having to re-visit a scene in the Courtroom, months later, they were attempting to banish from their minds.

And with up to one thousand people injured on the road every day - several with life-threatening or life-changing injury - many "Survivors" are in no fit state to get around to Victim Impact.

In Summary, England & Wales have steadfastly adhered to an *Adversarial* model of Hearing or Trial: one side prosecuting, one side defending - with the truth, if there is any truth, emerging somewhere in between those opposite poles. Gone - or not even attempted - is a more collegiate, round-the-table Court scene. And Youth Courts permit only a handful of outsiders in, usually a Social Worker or Probation Officer, maybe a parent. The nearest any Magistrates' Court gets to consensus, counter-intuitively, is when the perpetrator pleads Guilty. Many days in the dock or in front of a Jury are thereby avoided, at the penalty of the Proceeding then being horribly short, merely for Sentencing.

****

QUESTION SEVENTEEN :

WHY DO WE RARELY HEAR OF

THE LIVES & ACHIEVEMENTS OF PEOPLE

KILLED OR INJURED ON THE HIGHWAY ?

Unless the Driver or Passenger or Pedestrian who is killed or seriously injured on the Highway is very famous - or a star in their particular sport or vocation - their loss will be unrecognized, unless a local newspaper - fewer of those around! - gives them a few lines.

And even where a dead person is famous, strict *sub judice* laws prevent any newspaper attributing guilt, or even suggesting, let alone implying, guilt.

Only *after* the trial - if Criminal proceedings are initiated; also upon completion of the Inquest; can a local newspaper tell the full story. And even then: if the verdict has been "Not Guilty," nothing can be said to re-introduce the notion of guilt. So "news" of what we know or do not know has happened on the Highway is old and stale and highly speculative; curtailed by shortage of space or loss of "news interest."

That leaves the way open, one day, for a book titled: "Road Lives" giving miniature biographies of everyone who has lost either their life - or their ability to live as before the Collision that changed their daily routines forever. After all, every Casualty: each a Casualty of one single minute- at most 5 minutes - of unfolding drama, has had to be conceived ; then existed in one woman's womb for 9 months;

then learnt to walk & talk; then had a first day at School; then passed exams; then gone to work; then been on course to form adult relationships. And some Casualties have gone further & had birth- or adopted children before the Crash. Yet all this, and more, is ignored because it is *a road Crash*. So unless bereaved relatives ask for a 40-minute slot at the Crematorium, rather than 20 minutes - or request a proper Memorial Service on another day - most Victims of Collision go unrecognized.

In recent years, Road Peace or similar Organizations have held Church or Cathedral Services specifically for those killed by the motor car: complete with candles, poems, readings & the solemn calling-out of names. Even then there is howling; also many tears shed. It can be quite harrowing and emotional to attend right through. Nor are ordinary worshippers &outside Parties forbidden or restricted in their attendance.

****

QUESTION   EIGHTEEN :

WHAT   IS   THE   PUBLIC's   *EDUCATION*

SURROUNDING   ROAD   SAFETY ?

A quick answer to this question is Nil; Nowt; Nothing to See Here; RHINO: Rarely Here & in Name Only; Missing in Action; Back after Lunch. In other words, modern Road Safety education - except in a few diligent & inspired instances - isn't worth the Tarmac it's performed on.

So how did we as a Society get into a position where even big Comps do not teach Road Safety morning & afternoon? Nor are Parents much more attentive. Most Parents' Road Safety education is confined to the word "Don't!": "Don't run into the road;" "Don't go & fetch that ball!" or "Don't ask your friends till you're a bit more experienced behind the wheel" ; " Don't Cycle on the A46!" or "Don't scrape your Mother's car!"   Go and see what little Millie's doing and tell her not to.

But surely there's a kindly Pensioner - the Lollipop Man - ready to tell little children about the *Green Cross Code*? Surely the AA & RAC will be banging on about Road Safety in every lay-by? Surely there's a GCSE called *Roadcraft*?

And even if Teachers want to teach Road Safety, they're told it's not part of the National Curriculum. Then there is the flagrant dereliction of duty of dozens of Dads or Grandmas joining in 2 daily motor-scrums outside the school gates dropping off - or collecting - little Polly or Cousin Peter? "Do as I say... not as I do."

Roadcraft needs teaching at age 3, age 6, age 8, age 11, age 13, age 15, & age 17. And why so often? Because children of all ages have a habit of un-learning what they used to know. Each age of growing-up has its own danger: the 1st. time you're allowed to the sweet-shop on your own; the 1st. time you're allowed to walk to school with a friend your own age only? The 1st. time you cycle without stabilizers? The 1st. time you jog along a main road?

The truth is: not a few Teenagers have to wait till their Driving Theory Test before they get a half-decent Road Safety education. So why did their parents or step-parents or foster-parents not sit their children down and do it earlier? The answer is very simple: Parents are the *Drivers*, the Taxi-Drivers often, & do NOT welcome criticism or any negative feedback regarding their driving. Nor when their children play chicken on the road, or play ball on the Highway, or do wheelies on their bikes, do they welcome comment from the wider community. It's as if our motoring cannot be detached from our pride. We are too proud even to warn anybody aspiring to motor that death & injury are just round the corner.

My Wooden Cross Code is printed as an Appendix to this Book. The Roadcraft Charity BRAKE, in all but name founded 7 miles away from where I used to live, too has a proud record sending its well-tutored Volunteer Educators into Primary & Secondary Schools to take Assemblies & to address Driver behaviour, Pedestrian behaviour, Passenger behaviour. But it should be the Local Authority, or the Chain of Academies, doing this, not Charity.

＊＊＊＊＊＊＊＊＊＊＊

QUESTION   NINETEEN :

COULD   AUTOMOBILE   CLUBS   DO   MORE   TO

ENCOURAGE - & PROMOTE - SAFER   DRIVING ?

Yes!   The great Automobile Clubs had their heyday when Chauffering,   Motoring, Pleasant Sunday Afternoons were the exception not the rule; when ownership of a car was a novelty; when Drivers would salute the Roadside Rescue Man; when Automobile Clubs provided astonishingly detailed Itineraries for any Member undertaking a journey from Stoke-on-Trent to Exeter or from Basildon to Ayr.

And you depended on your Automobile Club to grade your overnight hotel; to lend you their roadside telephone; even to manufacture & erect your road-direction signs in an era when the Highways' Agency didn't. You could even earn the benefits of LIFE Membership.

But somewhere along the road, literally, some of the big Motoring Organizations perhaps became more interested in Pretty Villages, Sunny Seaside Resorts, Exotic Birds, Cruises, Holidays, L.P.s, Sweepstakes, Car Loan Agreements, Insurance, whatever... anything but Road Safety 1st., Road Safety 2nd., Road Safety 3rd.

****

QUESTION TWENTY :

WHERE WILL DEATH & INJURY

ON THE HIGHWAY BE IN YEAR 2030 ?

Forecasting is a difficult exercise at the best of times - but particularly a challenge looking forward to 2030, 2040, 2050. That's because Climate Change will one day severely restrict the sale of new motor cars unless they are electric. Diesels & petrol internal combustion engines will have been phased out by 3035 or 2040.

Therefore some years away from Year 2030 it's impossible to say much more than fewer cars will be sold ; also Drivers will learn to drive later into their 20s: a trend already embedded by Year 2020 - along with far later purchase of a house, far later marriages.

Deaths & injuries on the public Highway are increasingly difficult to bring down, now that the low-hanging fruit of hazard elimination has been eaten. Seat belts and, before that, drink-driving laws were great for bringing down the grim statistics. Strict speed limits &

clearer signage also helped. Also more working-from-home [especially during the Coronavius Pandemic] brought down the number of Commuters by car.

But what would happen if the figures now plateaued - or worse started to go *into reverse*: fewer safety features in the pipeline. Child casualties will increase as the next generation of Teenagers become so engrossed in their mobile phones that they are oblivious to the danger just behind them. They will also unlearn whatever they were told 8 years beforehand when they were not "grown-up."

And, crucially, Pedal Cycle deaths will possibly go up & up in proportion to the number of new Cyclists on the Highway - most of all Central London, Central Birmingham, Central Manchester. Nobody has yet devised an effective way of lorries or cars not colliding with Cyclists, most when the stronger Road-User turns Left in front of a cycle or creates a sort of wind-tunnel on the nearside.

Success is *Zero*. So by Year 2030, Zero deaths, 0 serious injuries should be the norm. One cloud on the Road Safety horizon is the invention of the "driverless car." One always needs a Driver: a guiding mind, because there are far too many unpredictable or surprise factors which an impact upon driving performance. A computer cannot respond quickly enough to avert death or injury - and were the "driverless car" to require a Guiding Mind as well, that rather defeats the idea of totally remote control.

So progress by the Year 2030 will look like far more footbridges, far more underpasses - and a clear defeat of the noisy 80mph. limit. For as soon as the Government agrees to 80mph., Drivers will do 90mph. - & so on. at least flexible work-hours, four hours of arbitrary "core time" for workers will get rid of the ruinous Rush Hour!

APPENDIX   ONE

THE [recorded] PREAMBLE

PRIOR TO EACH CAR JOURNEY

<< Good Day! Welcome on board this Vehicle

<< Your attention would be much appreciated before the engine is turned out for our Journey to-day.

<< Please check that your seat-belt isx securely fashtened & that young children are properly strapped in.

<< In the event of an emergency, please sound your horn if that might reasonably be hears by a Pedestrian or Passer-by. Then brake immediately and decisively - or take the safest possible route out of danger : whether that is a verge or even a ditch.

<< Passengers both at the front and the back of your vehicle should adopt the brace position to shield their heads.

<< When exiting the vehicle, make absolutely sure no other vehicle is passing nearside or offside. And do not attempt to move if your injury suggests that would do more harm than good.

<< Once away from your vehicle, try to stand behind a barrier if one is provided - & then ring 999... & Beware of fire!

<< Now wishing you a happy journey: driving defensively, then even more defensively. >>

APPENDIX TWO :

THE DRIVER OR RIDER'S PLEDGE

<< I _____ VOW THAT I WILL

AT ALL TIMES CONDUCT MYSELF ON THE PUBLIC HIGHWAY

IN SUCH A WAY THAT - CALM & COLLECTED -

ATTENTIVE & UNDISTRACTED -

I SHALL STRAIN TO CAUSE NO HARM TO

WHOMEVER I SHARE THAT HIGHWAY WITH >>

THE PEDAL-CYCLIST'S PLEDGE

<< I _____ VOW THAT I WILL

AT ALL TIMES RIDE MY CYCLE AS IF IT WAS A VEHICLE;

TO BE TOLERANT OF BAD DRIVERS;

TO BE COURTEOUS TOWARDS PEDESTRIANS

& TO BE READY FOR WHATEVER HAZARD BEFALL ME:

EVER READY TO DISMOUNT OR TAKE A DIFFERENT

OR SAFER ROUTE >>

THE PEDESTRIAN'S PLEDGE

<< I _____ VOW THAT

I WILL WALK RESPONSIBLY & CAUTIOUSLY:

RESTRAINING MYSELF FROM GETTING ANGRY OR

UPSET WITH CYCLES OR VEHICLES WHICH PROCEED

AS IF I'M NOT THERE; AS IF I DO NOT MATTER.

SO MAY I START OUT KEEN

& END MY TRIP CONTENT >>

THE WITNESS' PLEDGE

<< I _____ VOW THAT

I WILL ALWAYS TRY TO OBSERVE THE HIGHWAY

AS IF ANY MINUTE SOMETHING WAS ABOUT TO HAPPEN

OR NOT HAPPEN.

SO MAY I BE CONSTANT BUILDING UP A NARRATIVE

AND TRUE TELLING IT WHEN ASKED TO >>

APPENDIX THREE :

THE WOODEN CROSS CODE

FOR YOUNG PEDESTRIANS AGE 6 - 16

1) ALWAYS GO OUT ONTO THE HIGHWAY

   WITH EXTREME CAUTION ;

2) IMAGINE EVERY OTHER ROAD USER

   IS GOING TO HURT YOU IN ONE WAY OR ANOTHER ;

3) NEVER, EVER, TRUST ANOTHER ROAD USER -

   EVEN IF YOU ARE OFFERED A LIFT & TAKE UP THE OFFER ;

4) WHENEVER YOU CROSS ANY ROAD LOOK ROUND &

   ROUND IN ALL DIRECTIONS - THEN DON'T CROSS ;

5) TAKE IT THAT EVERY VEHICLE OF ANY SIZE HAS NOT

   SEEN YOU - EVEN ON A MARKED OR LIT CROSSING ;

6) IF THERE ARE VEHICLES BEHIND YOU, TAKE IT THAT

   THEY ARE NEVER GOING TO STOP FOR YOU TO CROSS ;

7) IF CROSSING ANYWHERE IS TOO UNSAFE, GO FOR A

DIVERSION : AN ALTERNATIVE WAY OF GETTING THERE ;

8) NEVER, EVER, RUN - BECAUSE IF YOU HAVE TO RUN

IT WAS NEVER SAFE TO CROSS IN THE FIRST PLACE ;

9) WHEN THERE ARE TWO LANES TO CROSS AT ONCE :

WAIT TILL BOTH LANES ARE COMPLETELY CLEAR ;

10) WHEN YOU TURN A BLIND CORNER, PRETEND THERE IS

A CYCLE OR MOBILITY SCOOTER ON THE PAVEMENT ;

11) CROSSING ANY ROAD IN THE DARK YOU ARE NOT

SEEN BY ANYONE ;

12) WHEN EVERYTHING IS COMPLETELY QUIET :

AN EMERGENCY VEHICLE IS ON THE WAY -

WITH SIREN BLARING.

BEFORE YOU TOOK TO THE HIGHWAY YOU WERE ALIVE;

AFTER YOU TOOK TO THE HIGHWAY YOU WERE DEAD ?

APPENDIX THREE :

THE << WALK-WIDE >> ….

The Walk-Wide came about by chance.

The tortuous country road that linked my house with the nearest Village a mile away had long perplexed me.

Cars and S.U.V.s approaching me as I walked on the correct side [Right, except on the Z-bend] of the unpaved tarmac - many of them on the School Run - just would not slow down for anything or anyone. Even though drivers could not possibly know who was ahead, child, pram, Driver, Pedestrian, Pedal-bike .

Over a period of 30 years, I was baffled. Should I wave at approaching Drivers? Should I use my Right hand to signal: "HALT!" ?   Would Hi-vis help me to be seen ? Or should I ostentatiously leap onto the verge or into a very wet ditch?

Then, one day, I chanced to have purchased some bulky pillows which I was carrying in my Left hand. Vehicles which would never have minded hitting *me* made elaborate efforts to avoid those pillows? Hence the Walk-Wide, based on simple 30" diameter rubber ring, available from any Seaside bucket-&-spade shop for between £1 & £3-50p. not inflated. A large *Sofa* Cushion has the same impact.

So does the Walk-Wide work? Astonishingly so! Drivers and the Riders of Motorcycles are *terrified* of that extra width on the Left-hand side of the Pedestrian striding toward them.

Equally, that Pedestrian can also revert safely to Pillows. Simply place two in a maxi-sized plastic carrier-bag!

****

ONE OF THE SUGGESTED *WALK-WIDES* WHEN INFLATED

<u>SELECT BIBLIOGRAPHY</u> :

There is a surprising shortage of good, modern, literature on Vehicle Collisions - especially for a non-specialist readership: this despite numerous films, plays, novels, short stories and radio broadcasts that rely upon the Vehicle Collision - or Car Crash - to move a story forward. Worse: despite Vehicle Collisions having an immeasurable impact on nearly every person, of whatever age, in every school, every hospital, every Court of Law, every workplace, every community.

1) Required Publications

Bingham & Berryman's Personal Injury & Motor Claims

Blackstone's Magistrates' Court Handbook

Fleet Management [*Robert & Michelle Currie*]

Know Your Traffic Signs [*Dept. for Transport*]

Motorcycle Roadcraft : The Police Rider's Handbook
[*Police Federation*] **KEY**

Murder Most Foul..by .J.S.Dean...[Road Peace Reprint]

Observational Before & After Studies in Road Safety :
Highway & Traffic Engineering Measures [*E. Hauer*]

Pass Your Advanced Driving Test [*I.A.M.*]

Roadcraft : The Police Driver's Handbook [*Police Fedn*] **KEY**

The Official DVSA Guide to Driving [*DVSA*] **KEY**

The Official DVSA Theory Test for Drivers of Larger Vehicles
[DVSA...2020 Edition] **KEY**

The Official Highway Code [*Dept. for Transport*] **KEY**

The *RoSPA* Bicycle Owner's Handbook

The Transport Manager & Operator's Handbook
[*David Lowe*]

Victim Support Handbook [*VS + Philippa Spackman*]

2) Other Publications Worth Tracking Down

A Road Safety Workbook for Young Riders [A.Pilgrim]

A Traffic Officer's Companion [Gordon Wilson]

Accident Black Spot [M. Austin] **KEY**

Advanced & Performance Driving [*Reg Local*]

Advanced Motoring [*I.A.M.*]

Back on Track [*Fiona Ford*]

Battle for the Roads of Britain [*Keith Laybourn*]

Car Crime [*Claire Corbett*]

Crash [*J.G. Ballard*]

Death on the Streets [*Robert Davis*]

Death Drive [*Stephen Bayley*]

Driving Spaces [*Peter Merriman*] **KEY**

Highway Engineering [*M. Rogers*]

How to Drive : *the Ultimate Guide* [*Ben Collins*]

Insurance Claim Secrets Revealed [*R.D. Longcore*]

Juggernaut [*John Wardroper*] **KEY**

Let's Go Out : *a Road Safety Activity Book* [*Sigsworth*]

Look Out on the Road [*Humphreys & Ramsay*]

On Roads [*Joe Moran*] **KEY**

Practical Road Safety Auditing [*Belcher & Proctor*]

Road Accidents : Prevent or Punish ? [*J.J. Leeming*]

Sentencing in a Rational Society [*Nigel Walker*]

Sentencing the Motoring Offender [*Roger Hood*]

The Impact of the Motor Car [*Barbara Preston*] **KEY**

Traffic : *Why We Drive the Way We Do* [*T. Vanderbilt*]

Vehicle in Collision [*Godfrey Holmes*] **KEY**

Please also read local Police or L. A. Road Safety Unit's literature ; &
BRAKE and Living Streets' own pamphlets and leaflets .

BIOGRAPHICAL NOTE
on the AUTHOR :
GODFREY HOLMES

Godfrey Holmes had many childhood Towns: from Bolton in Lancashire to Doncaster in South Yorkshire, from Longton in Stoke-on-Trent to Ruabon in Denbighshire. In between came a 4-year spell at Withernsea on the Yorkshire Coast where he is now based.

After studying Social Administration, Politics & Psychology at Nottingham University, Godfrey took his M.A. Econ. at the University of Manchester, so adding to the number of Cities he got to know so well, soon added to in Merseyside for his Post-Graduate Certificate in Education.

Some years of teaching in Corby New Town, then Chilwell Comprehensive School, Nottingham were followed with spells as a Social Worker concentrating on Children-at-Risk, also Fostering & Adoption, in Nottingham North-East, then Nottingham North-West, Derbyshire Dales, then Chesterfield.

Whilst in Chesterfield, Godfrey wrote over 70 detailed photographic Features on Derbyshire in general, Chesterfield in particular. But his work on Truancy, also on the subject of Alcohol Among Young People, was already published - in addition to a huge volume of essays & comment on Social Work principally for *Community Care* Magazine, but also for *Social Work Today*, *Youth in Society* & the *Times Educational Supplement*.

Godfrey has been President of Matlock Speakers' Club twice - and is often called upon to speak on the History & Mystery of Scarborough, Llandudno, Matlock Bath & Stoke-on-Trent; also on the Subjects of Church Architecture and the future of Britain's Seaside Resorts.

His interest in Highways & Highway Safety has been lifelong. Not only has Godfrey been a BRAKE volunteer Educator within schools & colleges; he has also been trained in specific counselling concerning bereavement & alcohol. His 2016 Book: VEHICLE IN COLLISION: *What Did YOU See?* broke new ground in appealing to Readers everywhere to work out how 100 Collisions on the Highway could be viewed, then understood, from several angles.

Year 2017 marked a new Chapter in Godfrey's output when he began writing Long Read Features for *The Independent* concentrating on Disaster, Social Exclusion & People-watching. In addition, Godfrey writes Poetry, including the country's longest Quintain on a single subject [in this instance: *Withernsea: A Sense of Place*], also the longest Hymn in public performance: *Cause for Wonder*.

His two pioneering Dictionaries first on *Oppression in the Workplace*, then *Truancy & School Exclusion* have, likewise, brought together an amazing number of strands of engagement & experience.

Apart from Pool and Ocean Swimming, Godfrey's hobbies include rambling, railways, photography, collecting coins & picture postcards, studying Architecture, & visiting Churches & Chapels near & far.

+ + + + + + + + + + +

OTHER RECENT BOOKS BY GODFREY HOLMES :

THE LINE- STORY
The Nation's Newest Pastime
978-0-9536016-2-2

YOUR CONVERSATION - OR MINE ?
200 Tactics When Talking
978-0-9536016-0-9

A DICTIONARY OF OPPRESSION IN THE WORKPLACE
978-0-9536016-5-3

A DICTIONARY OF TRUANCY
978-0-9536016-6-0

SANDCASTLES DO NOT FALL
New Holderness Verse
978-0-9536016-4-6

STILL STANDING AT FIVE :
A Complete Guide to Relations in the Workplace
978-0-9536016-7-7

TWIXT SCHOOL & DESPAIR :
A Complete Guide to Truancy
978-0-9536016-8-4

WITHERNSEA: A Sense of Place, A Place of Sense
Limericks for the Lighthouse
978-0-9934644-4-7

all available from Nethermoor Books, telephone : 01964-615258,
or from your Local Bookshop or from Amazon

ΩΨΩΨΩΨΩΨΩ

NOTES on ADDITIONAL TOPICS for
the CAUSE of COLLISIONS on the HIGHWAY

NOTES on ADDITIONAL TOPICS for

PREVENTING COLLISIONS on the HIGHWAY
